THE
NEW PROCLAMATION
COMMENTARY ON THE
GOSPELS

ANDREW F. GREGORY
DAVID BARTLETT
MORNA D. HOOKER
HENRY WANSBROUGH

Edited by

ANDREW F. GREGORY

new *The essential pastoral companion for preaching*
PROCLAMATION

New Proclamation Commentary on the Gospels

First Fortress Press Edition 2006.

Published in collaboration with the Society for Promoting Christian Knowledge, London.

Cover design: Laurie Ingram

ISBN-13: 978–0–8006–3752–1
ISBN-10: 0–8006–3752–6

09 08 07 06   1 2 3 4 5 6 7 8 9 10

Printed in Great Britain.

Contents

Contents

Foreword

I often get asked to take study days around Britain, and indeed give lectures abroad, for clergy and lay people on reading and preaching the Gospels today. You would have thought that after some two thousand years, the ways these four ancient texts could be read or taught would have been exhausted, and people would have moved on to other things. And yet the enthusiasm and appetite for these accounts of Jesus of Nazareth continues unabated, and I always come back encouraged from such events and often having learned something new myself. It is extraordinary that week by week, and even day by day, up and down the land and across the world, the Gospels are read publicly at the centre of Christian worship, often accompanied by a homily, sermon or some other form of explanation and application. Therefore, despite the multiplication of books and commentaries, any new aid to understanding the fourfold Gospel is to be encouraged – and I am happy to welcome this Commentary both from my own point of view and also for the wider Church.

Speaking personally, my own interest in communicating the Gospels began as a young Classics teacher trying to introduce seventeen-year-olds to the study of the Gospels in their literary context. Little did I realize that this would lead a few years later to researching a doctorate on the genre of the Gospels in comparison with Graeco-Roman biographies as part of my ordination training, later published as *What are the Gospels?*. Having concluded that the Gospels are a form of ancient biography, I was convinced of the need to read and teach them as coherent biographical narratives. However, the lectionary then used by the Church of England was thematically based, jumping from evangelist to evangelist each Sunday as the Gospels were ransacked for relevant passages, abstracted from their context. It was while I was lecturing on my work in the USA in the early 1990s that I first came across the phenomenon of clergy and preachers signing up for refresher courses on whichever Gospel was being used in their Common Lectionary that year. Sunday by Sunday, they would need to preach from the same Gospel, following it more or less sequentially throughout the year – and so investment in further training (and even buying the odd commentary!) was well worth while. So as I was writing my book *Four Gospels, One Jesus?* on how we should use these texts at the time, I concluded it with a plea that the Church of England should adopt this Lectionary as a way of listening to the distinctive voice of each evangelist in turn. A few years later, I was involved in the debates at our General Synod about this, and I even argued for a four-year cycle, rather than just three years, so that we could have a whole year devoted to John's Gospel, rather than squeezing it into the midst of the synoptic years, especially Year B on Mark. While I still think this would be absolutely right, I have to recognize that the fact that so many different churches around the world use the three-year cycle meant that my pleas were ecumenically doomed. Nevertheless, the adoption of the Revised Common Lectionary is a great step forward in letting each Gospel speak for itself within our worship – and any commentary which assists this process is to be warmly greeted. I even had to write a new edition of my book to remove my complaint about the Lectionary and update it to take account of the success of the Revised Common Lectionary!

The systematic reading of one particular Gospel over the course of a year in Christian worship allows several issues about the individual accounts and their fourfold nature to come to the fore. First, the concentration on just one evangelist Sunday by Sunday permits an appreciation of that particular account to grow in the minds of the worshippers. In Years A, B and C, the separate Gospels of Matthew, Mark and Luke are raided for passages to fit into the chronological sequence of the liturgical year with appropriate readings being chosen for Advent and the preparations for the coming of Christ at Christmas, his baptism and the call of the disciples for Epiphany, his temptation and some teaching for Lent, and then his passion, arrest, death and resurrection for the events of Holy Week and Easter. However, it is during the Sundays in Ordinary Time, between Trinity Sunday and the run up to Advent, that the Gospels are really allowed to give their individual message as readings follow more or less sequentially from the central sections of the Gospels about the ministry and teaching of Jesus. This means that their principal distinctive concerns, language and theology can begin to be appreciated by congregations, especially if they are served by preachers who explain such things to their hearers. This process can be assisted by extra teaching, through talks or study groups, about the particular concerns of each evangelist.

Nevertheless, the Lectionary never loses sight of the fact that there are four Gospels, with the interventions of John's Gospel, especially around Easter tide, and with readings from other Gospels chosen for services other than the principal worship each Sunday. This is surely correct and reflects the Church's instinct from earliest times to preserve the fourfold nature of the Gospel. The individual circumstances in which each Gospel was written and first produced may be lost to us today, despite the best attempts of both church tradition and academic scholarship to discover them – but what is clear is that very soon, within a generation or so and certainly by the middle or late second century, all four Gospels were being read and circulated together as a fourfold collection. This can be demonstrated from the defence written by St Irenaeus of why there are four Gospels, linking it to the four symbols of the human face, lion, ox and eagle of Ezekiel 1 and Revelation 4—5 (*Against the Heresies*, III.11.8–9).

The fourfold nature of the Gospel tradition presented a problem for the early Church – and was a gift to their early critics. Why not just have one 'authorized account'? Don't the differences suggest that none of them can be completely correct, much less divinely inspired? Such questions still arise today, both in debate with non-believers, as well as in inter-faith dialogue, especially with Muslims. Yet it is clear that the early Church resolutely set its face against both possible – and easy – solutions to this dilemma. Concentrating on just one Gospel, whichever was your favourite, at the expense of the others was not permitted. In fact, the need to keep all four together may well have been a driving factor behind the early Church's shift from scrolls (which could contain only one Gospel at a time) to the use of the codex, a book-like form consisting of many leaves, which was big enough to allow all four to be kept together. At the same time, the experiment of amalgamating them all together into a single account, tried by Tatian in his *Diatessaron* (i.e. 'one through four') was not successful either – even though it has given rise to many so-called 'Harmonies of the Gospels' at the back of various Bibles.

Instead, the solution of including four Gospels within the one canon of the New Testament has provided what Robert Morgan has called 'both a stimulus and a control' (Morgan, 'The Hermeneutical Significance of Four Gospels', p. 386). The fact that there are four portraits within our scriptures means that there can never be just one definitive representation of Jesus, one size fits all people, everywhere. It is a theological opportunity, for historical and doctrinal reconstruction as the Church has produced many different 'faith images' of Jesus, from the clean-shaven Good Shepherd of the catacombs' frescoes through the Byzantine Pantocrator, 'ruler of all the universe' and the Renaissance man of Michelangelo and Dürer to modern representations such as *Jesus Christ Superstar* or Mel Gibson's *The Passion of the Christ*. In every age, we have to preach and teach the 'one Jesus' afresh to each generation – and in doing so, we are following the way each evangelist told the same, old, old, story anew for his audience. And yet, there are four Gospels, not forty-four: the early church fathers rejected many other accounts which did not fall within the 'canon', or the rule, laid out by these four authoritative, inspired writings. So, too, we must preach and teach these four texts and bring to them any of our understandings of Jesus to see if they fit within these boundaries. In this way, four Gospels about the one Jesus provide both plurality and limits, stimulus and control.

I believe that a Lectionary Commentary like this one on the fourfold Gospel can help this process immensely. The sustained treatment of all the readings from one Gospel undertaken by a single scholar allows for the authentic voice of each evangelist to be heard clearly and explained for readers and preachers alike, especially with the helpful introductory essays that precede the commentary in each of the four Gospels. The fact that the readings are arranged sequentially according to the chronology of each Gospel, rather than the Sundays of the year, fits into the narrative biographical genre of the Gospels and allows for the story to flow as the writers intended. An added bonus is that the four commentators come from different Christian backgrounds in another expression of plurality within unity – four traditions, one Church. The ancient symbols of the human face, lion, ox and eagle come from biblical visions of the worship of heaven – and perhaps it is within worship that the four Gospels are best understood, read and taught. I welcome this commentary as an aid to that process, that we may all hear the four Gospels and worship the one Jesus.

Richard A. Burridge

Preface

For the past thirty years, Fortress Press has published a lectionary preaching resource that provides the best in biblical exegetical commentary for a variety of lectionary traditions. This resource, first published under the title *Proclamation* and now, *New Proclamation*, has become both a pioneer and a standard-bearer in its field, sparking a host of similar products from other publishers. Few, however, have become as widely used and well known as *Proclamation*.

Thoroughly ecumenical, *New Proclamation's* focus has always been on the biblical text first and foremost. On the conviction that the best resource for the preacher is the biblical text itself, *New Proclamation's* authors have asserted that those who are well equipped to understand a pericope in its historical and liturgical context are best prepared to compose meaningful and engaging sermons. To that end, *New Proclamation* has consistently invited the cream of North American biblical scholars and homileticians to offer their comments arising from their commitments to the text.

It is a great pleasure to offer to a North American audience *The New Proclamation Commentary on the Gospels* in collaboration with SPCK of London. Simultaneously published in England (under the title *The Fourfold Gospel Commentary*), this ecumenical undertaking by an international team of scholar-preachers offers continuous commentary on each of the four Gospels. Here the preacher will find the necessary context for all of the passages that appear in the Revised Common Lectionary for Sundays, as well as valuable grounding in the important themes of each Evangelist. (Because each commentary runs continuously through the Gospel, preachers who rely on the Episcopal Book of Common Prayer and the Roman Catholic Lectionary for Mass will easily locate discussions of passages appearing in those lectionaries where they differ from the RCL.)

We offer *The New Proclamation Commentary on the Gospels* with the same commitment that shapes the *New Proclamation* series: that of providing preachers access to the ideas of the best biblical scholars and homileticians of our day.

David B. Lott
Editor of *New Proclamation*

Contributors

David Bartlett is Distinguished Professor of New Testament, Columbia Theological Seminary, Decatur, Georgia, and Lantz Professor Emeritus of Preaching and Communication at Yale Divinity School. An ordained minister of the American Baptist Churches, USA, he has served congregations in Minnesota, Illinois, and California, and taught at a number of Divinity schools and seminaries. His publications include *What's Good About This News? Preaching From the Gospels and Galatians* (Westminster John Knox Press, 2003), *Ministry in the New Testament* (Wipf & Stock, 2001; originally published by Fortress, 1983), and commentaries on the Lectionary readings for Advent and Christmas in *New Proclamation Commentary, Series B 1999–2000, Advent through Holy Week*, Augsburg Fortress, 1999.

Richard A. Burridge is an Anglican priest and Dean of King's College, London. His publications include *What Are the Gospels? A Comparison with Graeco-Roman Biography* (Eerdmans, 2004), *Four Gospels, One Jesus? A Symbolic Reading* (SPCK/Eerdmans, 2005), *Faith Odyssey: A Journey Through Life* (Bible Reading Fellowship/ Eerdmans, 2003) and (with Graham Gould) *Jesus Now and Then* (SPCK/Eerdmans, 2004).

Andrew F. Gregory, an Anglican priest, is Chaplain and Fellow of University College, Oxford, and a member of the Theology Faculty of the University of Oxford, where he is involved in a research project 'The New Testament and the Second Century' for which he is preparing a critical edition of some non-canonical Gospels. His publications include *Four Witnesses, One Gospel? Reflections on the Fourfold Gospel and the Revised Common Lectionary* (Grove Books, 2005), *The Reception of Luke and Acts in the Period before Irenaeus* (Mohr Siebeck, 2003) and, as editor (with Christopher Tuckett), *The Reception of the New Testament in the Apostolic Fathers* (Oxford

University Press, 2005) and *Trajectories through the New Testament and the Apostolic Fathers* (Oxford University Press, 2005).

Morna D. Hooker, Lady Margaret Professor of Divinity Emerita at Cambridge University, is a fellow of Robinson College, Cambridge, and a former president of the Studiorum Novi Testamenti Societas. Much in demand as a Methodist preacher, she was one of the small group who translated the Revised English Bible, and is widely published in the field of New Testament studies. Her studies of Mark include *A Commentary on the Gospel according to St Mark* (A. & C. Black / Hendrickson, 1991 / 1992) and *The Message of Mark* (Epworth, 1983). Among her other publications are *Beginnings: Keys that Open the Gospels* (SCM Press / Trinity Press International, 1997 / 1998), *Endings: Invitations to Discipleship* (SCM Press / Hendrickson, 2003), and *Paul: A Short Introduction* (Oneworld, 2003).

Henry Wansbrough, a monk of Ampleforth Abbey, is Magister Scholarum of the English Benedictine Congregation, and a former Master of St Benet's Hall, Oxford. He is the only English member of the Pontifical Biblical Commission, Chairman of the Trustees of the Catholic Biblical Association, and is editor of the New Jerusalem Bible. His many other publications include *The Passion and Death of Jesus* (Darton, Longman & Todd / Abingdon, 2003), *The Gospel according to John* (Catholic Truth Society, 2002), 'The Four Gospels in Synopsis', in the *Oxford Bible Commentary* (Oxford University Press, 2001), and *The Lion and the Bull: The Gospels of Mark and Luke* (Darton, Longman & Todd, 1996). He lectures and broadcasts in England, in the USA and across the world.

Introduction: the fourfold Gospel and the three-year Lectionary

ANDREW F. GREGORY

The rationale of the Lectionary and the distinctiveness of this Commentary

The purpose of this book is to offer a commentary on the four Gospels as they are read in the three-year Lectionary that is used by millions of Christians across the world. The widespread ecumenical accept-ance of the three-year Lectionary – the *Roman Catholic Lectionary for Mass* (1969), the *Revised Common Lectionary* (1992), and its Church of England variant, the *Common Worship Lectionary* (1997) – is one of the most notable achievements of the ecumenical movement, and a helpful reminder of the place of the individual congregation in the worldwide Church. Modern biblical studies have contributed significantly to bringing churches together, so it is fitting that each contributor to this volume is a member of a different Christian tradition: Anglican, Baptist, Methodist and Roman Catholic.

Unlike most other commentaries on the readings in the three-year Lectionary, this book offers a cohesive, continuous and sustained commentary on each of the four Gospels as read in the Lectionary and proclaimed in the worship of the Church. Central to the three-year Lectionary is the reading of the canonical Gospels. This is stated clearly by the Consultation on Common Texts, the ecumenical body who produced the *Revised Common Lectionary*:

> The Lectionary provides a three-year plan or pattern for the Sunday readings. Each year is centred on one of the synoptic gospels. Year A is the year of Matthew, Year B is the year of Mark, and Year C is the year of Luke. John is read each year, especially in the times around Christmas, Lent and Easter, and also in the year of Mark, whose gospel is shorter than the others. The three synoptic evange-lists have particular insights into Christ. Each year, we allow one of

these gospels to lead us to Christ by a semicontinuous reading
during the Sundays in Ordinary Time. Passages and parables that
are unique to one evangelist are normally included as part of the
Sunday readings . . . The *Revised Common Lectionary* seeks to read
the four gospels during the liturgy in a manner which respects their
own varied literary structures. (*The Revised Common Lectionary*,
pp. 13, 16)

Whereas other Lectionary commentaries have tended to be written
by large numbers of people, each commenting only on parts of a
particular Gospel, this commentary allows four biblical scholars, each
of whom is also a preacher, to comment on one Gospel as a whole.
Each contributor offers an introduction to one Gospel, drawing
attention to the way in which it functions as a complete text, then
comments on each passage that appears in the Lectionary with
particular reference to the distinctive emphases that are found in
each evangelist's presentation of Jesus' life, death, resurrection and
continuing significance. Thus they hope to help preachers and other
readers of this Commentary to understand not only the content of
each Lectionary reading but also the context in which it appears
in the Gospel of which it is a part. Their use of the Lectionary is
not uncritical, and contributors draw attention to places where the
Lectionary omits material that is significant, or where it begins and
ends passages in ways that seem unhelpful.

Each introduction and commentary is intended to provide primarily exegetical rather than expository insights. They are academ-
ically rigorous, drawing fully on modern critical scholarship, but are
intended as a preparatory aid for those who preach on the Gospels
and the Jesus whom they portray. They do not offer model sermons,
but are intended to be of service for those who will relate these texts
to the communities of faith whom they serve, as well as for members of congregations in which the Lectionary is used. Thus the commentaries focus not on analytical methods concerning sources and
other historical questions but on the content of the passage or the
thought of the evangelist as reflected in the text of the Gospels as
they have been received and transmitted in the Church. Preachers
who use them will find them more helpful towards the beginning
of their sermon preparation as they try to wrestle with the text itself
rather than with its application.

All readings for Sundays and major festivals (as found, with minor variations, in each of these lectionaries) are included. They are printed in the order that they appear in each Gospel (not the order in which they appear in the Lectionary). This makes the book easy to use regardless of which version of the Lectionary a reader is using, and it also allows each commentary to serve as a useful introduction to what is distinctive in each Gospel for readers who wish to study the Gospels without reference to the Lectionary. Each reading is treated only once, even if it is used more than once in different liturgical contexts in the course of the three-year cycle of these lectionaries. On some occasions the beginning and/or end of a particular lection is altered in order to avoid duplication between and/or within different forms of the three-year Lectionary.

Four Gospels, one Lectionary

Although the Lectionary distinguishes between and seeks to learn from the related but different perspectives of the synoptic evangelists and the more obviously different perspective of the Fourth Gospel, it assumes that all testify to the abiding significance of one Jesus – risen from the dead, recognized as the Christ, and worshipped and served as Lord. The four Gospels were bound together from an early stage in their transmission, and the uniformity of their titles emphasizes the Christian belief that there is but one Gospel of Jesus Christ, although presented in four forms: the (one) Gospel according to Matthew, to Mark, to Luke and to John.

It was not always so, however. There were many Gospels in circulation in the early years of Christianity, yet the mainstream Church gave a privileged place to these four but no others. That some choice had to be made between the different presentations of Jesus found in these texts was perhaps inevitable; that four should be chosen rather than one was not. Early opponents of Christianity were quick to point to what they saw as discrepancies between them, and such differences – whether of perspective or of substance – have been seen variously as historically problematic or theologically fruitful ever since.

Two questions concerning the literary relationships between the four Gospels need to be noted before the question of the relationship between the four accounts and the one Jesus whom they portray may be properly addressed. The first concerns the relationship between Matthew, Mark and Luke, usually referred to as the synoptic problem. The pattern of similarities and differences between these three Gospels, both in their content and in the order in which it is presented, makes it all but certain that there is some literary relationship between them. At least one evangelist must have drawn on the work of at least one of the other authors.

For many years, Matthew was believed to have written first. Some scholars continue to hold to a modified form of Matthean priority, but the vast majority of scholars now believe that Mark was the earliest of the Gospels. Most of this majority believe that Matthew and Luke each used Mark independently of the other, and that they also made independent use of a shared source which contained some of the teaching of Jesus that is found in both their Gospels, but not in Mark. This postulated source is usually known as Q, which stands for Quelle, the German word for source. It is thought to stand behind material shared by Matthew and Luke, but not by Mark. Some of these scholars tend to think that Matthew and Luke each had access to other written materials or traditions that only one or other used in the parts of their Gospels that are without parallel in the work of the other. Other scholars prefer to think of such distinctive material as the creation of either evangelist. Thus this understanding of the relationship between the synoptics is known either as the two-document (Mark + Q) or four-document (Mark + Q + L + M) hypothesis. On the latter model, M and L are postulated as sources lying behind material found only in Matthew or Luke.

A rival hypothesis also affirms Markan priority, but maintains that the material shared by Matthew and Luke but not Mark is to be explained on the basis that Luke drew directly on Matthew. It therefore dispenses with any need to postulate the existence of Q.

Other explanations have also been canvassed; while there is a clear majority in favour of the two- (or four-) document hypothesis, debate over the synoptic problem is by no means resolved. In the commentary on the synoptic Gospels that follows, David Bartlett, Andrew Gregory and Morna Hooker all work on the basis that Mark wrote first, and that Matthew and Luke each drew on Mark and on Q. On this understanding of the relationship between these Gospels, aspects of the portrayal of Jesus that are distinctive to Matthew or to Luke can be seen not only in what is peculiar to their own accounts or in the overall shape of their narratives but also in the ways in which they appear to have used Mark (which survives independently of their texts) and Q (which does not).

The second question concerns the relationship of John to some or all of the synoptic Gospels. The scholarly consensus has swung backwards and forwards on the question of whether the author of John made direct use of one or more of the synoptic Gospels, and now tends to favour the view that he knew at least Mark. This may be seen either in terms of his use of Mark in the composition of his Gospel, or in terms of him writing his Gospel for other people whom he assumed to be familiar with Mark. A number of particular points of contact between the third and fourth canonical Gospels have led some scholars to argue strongly that John also used (or at least was familiar with) Luke, although the opposite case has also been made. There is no clear evidence to support direct literary dependence between Matthew and John, although both Gospels present similar perspectives on controversies between followers of Jesus and members of (other?) synagogues that are focused on christological debate. In the commentary on John that follows, Henry Wansbrough stresses that John is not to be seen as merely derivative, but may include tradition independent of and perhaps earlier than the synoptics, as well as material that is the result of reflection on one or more of the synoptic Gospels.

Four Gospels, one Jesus

That scholars have failed to find definitive answers that will command overwhelming if not universal assent, either to the synoptic problem or to the question of the relationship of John and the synoptic Gospels, may be problematic for the historian who wishes to delineate the precise way in which these Gospels developed. Yet it is much less of an issue for those committed to the fourfold Gospel as the definitive record and expression of the impact of Jesus on his first disciples. This is not to deny the validity or importance of questions that historians ask about the relationship between these texts, and about the events, sources and processes that lay behind them and shaped the understanding and belief of those who composed them. It is merely to recognize that our only access to Jesus and to his impact on those who met them is through the texts that are themselves the record of that impact – the outline details that we find elsewhere in the New Testament as well as the fuller but still selective and theologically motivated accounts in the Gospels.

These four texts show not only the impact that Jesus made on his earliest followers, but also the Jesus whom subsequent generations of Christians recognize as the one in whom God has most fully made himself known. It is the Jesus of the Gospels, not any reconstructed historical Jesus, whom Christian preachers proclaim as Saviour and Lord. Thus although it is our belief in the Word made flesh in space and time that drives us to want to know more of Jesus' life, it is the theological significance of that life that stands at the heart of our faith – a significance given definitive expression in these Gospels, not in the ever-shifting sands of historical research and the many different reconstructions of the historical Jesus which such research may produce.

It follows, therefore, that a commitment to the fourfold Gospel means not only that we recognize that our primary access to the initial impact of Jesus is through these texts, but that we refuse to see this as in any way a limiting factor. It also means that we acknowledge that our understanding of these texts is already coloured and shaped by the history of interpretation of these Gospels in the Church in which they continue to be proclaimed – the same Church which has arisen partly in response to its appropriation of these very texts, and has set them apart from other Gospels that do not convey its faith. Such a commitment does not remove the importance of historical and literary questions about the relationship of the Gospels in the period before they were transmitted as four complementary perspectives on Jesus as experienced and remembered by those who followed him in Galilee and Judaea. But to approach these four different and distinctive Gospels not only as discrete texts but also as constituent parts of the one fourfold Gospel of Jesus Christ relativizes the importance of such questions, for it focuses on Jesus as he is found in the Gospels rather than on a shadowy figure behind them.

Difficulties in getting behind these theologically laden biographical portrayals need not call into question the general outline of what we know about the life of Jesus of Nazareth. Nor need they call into question the conviction that the risen Lord to whom they bear witness is Jesus of Nazareth, the individual who stands as the goal of the continuing quest for the historical Jesus. What such difficulties may do however is to remind us that continuing uncertainty about the precise nature of the relationships between the Gospels may point more clearly not to an ever-changing and thus inaccessible historical Jesus somewhere behind these texts, but to the theological imperative of faith in the Jesus whom God raised and whom Christians believe to be alive and active by God's Spirit today.

Such an imperative calls neither for fideism, nor for naive and uncritical credulity in regard to the Gospels as historical sources, nor for the rejection of historical scholarship and its results. On the contrary, it notes merely that neither the historical methods nor the historical sources available at present are sufficient to penetrate beyond the fourfold Gospel as preserved by the early Christians in order to gain access to the Jesus behind them. Therefore any access to Jesus that we have is necessarily dependent on the already interpreted history that is presented for us first in Paul and then in the four canonical Gospels. Historical study remains important, not only for what it tells us of the world in which he lived and of the movement to which his life, death and resurrection gave rise, but also because it serves as a reminder that Jesus the Christ whom Christians worship is the risen Jesus of Nazareth, a human born in space and time whose human existence was taken into the life of God when the pre-existent Word took on Jesus' human flesh from the moment of his conception in what Christians describe as the incarnation.

Nevertheless, the Jesus with whom we are presented in the New Testament is found not behind those texts but rather when all four Gospels are read both in the light of the Spirit and in the light of each other and of other early witnesses to Jesus and his impact. It is my hope that this book will assist in that process.

The Gospel according to Matthew

DAVID BARTLETT

Introduction

The structure of Matthew's Gospel

We do not know for sure who wrote the Gospel according to Matthew, but its author was a devout believer in Jesus as Messiah and Son of God. Ancient traditions suggest that it was the tax collector whom Jesus called to be a disciple, a person called Levi in Mark and Luke, but Matthew in the Gospel that takes his name.

The author begins not by saying 'Here is my Gospel' but by saying 'The book of the birth (or the genesis) of Jesus the Messiah, the son of David, the son of Abraham'. His story is told by a third-person narrator who seems to know everything. He knows what Joseph sees, privately, in his dreams. He knows what Satan says to Jesus when Satan and Jesus are alone in the wilderness. He knows, before any of the characters in the Gospel know, a good deal about Jesus' identity, and he tells the readers at the very beginning that Jesus is Messiah, Son of David, and Son of Abraham (1.1).

The narrator also is trustworthy. There are clever novels today where we discover as we read that the narrator misleads. The narrator of this Gospel tells the truth at all times. In fact the three utterly reliable voices in Matthew are the voice of the narrator, the voice of Jesus, and the voice of God (which we hear only at 3.17 and at 17.5).

As with many good novels, Matthew has a protagonist, Jesus of Nazareth. Of the human characters in the novel he alone is unfailingly true and unfailingly trustworthy. Within the world of the story, we never have any reason to doubt the truth of Jesus' words or the appropriateness of his behaviour.

Arrayed against him are a host of antagonists, adversaries, enemies. The most conspicuous enemies are the leaders of the Jewish people. Scribes, Pharisees, and Sadducees not only misunderstand

Jesus, they oppose him outright. There are Gentiles who oppose Jesus too, most notably Pilate who is either an enemy or a dupe of the enemies. And it is Roman soldiers who mock Jesus, scourge him and lift him on the cross.

Satan, too, is an antagonist, and Satan's minions are enemies: the demons who destroy humans are themselves destroyed by this man, but not without protest, sound and fury.

Between the protagonist and the antagonists are the complicated and confused. There are two named groups who often appear as a group, defined by their attitude toward Jesus. The first group is the disciples. The disciples struggle between understanding and confusion, faithfulness and apostasy. The least faithful disciple betrays Jesus; the one who appears most faithful denies him.

The second group is the crowd. Sometimes they seem about to believe, sometimes nearly incapable of believing. The disciples are like the Christians of Matthew's time, whereas the crowds are like Matthew's contemporaries who can't quite make up their minds about Jesus. The disciples represent wavering faith; the crowds represent wavering doubt. The Gospel seeks to nudge both groups toward faithfulness.

In addition to the disciples and the crowds, there is also a whole host of 'minor' characters who interact with Jesus in such a way that he may show forth the truth of the kingdom. The healed demoniacs, the woman with the flow of blood, the blind men at the side of the road – all these provide the opportunity for Jesus to show the ways in which God demands mercy and not sacrifice, and shows mercy, too, through Christ himself.

In different ways John the Baptist and Joseph, the husband of Mary, are both heroes in this drama, and both foreshadow Jesus who follows. John preaches exactly what Jesus will preach: 'The time is fulfilled; the kingdom of heaven is at hand; repent and believe in the gospel.' John fulfils all righteousness by his willingness to baptize Jesus and foreshadows Jesus' death by his own. Joseph acts out the righteousness that Jesus will embody and enjoin. Like the Messiah he is obedient to the will of God at whatever cost to his own reputation.

God is a major character who makes only brief appearances. God does not speak much but is spoken of incessantly. When God does speak, God says the same thing twice: 'This is my Son.' When God acts, most decisively, God raises Jesus from the tomb. Sometimes a picture is worth a thousand words.

The plot of the Gospel includes conflict. We know there will be conflict in this story from the first realization that Herod, who pretends to honour Jesus, actually seeks to kill him. The conflict begins with disagreement, moves to plotting, ends with arrest and execution. There are subplots of conflict among the disciples or between the disciples and Jesus and of conflict between Jesus and the demonic forces. The conflict looks as though it is going to drive toward catharsis: a terrible death, like Hamlet's death in Elsinore, seducing us toward terror and pity. Instead it drives toward reversal: the tomb empty, the crucified one appearing, the authority he rejected in the wilderness now bestowed upon him for heaven and for earth.

Matthew's community: what's going on?

Each of the Gospels represents an attempt by the evangelist to address hopes and needs that are particular not only to the writer but to the community or communities for which he writes.

Most contemporary scholars seem to agree that the community for which Matthew writes lives in a very close relationship to the synagogue. Matthew was a Jewish Christian writing for other Jewish Christians who have moved from being traditional Jews to being Jews who thought Jesus was the Messiah to being a separate 'Christian' community.

Any theory tries, at least, to explain evidence that is hard to fit into a consistent picture. On the one hand there is evidence of an ongoing close relationship to the synagogue and its leaders: 'The scribes and the Pharisees sit on the seat of Moses. Therefore do and keep whatever they tell you. But do not act according to their works' (23.2–3). On the other hand sometimes 'the Jews' seem to be entirely distinguished from Matthew's own community. The false rumour about the disciples stealing Jesus' body is 'spread among the Jews even up till this day' (28.15). What seems clear from a reading of Matthew's Gospel is that the evangelist is particularly concerned to show both the continuity and the discontinuity between the traditions of (Hebrew) Scripture and the claims of the emerging Church.

Themes in Matthew's Gospel

There is a tradition that Matthew 13.52 provides the evangelist's self-description: 'On account of this, every scribe who is discipled for the kingdom of heaven, brings forth from his treasure store new things and old things.' We can find in this brief verse a number of the theological themes that characterize Matthew's Gospel.

New things and old things

We have already suggested that Matthew brings forth from his sources what is old – including the Gospel according to Mark and the hypothetical source Q (see above, p. 4) – and what is new: his own redaction (i.e. editing) and arrangement of the material. Whether or not Matthew here alludes to his own editorial techniques, he certainly alludes to the larger hermeneutical project that he undertakes. For the sake of the kingdom they bring forth the new, the good news of Jesus Messiah, and relate it explicitly to what is old: Jewish Scripture, what we call the Old Testament. We can see three aspects of this combination of old and new.

The first concerns Matthew's quotations. Many biblical quotations explicitly link the events that he portrays to the explicit or implicit prophecies of the Old Testament. Matthew is not concerned with what we would think of as the original historical setting of these texts. His concern is to use these quotations to interpret the activity and words of Jesus, and, we might add, he uses the activity and words of Jesus to reshape the meaning of the older texts. The first fulfilment quotation in Matthew is in 1.23. The introductory phrase is 1.22. 'All of this came to pass in order that there might be fulfilled what was spoken by the Lord through the prophet, saying: "Behold, a virgin shall conceive in her womb and bear a child, and they shall call his name Emmanuel."' Matthew uses the Septuagint, the Greek version of the text. He does not raise the question that excites contemporary scholars, whether *parthenos* (virgin) is an accurate translation of the Hebrew. And he does not ask what was going on in Isaiah's own context when Isaiah wrote these words. Matthew finds the prophecy he needs to illuminate the story of Jesus' miraculous conception.

A second way in which Matthew relates the old to the new is through typology. In typological interpretation a type (the old) is compared and contrasted with an antitype (the new). So, for instance, in Romans 5 and 1 Corinthians 15, Adam is the type who is compared and contrasted with Christ, the antitype. In Matthew's Gospel we are enabled to interpret Jesus' story in the light of the Old Testament types who foreshadow that story, and we are invited to reread the Old Testament in the light of the New Testament antitypes.

There is an obvious typological relationship between the Joseph of Genesis and Joseph, the husband of Mary. Both see and interpret dreams. Both travel into Egypt. Both prove to be upright. By reading the story of the latter Joseph through the lens of the former we see that this apparently humble man is part of God's plan for working redemption for Israel and indeed for the world.

There is probably also a typological relationship between Moses and Jesus. Herod's massacre of the innocents in Matthew 2 recalls Pharaoh's massacre of the innocents in Exodus. Moses goes up to a mountain to receive the commandments. Jesus goes up a mountain to deliver his first great sermon. Jesus not only replicates Moses, he succeeds him and deepens his message.

Third, Matthew takes up the theme of the old and the new in his presentation of the Law. As Jesus begins the Sermon on the Mount he makes clear his continuity with the first Moses and the Mosaic Law. 'Do not think that I have come to destroy the law or the prophets. I have not come to destroy but to fulfil' (5.19). Then, in the section of the Sermon called the antitheses, Jesus deliberately but euphemistically compares himself to Moses. 'You have heard that it was said to those of old, you shall not kill . . .' (5.21). The 'it was said' is simply a polite way around admitting: 'You have heard that Moses said . . .' Jesus then goes on to accept but also to expand that commandment. Not only are the listeners not to kill, they are not to grow angry. The antitheses do not represent the abrogation of the Law but its expansion. Intention counts as well as action. The evangelist brings forth from his treasure both what is old (Torah, the Jewish law) and what is new (the radicalizing of Torah for citizens of the kingdom of heaven).

The scribe who is discipled

According to Matthew, Jesus calls disciples at the beginning of his ministry (4.18–22; though Matthew does not call them disciples until 5.1). At the end of this Gospel, Jesus commands his disciples to make disciples (28.16–19). In the middle of the story Matthew says that the scribe of the kingdom is the one 'discipled' or 'taught' to bring forth from his treasure both the new and the old.

Matthew uses the noun 'disciple' and its cognates far more than any of the other Gospel writers. It is hard to know whether he uses the term 'disciples' as a foreshadowing of church leaders or as a foreshadowing of the larger community of believers in his own generation. The different contexts of the use suggest that both are possible. What is quite clear is that Matthew wants his readers and hearers to emulate the disciples at their best and to be warned by the disciples at their worst. For Matthew the term 'disciple' at least means this. To follow Jesus is to live under his discipline; to learn from him, and to obey him, too.

The scribe who is discipled for the kingdom of heaven

Matthew typically uses the phrase 'kingdom of heaven' where Mark uses 'kingdom of God'. This is probably because Matthew, as a Jewish Christian, is reticent to use the name 'God', and his audience would have understood 'kingdom of heaven' as an equivalent translation. That is to say the kingdom is the kingdom established by the heavenly king, the kingship that he exercises, not necessarily or exclusively a kingdom located *in* heaven.

The great charter for the kingdom is the Sermon on the Mount; the great map of the kingdom is the series of parables in Matthew 13 and 25. In the Lord's Prayer Jesus teaches the disciples to pray: 'Your kingdom come, your will be done, on earth as in heaven.' Notice the way the themes come in pairs. For God's kingdom to come is in large measure for God's will to be done. The kingdom that is coming is rooted in heaven but manifest on earth.

What's more, we do not need to guess what it looks like to live as a citizen of that kingdom, what it means to do God's will, because the whole Sermon on the Mount has given us a road map for discipleship in that kingdom. The parables of chapter 13 are extended

14

metaphors that describe what can only be described poetically, the presence and promise of the kingdom. The kingdom is like seed that despite all opposition and all odds bring forth harvest. It is like a very small seed that brings forth a great tree. It is a treasure so great that one should seek for it ceaselessly; it is like a treasure so surprising that it may simply pop up as we muddle through our lives without the slightest expectation.

The parables of chapter 25 provide a balance to the parables of chapter 13. The kingdom of heaven is also that consummation devoutly to be wished when faithfulness will be rewarded, hopefulness commended, charity blessed. Chapter 13 adumbrates the kingdom on earth; chapter 25 the kingdom coming from heaven.

The scribe is like the steward of a house

Whether or not Matthew sees 'disciples' as a code word for the Christian leaders of his day, he certainly sees 'scribe' as a term that can be used to describe Christian leaders as properly as Jewish ones.

Church and church order is another fundamental theme of Matthew, sketched out most fully in the fourth of Jesus' five discourses, chapter 18. Here at least it seems that the disciples do point ahead to the church leaders of Matthew's time. They are explicitly distinguished from the 'little ones' (18.6, 10) who seem to be the church members in their charge. The disciples are like shepherds; the little ones like sheep (18.10–14).

Church for Matthew is like family. When Jesus begins the discussion of the strategies of church discipline in 18.15 he refers to the fellow church member as a 'brother'. And in the larger context of the chapter, disciples are reminded of the will of 'your Father' (18.14).

As with any family, the structure of the Church depends on some kind of understanding of authority. Matthew seems to present two different understandings of church authority, somewhat in tension with one another. The first may be seen in chapter 16. In Matthew 16.16 Simon Peter confesses to Jesus: 'You are the Messiah, the son of the living God.' Jesus responds in this way: 'Blessed are you, Simon son of Jonah, because flesh and blood has not revealed this to you, but my Father in heaven. And I tell you that you are Peter (*petros*) and upon this rock (*petra*) I will build my Church and the gates of Hades will not prevail against it. I will give you the keys of the kingdom of heaven, and whatever you bind on earth will be bound in heaven.' Though a few verses later Jesus is calling Peter 'Satan' for attempting to dissuade him from his mission, Jesus never retracts the blessing, the naming or the authority he gives to Peter. However, in Matthew 18, the chapter on church discipline, Matthew suggests that Jesus understands authority in the Church somewhat differently. Speaking to all the disciples, he says: 'Amen I say to you, whatever you bind on earth will be bound in heaven, and whatever you loose on earth will be loosed in heaven' (18.18). It may be that between these two passages there is a tension that simply cannot be resolved. Or it may be that authority for Matthew's Gospel rests both in the congregation and in its leaders, and that Peter represents not only an historic 'rock' for the Church but a foreshadowing of the on-going leadership that makes both church teaching and church discipline possible.

Matthew understands Church, not just as a temporary movement, but as an established community waiting for Christ's return. To be faithful is not only to wait for the fullness of the kingdom, it is to live out God's will on earth as part of a particular family, the Church.

Jesus Messiah, fulfilment of the Old: promise of the New

Matthew uses a number of titles for Jesus in his Gospel. At the beginning of the story Jesus is Messiah, Son of David, Son of Abraham. At the end of the story (and whenever the divine voice speaks) Jesus is recognized as Son of God. He is also the teacher greater than Moses and the wonder-worker whose wonders are signs that the kingdom of heaven is breaking in.

In the last part of the story, in chapters 26 to 28, we also see him as tempted but faithful, crucified but victorious.

Christ as tempted but faithful. Matthew records three times when Jesus is put to the test. In the wilderness Satan tempts him. 'If you are the Son of God, throw yourself down.' Jesus, tested, refuses to test God: 'Again it is written, "You shall not test the Lord your God"' (4.7). When he is on the cross, the passers-by cry out: 'If you are the Son of God, come down from the cross' (27.40). In the middle of the story, Peter tries to test Jesus, too. Jesus predicts his own passion and Peter pulls him aside and begins to rebuke him: 'Mercy no, Lord. This must not happen to you.' Jesus names Peter and labels the occasion: 'Get behind me, you Satan' (16.22–23).

The fundamental temptation for Christ is the temptation that he will test God by backing off from the ministry of suffering and loss to which God calls him. His fidelity is the fidelity that resists temptation in the wilderness, at Caesarea Philippi, and finally at Calvary.

Christ as crucified but victorious. For Matthew, more clearly than for any of the other Gospel writers, Jesus' crucifixion is itself the beginning of the final arrival of the kingdom. When he dies the signs are eschatological signs: the temple curtain torn asunder, an earthquake, the dead rising from their tombs. In Mark it is Jesus' death itself that causes the centurion to say: 'Surely this was the Son of God.' In Matthew it is the signs that the kingdom of heaven begins to invade the kingdoms of this world in the death of this man.

The resurrection is the fullest sign of that triumph. Only in Matthew is there such emphasis on the fact that Christ rose again, body and bones. The constant polemic against rumours that the disciples stole the body is part of the ongoing struggle with the synagogue (28.11–15). However, it is also a way of saying concretely, firmly, that resurrection is the real resurrection of the real Jesus. God robs the tomb of Christ's body, death of its apparent victory.

At the very end Jesus shows the fullness of the authority that we already saw at the end of the Sermon on the Mount. Now it is not only the authority to teach and the authority to heal, it is the authority to direct the disciples and through the disciples the Church, to take on its mission of discipling.

The resurrection proves that the promise of chapter 1 was not vain. Out of the kingdom's treasure house God has brought forth the old promise of Isaiah, God with us, and has also brought forth this astonishing new thing: Christ risen, kingdom begun.

At the beginning the angel says to Joseph: 'And they will call his name Emmanuel, God with us' (1.23). At the end, Jesus says to the disciples, to the Church: 'Look, I'm with you always, till the end of the ages' (28.19).

Commentary on the Sunday readings from Matthew

Matthew 1.18–25

Here Matthew focuses on Joseph, whereas Luke in his birth narrative focuses on Mary. Names matter to Matthew. To understand a person's name is to understand something of who that person is. Joseph's name recalls Joseph in the Genesis story. Notice how closely the new Joseph emulates the old. He too reads dreams to receive God's revelation. He too travels into Egypt in fulfilment of a divine plan he does not altogether understand. He too is a 'righteous' man.

The names for the newborn child also matter. He is called 'Emmanuel' because he fulfils the prophecy of Isaiah 7.14. We now know that in the Hebrew of Isaiah 7.14 Isaiah prophesies that a young woman, not a virgin, will conceive and bear a son, but Matthew would have known the Greek translation which did say 'virgin'. In any case what counts for Matthew here, as so often elsewhere, is not so much the surprising biological claim about Jesus as the scriptural claim. What happens to Mary, Joseph and their son fulfils the promises of God. In many ways the whole purpose of Matthew's Gospel is to show how Jesus is 'Emmanuel', God with us, and at the end of the story Jesus will promise to be Emmanuel for the rest of human history as well (28.20). What happens to Mary, Joseph and their son fulfils the promises of God.

The name 'Jesus' is our English version of the Greek version of the Hebrew word for Joshua. That name refers to the salvation God works among us, and so Matthew reminds us that to name this child Jesus is to claim him as 'the one who saves the people from their sins' (1.21).

We are not sure exactly what shame Joseph was trying to avoid by determining to end his engagement to Mary secretly. What we do know is that Joseph's intentions were just, righteous, upright (1.19), and we know that his willingness to do as God commanded showed forth an even richer righteousness.

Matthew 2.1–12

We are not quite sure how best to translate the Greek term *Magoi*, in this passage, but the visitors were not kings. They were seers and perhaps even astrologers. Astrology was an honourable science in the ancient world, and if that was their vocation it would explain their interest in the odd star that moved through the heavens toward Bethlehem.

The contending kings in this passage are Jesus and Herod. The infant, we shall see, grows into a man who speaks only truth. The pretender is a liar from the start, pretending both to be a real king and to desire to pay homage to his divine usurper. The story will reach its climax only years (and chapters) later, when even the Romans themselves wittingly or unwittingly settle the dispute on kingship by placing a title above Jesus' cross: 'This is Jesus, the King of the Jews' (27.37).

There is no harm in meditating on the meaning of the three gifts – gold for the rich one now humbled, frankincense as a sign of worship, myrrh as a foreshadowing of the tomb. If Matthew is thinking of such symbols he does not give us further clues. The clue he does give us is the one we pick up in using these texts for Epiphany. Here at the very beginning, when the only 'righteous' Jewish believers we have seen are Joseph and Mary, the first righteous Gentiles appear. Again the beginning foreshadows the end when the babe, grown, crucified, risen, says to his disciples: 'Make disciples of all nations', which can equally well be translated 'Make disciples of all Gentiles.'

Again Matthew tells us why these things must be. Scripture tells us so. Again God speaks in dreams, to the righteous Gentiles as to Joseph, the righteous Jew. The Magi go home by another way because they are prudent. Many a sermon recalls that when we have worshipped the infant we are bound to find a new way home.

Matthew 2.13–23

We have already seen that Herod is a liar; now we see that he is a murderer as well. Once again the text is full of foreshadowing. Herod, so-called King of the Jews, now visits upon his people what Pharaoh, the great enemy, had visited before. Death to the children. 2.17 is one of Matthew's many fulfilment quotations, showing how what happens in the story of Jesus has been predicted in the Hebrew Scriptures. Matthew is not worried about magic, he is worried about providence. The way to explain the story he tells is to show how God has foretold this story through the prophets.

19

In a moment of tragedy like the slaughter of these children it is essential not to let go of faith in the providence of God. That will become essential again when Matthew tries to help us understand the slaughter of the innocent Jesus. Every preacher knows that there is no sufficient answer to the question of why the innocent suffer. Every preacher also knows that we can only begin to reach out to that suffering by starting with the cross.

This particular fulfilment quotation is pertinent not just because it foreshadows the weeping of these first-century mothers. It is pertinent because this story is the continuation of a story of loss and exile for Israel over generations. It is pertinent because it recalls the reason that Rachel wept (in Jeremiah 31.15). Her children are in exile. This slaughter of the innocents recalls and outdoes that awful exile. Jesus and his family will soon be exiled, and for them, too, slaughter lies ahead.

This is one of those texts whose peculiar power is its power to chasten our cheerfulness. When God works among us, when God comes among us, Emmanuel, we are confronted not only with bowing Magi and great gifts. From the beginning there is opposition; from the beginning the way to life lies through death.

Matthew 3.1–12

John the Baptist fulfils and foreshadows. He is the prophet who is prophesied. He fulfils the prophecy of Isaiah 40.3. No wonder some will think that he is Elijah returned from heaven. John is the great link between what God has done and what God is about to do.

John's preaching foreshadows Jesus' preaching. He proclaims: 'Repent for the kingdom of heaven has come near' (3.2). In Matthew 4.17 Jesus begins his ministry by proclaiming exactly those words. John's baptism foreshadows Jesus' baptism. The water of repentance points ahead to the fire of judgement. Soon, John's execution will foreshadow Jesus' death.

The way of the Lord that John prepares is a straight way, and many will fall aside. Genealogy does not guarantee redemption. God used Abraham but does not need Abraham's children. So powerful is the God of Jesus Christ that stones will suffice to sing God's praise.

In all the Gospels the way to Jesus leads through John the Baptist. God with us is not only God for us but also God against us – against the old pretensions and securities that prevent us from faithfulness.

For the first time, but not the last, in this Gospel, the readers are called to be fruitful. In many ways, the rest of the Gospel is written to help us see what the fruits of repentance look like – to perceive the righteousness Christ embodies and enjoins.

In Matthew, 'the kingdom of heaven' is another way of saying what Mark says in the phrase 'the kingdom of God'. Perhaps Matthew, who was almost certainly a Jewish Christian, shares the reticence orthodox Jews still use in writing only of G—d. In any case the kingdom of heaven is not limited to some heavenly realm; it encompasses the heavens and the earth; it is present and it is on the way. That is what John the Baptist means when he says: 'the kingdom of heaven is drawing near'. God's reign has one foot in the door.

Matthew 3.13–17

This is a surprise. John has just told us that Jesus is the greatest baptizer and now Jesus comes to be baptized. Behind this scene lies the somewhat tricky problem of explaining why the greater was baptized by the lesser.

In Matthew, Jesus explains that the reason for the baptism is for Jesus to fulfil all righteousness. In part this means that he acts like a righteous person, living out the commitment God requires of all. In part it means that he lives out the righteousness of God; this is part of God's right plan for the redemption of the world. The baptism is more than a baptism, however. It is also a coronation. God's proclamation, 'This is my beloved son', surely recalls Psalm 2.7, where the enthroned king is declared as God's son. But it also recalls the promise of the birth to Mary the virgin in chapter 1, and the claim in Genesis 22 that Isaac is Abraham's beloved son. God's claim affirms the depth of God's love and foretells the depth of Christ's sacrifice.

God speaks aloud only twice in Matthew – here and at the transfiguration. In each case God makes the same claim: 'This is my son.' Whoever else Jesus proves to be in this Gospel, we now have God's unshakable claim that the one who is with us is God's own son. In Mark, God speaks this claim to Jesus alone. In Matthew, apparently all can hear.

The Spirit rests upon this Son as reminder of the prophecies of Isaiah 42.1 and 11.2. What God has promised is fulfilled in Jesus, who will promise even more.

Though there is no full doctrine of the Trinity in the New Testament, it is striking that at this moment when Jesus' ministry begins, the Father speaks, the Spirit descends, the Son fulfils all righteousness (compare also the triadic formula in 28.19).

Matthew 4.1–11

The Spirit that descended on Jesus at his baptism now drives him to the wilderness to be tempted. The Spirit is not only the sweet heavenly dove; the Spirit is also the driving, strenuous power of God. For Jesus as for Job, Satan is the tempter but he tempts under the Spirit's auspices.

We note that the struggle between Jesus and the devil is in large measure a struggle over exegesis. Like duelling rabbis they hurl texts at one another. The texts Jesus cites all come from Deuteronomy, that great retelling of Israel's forty-year test in the wilderness. Again Jesus recapitulates and completes Israel's story.

For Matthew this is primarily a story of Messianic temptations. What does it mean for Jesus to be Son of God? If, as Matthew suggests, these are real temptations then Jesus really has to choose.

In the first temptation Jesus chooses to trust God rather than to rely on his own wonder-working powers, and in particular he chooses to trust God's word. In the second temptation Jesus chooses to honour God as God, the one who disposes, not some little god at our disposal. In the third temptation Jesus chooses to worship God: all his allegiance is due to the one who calls him 'Son'.

Each of the temptations will find its echo later in the Gospel. In the feeding stories Jesus does bring forth bread for the hungry, but even there he makes clear that it is God's word that feeds even more richly than food. In the crucifixion those who taunt him echo the devil: 'If you are the Son of God, come down from the cross.' Again Jesus resists this temptation, to remain faithful to death. Beyond death Jesus does receive all authority, not just on earth but in heaven, too, but it is still not the authority of princes and principalities. He receives the authority by which he sends his disciples forth to make disciples and to baptize, the authority of presence.

Matthew 4.12–23

Again our story is shaped by continuity. Even Jesus' location in Capernaum lives out the prophecy of Isaiah 9.1–2. And again John the Baptist provides the link between what is old and what is new. Jesus' ministry begins only after John has been arrested. John's arrest foreshadows Jesus' own fate (the verb for 'arrested', *paradidomi*, can also be translated as 'handed over' or 'betrayed'). The same verb is used to describe Jesus' destiny in Matthew. When Jesus begins to preach he says just what John said in Matthew 3.2. The old is fulfilled and recapitulated in the new.

The reference to Galilee of the Gentiles in the fulfilment quotation from Isaiah hints at what the end of the story will confirm: this light is for all the nations, not just for Israel.

Matthew slightly shifts Mark's report of Jesus' first preaching. In Mark 1.15 Jesus says, 'The time is fulfilled and the kingdom of God is at hand; repent and believe in the gospel.' Matthew's account of the same proclamation is this: 'Repent for the kingdom of heaven has come near.' The presence of the kingdom is the gift and obligation that provide good news first to Israel and then to the world.

The mission to Israel begins with the calling of the disciples. We do not know whether the disciples had ever seen Jesus before or even heard of him. What we have is a clear sense of the pure authority by which Jesus can command and the disciples obey.

We will see as the Gospel continues that these disciples fill a variety of functions. The twelve disciples represent twelve tribes of the new Israel. They also represent church leaders of Matthew's own time. And they represent surrogates for all of us who hear or read this story – the blessings and the challenges bestowed on them are bestowed on us as well.

They begin well, not counting the cost, leaving everything. He says 'Follow.' They follow.

Matthew 5.1–12

Matthew has organized material in his sources into five great discourses: the Sermon on the Mount in chapters 5–7, the commissioning of the disciples in chapter 10, the parables in chapter 13, the discourse on church order in chapter 18 and the eschatological sermon in chapters (23)24–25.

In the Sermon on the Mount Jesus speaks to the disciples in the presence of the crowds. The Sermon seems to be intended primarily for those who are committed to following Jesus, but its picture of the faithful life invites the curious and the seeking to listen too (see 7.28–29).

The Sermon begins with blessings. The Greek word translated 'blessing' is probably borrowed from the Septuagint translation of a Hebrew word that can mean either 'happy' or 'blessed'. There are Old Testament beatitudes in Psalms 41.1 and 65.4.

Note that these are blessings and not commands. This text is primarily descriptive, not prescriptive.

There is some indication that Matthew, using the same source as Luke, makes the Beatitudes more explicitly 'spiritual' and less explicitly 'material'. In Luke Jesus blesses 'the poor'; in Matthew he blesses the 'poor in spirit'. (Compare Luke 6.20 with Matthew 5.3 and Luke 6.21 with Matthew 5.6.)

These are eschatological blessings. Those who are merciful have not yet obtained God's mercy, nor are those who hunger and thirst for righteousness yet satisfied. Yet there will be signs throughout the Gospel of mercy in the present age, prefiguring the kingdom to come.

These blessings are all promises from God and about God, but the rest of the Sermon on the Mount will give important clues to the ways in which faithful people can share in God's eschatological work of blessing. Jesus is himself the first fruits of the blessings yet to be consummated. The promise is not yet complete, but in Jesus and those who follow him, the days of blessedness have begun.

Matthew 5.13–20

Matthew 5.13–16 concludes and illumines the meaning of the Beatitudes. 5.17–20 provides the explanation and framework for the 'antitheses' that follow.

The Beatitudes describe for us what it means to be the earth's salt and the world's light. Here are the kind of people who give savour to the earth and who illumine the world's darkness. Without these the earth grows dull and the world stays dark.

Matthew is much less concerned about 'works righteousness' than those of us shaped by Luther's powerful concern. John the Baptist has told us that fruits matter, and the light and salt the faithful bring are the fruits of their repentance and fidelity. Note, however, that the purpose of doing good works is not to add to our glory, but to God's.

Whether or not Matthew has read Paul's letters, his next claim stands at least in tension with, if not in contradiction to, much of what Paul writes in Romans and Galatians.

Matthew, writing for Jewish Christians and in tension with the synagogue, wants to insist that Jesus does not replace the Law. Jesus fulfils the Law. The righteousness illustrated and commanded by Jesus is not the Law's end but its consummation. Though the passage about light ends with humble attention to the glory of God, it is hard to miss the competitive note that helps move us toward the antitheses: 'Unless your righteousness is greater than that of the scribes and Pharisees you will by no means enter into the kingdom of heaven.'

A theme emerges that we will see throughout the Gospel. As for master, so for disciples. Jesus is the light of the world (4.16). The believers are lesser lights, standing with Jesus against the darkness. Jesus is the fulfilment of the Law – its truer interpreter than Moses. Believers are obedient to that richer law – clearer and stronger in their devotion than Moses' supposed followers, those annoying scribes and Pharisees.

Matthew 5.21–37

This passage is the first half of the so-called antitheses which make a contrast between the old and the new: 'you have heard that it was said to those of ancient times . . . *but* I say to you . . .'

'You have heard that it was said . . .' is a kind of euphemism. Every reader of Matthew's Gospel will know *who* said these things. It was Moses. Jesus makes an astonishing claim. 'Moses had authority . . . but my authority is greater.'

Yet the preceding passage (5.17–20) has also made clear that Jesus preaches, not to contradict what Moses says, but to complete it. By setting up the antitheses in this way Matthew makes clear that Jesus teaches the fuller and richer application of a Torah which stands till the end of time.

5.21–26 deals with the first commandment of the second tablet of the Law: 'You shall not kill.' For Jesus' followers it is not enough not to kill the other, one must not wish the other dead. If we wish the other to go to hell, we stand in danger of hellfire ourselves. The question of whether Matthew (or Jesus) thinks of hell literally as an eternity of fire, or uses the image of Gehenna, the fiery trash dump outside Jerusalem as a metaphor, is unanswerable. What is clear enough is that intention counts, eternally.

5.27–32 applies a similar standard to marriage. Here the first question is not only whether one physically violates the marriage vows but whether one wishfully contemplates such violation. True lawfulness is a whole-hearted matter. The second question is whether officially legal divorce might still violate the deeper intention of the Law, which reminds us that true marriage is a whole-hearted matter, and a lifelong matter, too.

5.33–37 tells the hearers that oath-taking is a way of tinkering with God, using words to manipulate God into serving our desires. 'Speak straight.'

Matthew 5.38–48

This passage continues and concludes the antitheses.

Jesus expands on the law of retribution found in Leviticus 24.19–20: 'Anyone who maims another shall suffer the same injury in return; fracture for fracture, eye for eye, tooth for tooth; the injury inflicted is the injury to be suffered' (see Exod. 21.24; Deut. 19.21).

In the Torah the concern for proportionate justice is in part a protection against disproportionate revenge. The death penalty is not an appropriate punishment for knocking out someone's tooth.

Jesus calls for disproportionate mercy. He gives examples of what he means. Only the first relates directly to the question of retaliation, the call to 'turn the other cheek'. The other three examples – giving the cloak, going the second mile, and giving ungrudgingly – expand the range of Jesus' concern from questions of punishment to questions of generosity. The commentaries give some of the probable background for the injunctions in the Roman practices of the time, but the application is clear enough: give more than is asked or give whatever is asked ungrudgingly.

In the final antithesis Jesus, or Matthew, uses homiletical licence in the citation of Scripture. The command to 'love the neighbour' is found in Leviticus 19.18, but there is no corresponding command there, or anywhere else, to hate the enemy. Such hatred is so much a part of the human condition that we hardly need a command to enforce it.

Jesus again takes the intention of the command and drives deeper. If love is the rule, we cannot limit love to those closest to us. Jesus calls us to *imitatio Dei*, the imitation of God. God's great impartiality, that mercy that sends sun and rain, is a model for our impartiality. There are no tests by which to limit our obligation of love.

In this context, at least, to be perfect as God is perfect is to be perfectly impartial.

Matthew 6.1–6, 16–21

It is odd to leave the Lord's Prayer out of the reading, because that prayer provides both the model and the motivation for avoiding the kind of pretentious piety Jesus here opposes. To place oneself entirely in the will of God is to guard against the ongoing temptation to show off our faithfulness for the sake of others.

Showing off is what's at stake here. Jesus assumes that his faithful followers will pray, give alms and fast. However, he makes a strong, even a harsh claim. We can choose between human approval and God's approval. People see what's obvious – visible generosity (the plaque on the new building; the list of 'Friends of the School' in the alumni magazine). God sees what is secret: the cost or ease of the giving. People hear what's obvious: loud prayers. God hears what's silent, the One to whom all hearts are open, all desires known, and from whom no secrets are hid. People are impressed by the visible: the outward signs of ascetic practice. God honours the invisible: the cheerful face that hides the contrite heart.

There is some irony in the fact that in many Christian churches, we usually read this text on Ash Wednesday morning and then undergo the imposition of ashes so that our piety can be entirely visible, if puzzling, to our friends and fellow workers for the rest of the day. The text reminds us, of course, that the deepest repentance comes from the heart, and bears fruits of righteousness.

The last part of the passage is a Proverbs-like reminder that the treasures we store up will pass away (as, of course, will we). The alms, prayers and fasting we entrust to heaven will endure. It is a cautionary note that often the best way to check on the state of our hearts is to look at the priorities in our budgets.

Matthew 6.24–34

We start with the end. Matthew 6.34 seems a kind of prudential tag-on to a homily on providence. It may reflect an original word of Jesus, but if so he was having a more cynical day than usual. More likely it's a kind of popular saying that Matthew adds to the text because it seems to fit thematically, if not theologically.

Matthew 6.24 also sounds a note that recalls wisdom literature. Wisdom literature is literature that encourages us to look at the world as it really is and to see in ordinary consequences the hand of God. Here Jesus says, 'Here's how it is. You can't serve two masters because to do so would be to divide your heart, and the broken heart won't long endure.'

The heart of the passage is a kind of argument common to Jewish teachers of Jesus' time – 'how much more'. If God feeds the birds and clothes the flowers, how much more will God clothe the people God loves? Logically the indicative precedes the imperative: this is the kind of God we have, therefore do not worry about your life. Taken literally such advice might force us to empty our savings accounts and cancel our insurance policies. Taken seriously the words about the birds and the lilies push us away from anxiety to what is very nearly its opposite – trust.

When Jesus says that if we seek the kingdom of God and God's righteousness 'all these things will be given to you as well', it is clear that he is not preaching a prosperity gospel. In a sermon damning mammon, Jesus hardly means that those who seek God's bounty will receive mammon's rewards. Rather what we are promised is just what the passage says: food enough, clothing enough, time enough. Bread for the day. Our daily bread.

Matthew 7.21–29

The first great sermon of Matthew's Gospel draws to a close. When the crowds acknowledge in 7.29 that Jesus 'taught them as one having authority, and not as their scribes', it is clear that they are beginning to understand what God is doing among them in Jesus. What they do not yet acknowledge is that Jesus teaches with an authority greater than that of Moses, too.

Verses 21–23 need to be understood in the context of Matthew 7.15–20. Jesus is concerned not only with ordinary Christians but especially with Christian leaders who talk the talk but do not walk the walk. The reminder that not everyone who names Jesus as Lord will enter the kingdom recalls the condemnation of visible piety in chapter 6. It may be that saying 'Lord' loudly and often enough can get in the way of serving Christ's righteousness, softly and persistently.

Matthew 7.24–27 recalls the imagery of Psalm 1. In the psalm those who delight in God's Torah are like trees planted by streams of water, and those who ignore God's Torah are like chaff, blown away. In the sermon those who delight in serving Jesus' Torah are like those who build their house upon a rock; those who ignore Jesus' Torah are like those who build upon the sand. The storm is both a metaphor and an eschatological promise. The consummation of all things is coming: those who follow Christ build on the rock that will not be shaken.

The end of the sermon recalls the sermon's beginning. Those who do build on the rock of Christ and seek his righteousness are the blessed. The Beatitudes pronounce a blessing on those who hunger and thirst for righteousness. The rest of the Sermon on the Mount helps us to see what that longing looks like.

Matthew 9.9–13, 18–26

Because tax collectors were hired to collaborate with the Roman occupiers and were notorious cheats, their fellow Jews despised them. Now as in chapter 4, Jesus calls a disciple, without forewarning but also without precondition. Here, however, he calls a man rejected and despised.

The call sets up the dispute story that follows. In Matthew's narrative world the Pharisees have become surrogates for Matthew's own opponents.

Jesus defends with three related sayings the ungrudging hospitality that the Pharisees begrudge. First there is the proverb that the sick, not the well, need a physician. The irony of course is that as the Gospel unfolds it will be clear that the Pharisees suffer a kind of sickness unto death.

Second there is the quotation from Hosea 6.6, 'I desire mercy and not sacrifice' (see also Matt. 12.7). Here presumably mercy is what Jesus shows and his followers will show; sacrifice is the devotion to narrow piety.

Third there is the claim about Jesus' own vocation. He has come to call sinners not the righteous. Of course Jesus calls the sinners to *be* righteous (see 5.20).

Matthew takes the combined stories of the ruler's daughter and the woman suffering from haemorrhages from Mark. In the one case it is the woman's own faith that opens the way for Jesus' healing. In the other case it is the faith of the girl's father. It may be, as some of the freer translations suggest, that the father is a synagogue leader (the Greek has only 'leader') and if so his attitude is contrasted to that of the Pharisees. Jesus reaches out to heal the young girl; the woman reaches out to be healed by Jesus.

In the two passages for today Jesus reaches out to three people judged unclean by their compatriots – a tax collector, a woman with a flow of blood, a child who is (or appears to be) dead. What he provides is 'mercy and not sacrifice'.

Matthew 9.35—10.8 (9–23)

In Protestant churches in the United States, the concluding verse of this section is often used as a call to the offering. 'Freely you have received, freely give.' This limits too narrowly the scope of Jesus' words to his disciples. What they have freely received in Matthew is the astonishing gift of discipleship, and discipleship is what they are to give.

Matthew 10 is the second great discourse in the Gospel, the first being the Sermon on the Mount. The Sermon on the Mount seems to be directed to all believers. This sermon is directed to the twelve who are the closest circle of Jesus' followers. Through them we may guess that it is directed to Christian church leaders and missionaries of Matthew's own time.

Of course Matthew did not use our chapter and verse numbering, and the end of chapter 9 provides the setting for the beginning of chapter 10. The people who come to Jesus for direction and healing foreshadow those who will come to church leaders after his death and resurrection. They are to be shepherds for his sheep; they are to be workers for his harvest.

The first responsibility of the shepherd and the worker is to declare what Jesus, and before him John the Baptist, have declared. 'The kingdom of heaven is at hand' (see 3.2 and 4.17).

The authority of the disciples replicates the authority of Jesus himself. The next verses (10.9–23) make clear that the danger to the disciples will replicate Jesus' story, too.

Here Jesus states that the mission of the disciples extends only to Israel. Is this an historical reminiscence that the mission to the Gentiles begins only after the resurrection (as seen in 28.16–20), or is there some kind of contrast between the earliest mission of the disciples and the broader mission of those who will follow?

In either case what we see clearly here is what Bonhoeffer called 'the cost of discipleship'.

Matthew 10.24–39

I know a number of American and European Christians who have annoyed their families by their decision to follow Christ. But not many have had to choose between Christ and family. Some Asian and African friends, however, tell difficult stories of being disowned and having to find a new family in the community of Christ.

Matthew's Gospel was written in part to encourage synagogue members to risk separation from family and friends in order to follow Jesus. Christianity was not just counter-cultural; it was dangerous.

Matthew 10.24–25 sets the context. If the disciples are not greater than the master, then they should expect the same mistreatment that their master received. That is the hard news. The good news is that they *are* related to Jesus; they are disciples of the one great teacher and servants of the one true Lord and members of his household. (Incidentally this is one of the few places in Matthew where the term 'disciple' is used rather narrowly to refer to the student of an authoritative teacher.)

The rest of this passage sets the call to courage within both a theo-centric and an eschatological context.

The theocentric context includes the strong affirmation of God's providence. It is God whose eye is on the sparrow and who counts each hair on the believer's head. Persecution and slander cannot separate believers from the providential care of God.

The eschatological context calls people to courageous proclamation and service because at the end of history, Jesus himself will stand as advocate for the faithful. Verse 39 underlines the eschatological promise and threat. If you try to hang onto your life and let go your faithfulness, you will also lose your life, eternally. If you are willing to let your life go for the sake of the kingdom you will have your life given you again, richly, eternally.

Matthew 10.40–42

Though we have to guess about the details behind this text, Matthew seems to envision a church that is comprised both of those who travel for the sake of the Gospel and of those who stay put. It is always tempting to think that the more heroic the service the greater the reward in the Christian life, but Jesus here insists that God's reward is not graded (a first for prophets; second for righteous people, and so on) but is entirely generous and gracious.

The promise of the passage depends on a theme that is also evident in the gospel according to, and in the letters of, Paul. Within the world of Jesus and Matthew's time, the one who is sent takes on all the authority of the sender. The Greek word for sending is *apostello*, and an apostle is one who is sent. Jesus is sent by God; the disciples are sent by Jesus. First Jesus and then Christian missionaries share in the very authority of God; all are apostles.

In the first century there were Christian prophets who went from town to town preaching the gospel. They depended on the hospitality of more settled Christians to provide for their well-being. It's less clear whether the term 'righteous' refers to a particular group of missionaries (10.41b). In Matthew all Christians are called to be more 'righteous' than the scribes and Pharisees. The 'little ones' are almost certainly those Christians who do not have special responsibilities, authorities or titles but who also are sent out for the sake of the gospel (see 18.6–10).

In preaching this text one might want to attend to ideas of hospitality, interdependence, the variety of gifts and the promise of God's eschatological reward for the 'great' and the 'small' alike.

Matthew 11.2–11

Theologically it makes perfect sense for Matthew to record this query by John the Baptist at this point in his Gospel. John's question becomes the occasion for Jesus to reaffirm the nature of his ministry as a sign of God's arriving kingdom. Homiletically the placement in the narrative may also make sense. When John the Baptist is free he can honour Jesus as the Messiah, but when John is imprisoned it looks as though Jesus hasn't lived up to his press. If this is the Messiah, where's the messianic age?

Jesus' answer reminds us that we will be able to tell the true Messiah from pretenders by looking at his fruits (7.15–20). Jesus acts out the signs that mark the kingdom's beginning. Jesus' speech ends with the tenth beatitude (the other nine are in Matthew 5.3–12). 'Blessed is anyone who takes no offence at me.' Applied to John this is a modest blessing for a modest virtue.

We see in vv. 7–11 that John is part of the preparation for God's kingdom but he is not yet a citizen of that kingdom. Those whom Jesus blesses in chapter 5 are already participants in the realm of heaven. John foreshadows many believers from the first century until now. He receives the blessing that falls on those who honour Jesus but do not yet follow him.

It is unfortunate that the Lectionary cuts off Jesus in mid-sentence. Jesus not only calls attention to John's greatness, he calls explicit attention to John's role. John is Elijah. Perhaps Jesus means this metaphorically. More likely the text reflects the belief in first-century Palestine that since Elijah had not died on earth but been lifted bodily to heaven, he would return to be the forerunner of the Messiah. For Matthew and for Jesus John may not just have been Elijah-like, he was the real Elijah pointing the way to the real King of the Jews.

Matthew 11.16–19, 25–30

We start at the end. In this passage Jesus sounds very much like Sophia, Wisdom, the gentle presence of God who calls people to herself. A yoke makes it possible for the oxen to bear the burden that would otherwise be too heavy. The burden is light only because the yoke is easy. Frequently the rabbis refer to the yoke of the Law as the way of bearing and easing the burden of responsibility to God. It seems odd, after we have heard the Sermon on the Mount and the instructions to the disciples in Matthew 10 to think of Jesus' yoke as easy. Yet precisely because Jesus gives us signposts on the road of obedience he makes the way of obedience accessible. Were it not for this passage we would be hard pressed to believe that the Jesus we have seen in this Gospel is either gentle or humble in heart. Perhaps his humility is simply his generosity. He shares with his disciples the markers that will enable them to follow him on the way.

The little parable with which our passage begins is hardly gentle or humble, either. Here Jesus implicitly identifies himself with Wisdom. He points to the deeds he performs in order to call his hearers to repentance. He accuses them of playing the familiar game of 'damned if you don't and damned if you do'. John is criticized for being too ascetic; Jesus for not being ascetic enough. Maybe when Wisdom comes to call she is forever surprising us, looking like restraint one day and like abundance the next. Verses 25–27 seem almost to have been cut and pasted from the Gospel according to John. The unity of the Father and the Son is fulfilled in the unity of the Son and those whom he chooses. Through Christ, the Wisdom of God is brought into the life of disciples, and hard-pressed as they may be, they find rest for their souls.

Matthew 13.1–9, 18–23

Here begins the third great sermon in Matthew, the chapter of parables. The Lectionary joins together what St Matthew puts asunder – the parable of the sower and its explanation. What comes between our two passages is Jesus' explanation of why he tells parables (13.10–17). He tells parables, not to make the kingdom clear to all, but to make the kingdom just as mysterious as it really is. This explanation of how hard it is to understand parables prepares us for what seems a disjuncture between the fairly straightforward parable of 13.1–9 and its fairly complicated explanation in 13.18–23.

Though Matthew borrows heavily from Mark in his telling of this parable, he adds his own nuances to the story. Both subtle and clever is the way in which Matthew introduces the story: Jesus 'goes out' from the house to teach just as in the parable the sower 'goes out' to sow. It is clear from the very setting of the story that for Matthew Jesus is the sower, and that what he sows is the word, indeed the very word of these parables. Before our very eyes the word is sown and grows on some soil, dies on other. Jesus' word to the crowds: 'Whoever has ears, let him hear' also means 'be good soil'.

One reason that many scholars have thought that the explanation of the parable is a secondary addition to the parable itself is that the reference seems to have shifted. In the parable the seed is surely the word that Jesus sows in his preaching. In the explanation the different kinds of seed are the different kinds of people who hear and either do or do not keep the word.

The explanation is both a call to evangelism and a cautionary note. When the word is faithfully preached it will indeed bear fruit, but outsiders will be fruitless soil. Our business is to follow Jesus in sowing the word. What becomes of our sowing is in the hands of God.

Matthew 13.24–30, 36–43

Again the Lectionary leaves out the middle (13.31–35) that provides some of Matthew's interpretation of the parable of good seed and weeds. The parables of the mustard seed and of the leaven remind us that, weeds or no weeds, the promise of God is for generous, surprising, overwhelming abundance in the kingdom. The quotation from Psalm 78.2 provides the Matthean reminder that Jesus' use of parables acts out the clear intention of God, as foreshadowed in the Old Testament.

There are two competing interpretations of what the parable of the weeds and its explanation signify in Matthew. The first interpretation is that this is Matthew's way of dealing with the problem of a 'mixed' Church in his own time. Matthew's churches apparently contained both true disciples and those whose discipleship was much less certain. Perhaps Matthew here thinks of the kinds of seed in the preceding verses: those who don't understand, those who are scared, those who turn aside to earthly treasures. Matthew shifts the metaphor. Such seed produces only weeds. The way for the Church

35

to deal with the weeds is not through an annual pruning of the membership rolls. Leave the pruning to God.

The second interpretation is that this is Matthew's way of dealing with the reality of a 'mixed' world. While the Church may consist almost entirely of faithful disciples, the world is full of those who fail to understand. It is not the Church's job to impose its vision of fidelity upon the world. It is the Church's job to live out its own fidelity and to trust the final judgement of the world to God.

Both explanations acknowledge the fundamental apocalyptic framework in which Matthew sets these parables. The end of this struggle comes at the end of history, not in its midst. The end of struggle includes strong judgement. For Matthew real disobedience has real (and eternal) consequences.

Matthew 13.31–33, 44–52

We already noted our puzzlement that the Lectionary largely ignores the order of the parables in Matthew in order to make its own connections. This is a profoundly anti-canonical way to assign lections.

Matthew 13.31–33 presents us with two parables that stress the astonishing, superabundant generosity of the kingdom of heaven. Jesus takes two items familiar from the lives of his hearers and uses them as metaphors for God's reign. A small seed becomes a tree so great that the birds of the air can nest in its branches. Surely the hearers are meant to recall Ezekiel 17.23 where God promises that a remnant of the House of Israel will be saved like a spring from a cedar tree. The small seed sown in Jesus' word will grow into a towering tree serving like Israel as the sign of God's kingdom.

We do not know how much leaven is used to make dough of all that flour, a great deal no doubt. What we do know is that leaven works secretly, hidden in the midst of the dough as the kingdom is hidden in the midst of the world, but working toward its astonishing transformation.

I have heard sermons that suggest that the mustard seed was notoriously unruly and the leaven excessively smelly. The kingdom of heaven does not always grow politely or pleasantly, but recklessly and annoyingly. That is certainly true of the kingdom whether or not these parables say so.

The parables of Matthew 13.44–45 run roughshod over our careful distinction between grace and works. One person stumbles upon a treasure in sheer serendipity. Another seeks and seeks until he finds. What both receive is treasure, sought or unsought, equally precious for both.

This treasure, sought or unsought, demands response. The gift of discipleship is immeasurable; the cost of discipleship is giving up everything – every thing – for the sake of that treasure. Good news is hard news, and vice versa.

Matthew 14.13–21

A quick note on the end of the story. 'Five thousand men, not counting women and children . . .' does not mean that there were no women and children there to count, but rather that in addition to the men there were women and children.

This story of God's generosity in Jesus is preceded by two reminders of the way in which the kingdom still has to work against great opposition. Jesus is rejected at Nazareth; John is beheaded in the prison. The devil is at work in the field (see 13.36–43).

Yet this miracle story also acts out the more promising parables of chapter 13. The fish and loaves are like mustard seed. A little food turns into an overwhelming feast. They are like the leaven hidden in the loaf; the disciples fail to see the food hiding almost secretly in the midst of the crowd (see 13.31–33).

The disciples who are supposed to be insiders fail to know the mystery of the kingdom of heaven, that in the providence of God Jesus can take little and make it into much. In the light of his promise he calls them to their responsibility: 'You give them something to eat.' He acts through their service.

Notice that Jesus' compassion for the crowd is shown in two ways. He feeds them, and he heals them (14.14).

The feeding of all these people foreshadows the Eucharist. Jesus blesses the bread in 14.19 as he will bless it at the Last Supper in 26.26. Thinking of the Eucharist in the light of this passage, we can know that Christ takes what is apparently little and turns it into much.

The passage also reminds us that the table is not only a sign of Christ's spiritual compassion. Fed at the table the faithful work and serve in a world where sharing is one way that we show our willingness to give up everything for the treasure that surprises us, for the pearl we have sought and found (13.44–46).

Matthew 14.22–33

In much of Matthew, Peter serves as a paradigmatic disciple and a prototype of Christians in Matthew's own time. While in Mark Jesus often accuses the disciples of lack of understanding or faith, Matthew has apparently coined the term he uses more often: 'You little faith'.

Little faith is not faith that starts off in doubt. Peter starts off faithfully. 'If it is you, command me to come to you on the water.' Little faith is not half doubt; little faith is faith that starts in trust and dissipates in fear. Jesus calls Peter 'little faith' only after Peter has 'become frightened', and when Jesus rebukes Peter what he asks, literally, is not (as in the NRSV) 'Why did you doubt?', but 'Why did you hesitate?'

When Matthew says in v. 25 that the boat is being 'tormented' by the waves, the text begins to move toward allegory. Waves do not literally torment boats, but faithful people are tormented by hardship, persecution, loss.

Jesus' peculiar power is affirmed in two ways. First, when he speaks to the fearful disciples he says: 'Take heart, it is I.' 'It is I' translates the Greek *ego eimi*. Surely the reader is meant to recall Exodus 3.14 and Isaiah 43.3. 'I am' is God's self-designation, and readers remember the God who was revealed to Moses and who brought Israel through the waters (see also Psalm 77.19).

Second, the disciples 'worship' Jesus and say of him, 'Truly you are the Son of God.' This is the claim Peter himself will repeat and enrich in Matthew 16.16, just before sinking once again into little faith. Matthew's narrative is not so much a Gospel of progressive insight as a Gospel of repeated fits and starts; now they get it, now they don't. Now they are brave, now afraid.

Matthew 15.(10–20) 21–28

Much of Matthew's Gospel is concerned with drawing the distinctions between the way in which Jesus and his followers interpret the Law and the way in which Pharisaic Jews obey the Law.

In Matthew 15.1–20 Jesus puts his opponents to the test. Their attention to culinary cleanliness stands in the way of the deeper concern. It is not what people eat that defiles them but what people say.

In Matthew 15.21–28 Jesus himself is put to the test. He has just given permission to his disciples to break traditional boundaries between what is clean and what is unclean. Now a Canaanite begs Jesus to expand his own vision (remember 10.5–6, 24).

We can guess what is going on in Matthew's own community. Here and elsewhere in the Gospel we can see the beginnings of the pressure or the call to bring non-Jews into the Church. When Matthew shows Jesus changing his mind about dealing with this woman, he gives permission to his own Jewish Christian community to reach out more broadly. The resistance of the disciples to the woman is transparent to the resistance of some of Matthew's community to a broader Church.

Within the narrative, however, we are still left with the astonishing moment when the woman out-teaches the teacher. She provides her own antithesis (see 5.21–48): 'You have said that it is not fair to take the children's food and throw it to the dogs, but I say to you, even the dogs eat the crumbs that fall from the masters' table.'

Attempts to water down the harshness of Jesus' reply, suggesting that he doesn't really mean Samaritan dogs but cute little puppies, water down the astonishing denouement of the story. Jesus is out-argued.

The woman shows faith from beginning to end. With faith she addresses Jesus both as Lord and as Son of David and in faith she cries out for her daughter with what may already be a liturgical formula: 'Eleison . . . Kyrie', 'Have mercy . . . Lord'.

Matthew 16.13–20

As in Mark's Gospel, Peter's confession at Caesarea Philippi is a central moment in the development of the narrative. Jesus uses the term 'Son of Man' for himself as a kind of cipher. The sentence comes very close to meaning what Mark's version says: 'Who do people say that I am?' (Mark 8.27). Matthew's list of the answers the disciples provide echoes Mark's with the exception of the addition of the name 'Jeremiah' with 'one of the prophets'. Clearly 'people' say that Jesus stands in the great prophetic tradition.

Matthew's representative disciple is always Peter. Here he refers to him as Simon Peter probably to emphasize that Peter is a nickname for the sake of the pun that follows. Peter provides a Matthean expansion on the confession in Mark. 'You are the Christ, the Son of the Living God.' It is Jesus' sonship, not just his messiahship, that is central to this Gospel (cf. 3.17; 14.33; 17.5; 27.54). Only in Matthew does Jesus pronounce a beatitude on Simon. By referring to 'my Father in heaven' Jesus underlines the claim that Peter's claim is right. By insisting that it is God who has made this revelation to Peter, Jesus emphasizes that such faith is always a gift.

Now Jesus names Peter as the Church's rock. My own very Protestant interpretation is that Peter here receives authority as representative of the disciples. The term 'church' appears for the first time in this Gospel. This shows a shaping of the text after the resurrection when community had become 'church'. Peter is given the authority to 'bind and loose'. When rabbis 'bind' and 'loose' they provide helpful interpretations of the Torah. For Matthew the job of the disciples and of the teachers who will succeed them is to interpret what is binding in the Torah for Christian people.

There are two astonishing promises here. Church will prevail against all the powers of hell. What church does faithfully on earth, God confirms in heaven.

Matthew 16.21–28

Peter has taken two steps forward and now takes one step back.

In this first passion prediction, Jesus says that it is 'necessary' that he suffer in this way (Matthew uses the impersonal verb *dei*, 'it is necessary', often associated with the divine plan). For Matthew necessity is not a matter of fate but of providence. It is necessary for Jesus to suffer this way to live out the story that Matthew has been presenting from 1.1. The way we know that Jesus must live out this story is that the Old Testament confirms it time after time.

In the preceding passage Peter spoke what the heavenly Father had revealed. Now he has deserted heaven's cause entirely and no longer thinks God's thoughts but cowardly human thoughts. Indeed he plays Satan in the manner of Satan in Job 1.6–12 and Matthew 4.1–11. Jesus' words to Peter echo his words to the devil in 4.10. 'Go away, you Satan', there; 'Get behind me, you Satan', here.

We can gather from the end of our passage why Peter has rejected Jesus' prediction. In 16.24–26 Jesus makes clear that his suffering will be shared by those who follow him. Peter protests not only for Jesus' sake but also for his own, a little faith whose commitment is hampered not by doubt but by fear.

Our whole passage makes clear that for Matthew the gospel is good news and hard news both. Though we love to preach this text metaphorically, showing how great sacrifice can result in great spiritual riches, Matthew uses the story eschatologically. To gain one's life is to hold onto life in the judgement day that is coming.

Verse 28 may reflect the early Christian hope that Jesus would return within the lifetime of the first generation of believers, in which case the most honest way to deal with it pastorally and homiletically would be to admit that this particular hope was disconfirmed. Such disconfirmation would not negate the call to discipleship or the promises of God.

Another possibility is that it refers to and is fulfilled in the transfiguration, to which Matthew turns next.

Matthew 17.1–9

The story foreshadows the resurrection, since Peter, James and John are instructed to tell no one until 'after the Son of Man has been raised from the dead' (17.9). It foreshadows the Parousia ('the second coming'), and begins to fulfil the difficult promise that immediately precedes it: 'Truly I tell you, there are some standing here who will not taste death before they see the Son of Man coming in his kingdom' (16.28).

At three climactic moments in Matthew's narrative Jesus ascends a mountain: at the beginning of his first discourse – the Sermon on the Mount; at the end of the Gospel for the great commission; and here at the Gospel's centre. The mountain represents a place of particular authority. Unlike Mark, Matthew says that Jesus' countenance shone as well as his garments. Surely this reminds the reader of Moses on the mountain, too (see Exod. 34.29–35 and 24.16; cf. 2 Cor. 3.7–18).

Now Moses himself appears as representative of the Law. Elijah appears as the greatest prophet. Law and prophets witness to Jesus but are subordinate to him. The voice from heaven tells the disciples

41

'Listen to Jesus' – not listen to these three. And when the scene fades the disciples stand with Jesus alone.

On the mountain the disciples not only hear God, they see God with us. In Mark the disciples are terrified of the astonishing apparition (Mark 9.6); in Matthew they fall before Jesus in godly fear and are encouraged by his touch.

Peter wants equal treatment for the three sages, only one of whom is really Emmanuel, and he wants to turn a resting-place into a stopping-place.

God's voice says what God's voice said at the baptism (3.17), recalling especially Psalm 2.7. Rightly read Law, prophets, psalms all point to this one, God's true beloved son.

The command 'Listen to him' comes straight from Mark, but it is especially appropriate to Matthew where Jesus brings God's new law.

Matthew 18.15–20

Matthew 18 is the fourth of Jesus' long speeches in Matthew. He is speaking to the disciples. They are prototypes of the church leaders of Matthew's own time.

Matthew 18.15–20 is a remarkably straightforward prescription for appropriate church discipline. Note that the issue is one church member sinning against another, not the question of more general offences against outsiders or against society.

The instructions begin at the most hopeful point. If one believer sins against another let them try to work out restitution and reconciliation with each other. The Greek word here (*elenko*) however does not just mean have a friendly chat. It is a matter of convicting and perhaps even reproving. If reproof fails bring in witnesses, presumably both to strengthen your case and to provide testimony to the Church (see Deut. 19.15). If the disciplinary committee fails, bring the issue before the whole congregation.

The penalty for an unreconciled offence against a fellow Christian is that the offender should be treated as a Gentile and a tax collector. Does this mean that the offender should be forever shunned? Or does it mean that, like other tax collectors (see Matt. 9.10–13) and other Gentiles (see Matt. 28.17) the offender now becomes the object of appropriate evangelical zeal?

As binding and loosing were promised to Peter at Caesarea Philippi, so here binding and loosing become the gift and responsibility of the whole congregation. Here binding and loosing have less to do with right interpretation of Christ's Torah and more to do with counting or forgiving trespasses. But again the astonishing claim is that what the faithful do on earth binds God in heaven.

Jesus' promise to be with 'two or three gathered in his name' is not made as a promise for prayer groups or even for family devotions. It brings the authority of God with us to bear on the disciplinary problems of congregations. In this case God is with us as judge.

Matthew 18.21–35

Peter asks for an explanation of the demand for Christian discipline and at the same time helps shift the focus of the injunction from justice to mercy.

The context is still clearly within the Christian congregation. Whether the Greek term in Jesus' response to Peter should be translated 'seventy seven' or 'seventy times seven', it is clear that Matthew uses hyperbole; Jesus is saying there is no end to the obligation to forgive.

The parable does not really illustrate the demand for unending forgiveness, but lifts up a related aspect of forgiveness. It recalls the petition of the Lord's Prayer: 'Forgive us our debts, as we forgive our debtors' (6.12). In the parable the steward has already been forgiven his debts and fails miserably to forgive his debtors.

The parable is also full of hyperbole. The servant owes an inconceivably large amount, and the lord forgives with unlikely generosity. The kingdom of heaven pushes beyond our limits to the hyperbolic mercy of God.

Some of the features allegorically remind the hearers that the man who is a king is like the true king of the kingdom of heaven, the kingdom that this story purports to show. The servant bows down before the king in a gesture appropriate to worship, and beseeches him to 'have mercy' (v. 26). The 'lord' of the servant 'has mercy' and 'releases him' (v. 27). The language is psalm-like and liturgical.

The fundamental point of the parable is found in v. 33. 'Was it not necessary for you to have mercy on your fellow servant, as I had

43

mercy on you?' The Lord who was filled with compassion in v. 27 is now filled with anger.

The sentence imposed on the unforgiving servant again points to judgement both divine and eternal. There is no way in heaven or on earth that the servant will be able to repay everything he owes the master, or that the believer will be able to repay everything owed to God.

Matthew 20.1–16

This parable, found only in Matthew, puts the lie to the claim that Matthew is fundamentally concerned with fair return for steadfast obedience. The Gospel according to Matthew does again and again enjoin obedience, but it also shows that the kingdom is not a matter of fair play but of astonishing generosity.

Matthew probably uses this parable in part to encourage his own Jewish Christian community to be more open and welcoming to Gentiles who are now beginning to come 'late' into God's vineyard. (The vineyard recalls God's care for Israel in Isaiah 5.1–10.)

Matthew 20.16 looks back to Matthew 19.30. The parable therefore becomes for Matthew an illustration of the claim that in the kingdom expectations will be reversed: first will be last, last first. Peter will be blessed but others will be also (19.27–30). Jewish Christians will be given the promises, but Gentiles will, too.

The key verse, which the NRSV translates: 'Or are you envious because I am generous', can be more literally translated: 'Or is your eye evil because I am good' (20.15).

The scene is set dramatically. We stand with the early workers, promised our daily wage. When we see the late workers get just what we were promised, we are filled with expectation. Twice the hours, surely twice the wage.

The story makes clear that the business of the kingdom is not business.

No one is cheated in this parable. The landlord gives precisely what the landlord promises. The covenant is kept absolutely. The problem for the long-time workers is not that the owner has been ungenerous to them but that he has been so generous to others.

Some days that is truly annoying. How did those people receive such mercy? Some days it is truly comforting. How did we receive such mercy, latecomers that we are, every one?

Matthew 21.1–11

For Matthew the Old Testament is the telling (not just the fore-telling) of Jesus' story. Matthew's major contribution to the telling of the story of Jesus' entry into Jerusalem is the mixed citation from Isaiah 62.11 and Zechariah 9.9.

This is not a story of people astonished to discover that the so-called King of the Jews rides into town on a donkey. Rather Jesus shows just exactly what readers of Zechariah would expect him to show. He is a king, and his riding on a donkey is proof of that claim. Further, he is a humble king. Remember that when Jesus presents himself as God's wisdom come to humankind he says of himself: 'I am humble and lowly of heart,' using just the same adjective (*praus*) that Zechariah uses in Matthew's quotation (cf. Matt. 11.29). Now God's Wisdom enters a city that will soon enough reject it.

The unique claim that Jesus took both the donkey and its colt probably also derives from Matthew's concern to show Zechariah's claim lived out. It looks as though Matthew didn't know as much about Hebrew poetic parallelism as we do. He certainly knew enough about transportation to know it unlikely that Jesus straddled two beasts, so we are probably to imagine Jesus riding on the donkey with the colt tethered alongside.

We note that as usual Jesus is in command of the situation. He knows what the disciples will find and he tells them how to find it. He acts out the acclamation of the crowds: 'This is the prophet Jesus, from Nazareth in Galilee' (21.10).

The term that the crowds shout, 'Hosanna', is a transliteration of the Hebrew word that originally meant 'Save, we pray.' By Matthew's time it seems to have become a term of acclamation, but for Matthew who loves the hidden meaning of familiar words, the acclamation may also be petition. 'Lord, save.' That, of course, is what we will see Jesus do in the events that follow.

Matthew 21.12–16

In Matthew 21.12–13 Matthew picks up themes from Mark. The issue seems not to be the worth of temple worship in itself but the abuse of the Temple that is at stake here. Like Mark, drawing on Isaiah 56.7, Matthew says that the money changers and those who sell doves have made what should be a house of prayer into a den of thieves.

Matthew's 21.14–16 is our evangelist's addition to the material on the temple cleansing that he takes over from Mark.

The healing of the blind and lame continues the messianic healings that have marked Jesus' ministry from beginning to end. The cry of the children prolongs the triumphal entry. The quotation, from Psalm 8.3, is from the Septuagint version of the psalm. Psalm 8, with its reference to the Son of Man and the subjection of all things under his feet, is used elsewhere in the New Testament as a christological psalm, and Matthew may reflect that usage (cf. 1 Cor. 15.27, Eph. 1.22).

The opposition of the chief priests and the scribes becomes one more example of the mounting opposition that will all too soon lead to Calvary.

The fact that the Roman authorities considered Jesus dangerous enough to be executed, and the continuing references to the threat to destroy the Temple in the various trial scenes of the Gospels, may suggest that what seems to Matthew a messianic narrative seemed to the Roman authorities a threat to the uneasy status quo that kept Roman authority and temple piety in an uneasy alliance.

In this passage Matthew shows Jesus claiming his rightful lordship. As David's son he can claim the Temple, rid it of those who would corrupt it for money's sake and restore it, if only temporarily, to its rightful role as a house of prayer. The kingdom of heaven is always breaking in.

Matthew 21.23–32

In Matthew, Jesus consistently outwits his opposition. Often he does this by posing a question that it is imprudent for them to answer. This passage is an example of that. Here the opponents are apparently trying to trap Jesus in admitting his sonship in such a way that they can accuse him of blasphemy.

In all three synoptic Gospels this dispute takes place in the Temple where Jesus has just demonstrated his own messianic authority.

The passage takes us back beyond John's queries from prison to the beginning of the Gospel where John presents Jesus as the eschatological figure who will baptize in the Holy Spirit and in fire and will bring God's judgement on earth (3.11–12).

The contrast between heavenly and human authority recalls Jesus' rebuke to Peter in 16.23 where Peter is thinking 'human' instead of 'Godward' thoughts. John the Baptist clearly has his mind set on God's truths. The opponents show that their authority is derived from human beings by worrying precisely about what human beings will think of them if they belittle the popular opinion of God.

In Matthew, Jesus is a great divider. Everyone has to decide where his authority comes from. Ignorance, evasion, self-interest are no excuse. To those who seek to avoid his authority he gives no answers; he shows forth the authority to refuse.

The parable that follows is found only in Matthew. The parable doesn't work quite into the neat allegory that we might have expected. In the history of salvation it would be the scribes and high priests who are asked first to work in the vineyard and the outsiders (tax collectors in Jesus' and John the Baptist's time, Gentiles in Matthew's time) who would first refuse but then go. The parable is bound to recall the vineyard of Isaiah 5. The expectations of the audience are reversed. Those who seem to be devoted to the divine are slaves to human expectations.

Matthew 21.33–46

Matthew adds 21.34 to his source. The verb *eggizo* is the verb that announces the drawing near of the kingdom (see 3.2; 4.17; 10.7). 'When the harvest was at hand . . .' makes clear that for Matthew this is a parable of the inbreaking of the kingdom.

The implicit allusion to Isaiah 5 in the preceding parable is here made explicit with the phrases quoted in 21.33. This is a story about Israel, God's own vineyard.

In Matthew the story is an allegory whose meaning depends on Jesus' death and resurrection. The quotation from Psalm 118.22–23 in 21.43 is a familiar Christian testimony bearing witness to the meaning of the resurrection. Christ is the rejected stone and after his resurrection becomes head of the corner (see Acts 4.11 and 1 Pet. 2.7).

Matthew makes clear in 21.45 that this parable is not directed against Israel as a whole but against the leaders. The crowds regard Jesus as a prophet but they still do not fully know how to place him in his own allegory: he is, after all, the son.

We note the dogged persistence of the landlord in claiming his own. The servants who are sent to the vineyard are the prophets, perhaps including John the Baptist. The son is Jesus, who will be killed outside the city as the son in the parable is killed outside the vineyard. The landowner is God, and the final threat within the parable points toward eschatological judgement and perhaps to the fall of Jerusalem in AD 70.

The 'other tenants' of the parable and the 'nation' of 21.43 may refer to the Gentiles, or perhaps more likely to a new generation of faithful leaders within Israel – Christian Jews. As is so often the case with faithful people, these new tenants bear fruit (see 3.8; 7.16–20; 23.33; 13.8).

(Note that the early manuscript evidence is divided on whether v. 44 should be included in this text.)

Matthew 22.1–14

This is a parable that Matthew and Luke share in common but do not borrow from Mark. For Matthew this is the third 'conflict' parable in a row and the third parable that deals with the question of who will and will not inherit the kingdom.

The parable begins with the guests who were too busy with the matters of this world to come to the wedding feast. They not only refuse the invitation, but like the tenants in the preceding parable, some of them even mistreat and kill the king's servants. Again we think of the prophets. In response to this refusal, the king sends out and gathers a crowd from the highways and byways. (Presumably the tax collectors and sinners were as surprised to be included in Jesus' banquets as the leaders were to have them included.) Those who refused the invitation have their city burned – probably a reference to the destruction of Jerusalem. This detail is found only in Matthew.

Matthew edits the parable in interesting ways. He identifies the wedding banquet as a banquet for the son, allegorically for Jesus (see 25.1–13). He gives a list of the excuses the first invitees use for refusing to come, opening up a treasure of homiletical possibilities.

It is Matthew who adds to the parable the whole sub-plot of the guest who comes without a wedding invitation. One suspects that this is one of those places where Matthew is worried about the mixed nature of his own congregation. Whatever Matthew has in mind it is clear that being the last invited is in itself no guarantee that you'll be invited to stay. The invitation to the kingdom is the beginning, not the end of the story. Since this is the Gospel according to Matthew, we can be quite sure that Jesus wants latecomers to bear the fruits of their faithfulness.

Matthew 22.15–22

We now notice that the Pharisees seem to have learned a trick from Jesus. (No one knows just who the Herodians were.) Just as Jesus' question to the opponents about John the Baptist could not be answered without making trouble, so their question to him cannot be answered without making trouble.

Iago-like they try to flatter themselves into his favour and then ask: 'Is it lawful to give taxes to the emperor or not?'

If he answers yes, he will incur the wrath of the more radical Judaeans who want to refuse the poll tax owed to the Romans. If he answers no, he will incur the wrath of Rome.

Jesus knows and outsmarts them. They hold up a coin: 'Whose image and whose epigraph is this?' he asks. What Matthew probably describes is Jesus holding up the denarius with Tiberius' picture. When they answer 'Caesar's', he has them caught: give to Caesar what belongs to Caesar, to God what belongs to God.

There are at least two ways of interpreting this. (1) Perhaps it does give a rationale for paying the tax, no matter how much one opposes Rome. The coins are Caesar's business and he can lay claim to them. The verb Matthew uses might suggest this: 'Give back to Caesar what (you got from) Caesar.' (2) Perhaps Jesus' word leaves us pondering what really does belong to God and what really does belong to Caesar. Perhaps this it not a one-rule-fits-all maxim, but a kind of parabolic guideline for deciding our loyalties.

One thing is clear to anyone who knows Scripture. The coin may bear Caesar's image, but the listeners bear God's image (Gen. 1.26). Whose image is on the coin? Caesar's. Whose image is on us? God's. If you can give Caesar the coin without giving some of yourself with it, all right. But everyone knows that that's not as easy as it sounds.

Matthew 22.34–46

In these two passages Jesus shows himself again to be a master interpreter of Scripture. In the passage on the great commandment both Jesus' texts are taken from Hebrew Scripture – Deuteronomy 6.5 and Leviticus 19.18. What is striking is that he brings the two together and makes them equally important.

In 22.37 Matthew and Mark add to the passage from Deuteronomy the requirement that we love God with the understanding as well as the heart and soul. Matthew also adds to Mark that the whole Law 'hangs' from these commandments, so they become not only a summary of Torah but its basis and grounding.

Despite our contemporary attempt to turn the dual commandment into a trifold commandment: Love God, Love yourself, Love your neighbour, Jesus seems to assume that we love ourselves well enough.

The passage on the son of David is particularly tricky because one of the major purposes of Matthew's first chapter has apparently been to show precisely that Jesus is son of David (1.17, 21, 25). Here Matthew deepens the tradition about Davidic sonship; he does not deny it. There is a kind of parallel with the antitheses, where the Mosaic law is not abrogated but deepened and expanded. The text Jesus draws on is Psalm 110.1. Like Psalm 8 (see above, on p. 46), Psalm 110 is much used as a christological text in the early Church (see Acts 2.34–35; 1 Cor. 15.25; Heb. 1.13). Jesus simply assumes that Psalm 110 was written by David under the inspiration of the Spirit (see 2 Sam. 23.2). The text can be glossed in the following way: 'The Lord (God) said to my (David's) Lord (Jesus), "Sit at my right hand."' If David foresees Jesus' enthronement and calls Jesus Lord, Jesus cannot (simply) be David's son.

This answer is apparently so authoritative (or so puzzling) that the oral opposition of the Pharisees comes to an end. They will find other ways to get at Jesus.

Matthew 23.1–12

Matthew 23 helps us reconstruct the social context of the Gospel according to Matthew. Matthew is providing guidance for Jewish Christians who are trying to find their own identity in relation to the synagogue. According to Matthew 23.1–3, the scribes and Pharisees are still interpreters of the true Law. Because they sit on the seat of Moses, their interpretations demand attention.

However, their lives do not bear imitating. What is at stake here is not false teaching; it is right teaching and false living.

Matthew writes in a context of serious friction between Jewish and Jewish Christian leaders. The passage has all the polemical power of a family feud. The scribes and Pharisees would hardly recognize themselves in this description.

The warnings against hypocritical leaders, however, have a pertinence that transcends confessional differences.

Here are the places where religious leadership can go wrong:

1 Religious leaders can ask much of others and do little to help others with the burdens they impose (23.4).
2 Religious leaders can practise conspicuous piety (23.5).
3 Religious leaders can love publicity, hurrying to stand beside the famous politician just in time for the press to take the picture (23.6).
4 Religious leaders can love their titles (23.7).

Jesus describes a different kind of religious community and envisions a different sort of religious leader. In this community only God and God's Christ have positions of honour.

The passage concludes with two brief sayings, probably originally independent of each other. Both claim that greatness depends on service. The world is turned upside-down. Matthew 23.12 is a variation on 23.11 and again becomes an exhortation especially for Christian leaders.

The tricky thing, of course, is that if one is busily humbling oneself in order to be exalted that is not true humility at all.

Matthew 24.1–14

Matthew relies heavily on Mark. For both of them the impending destruction of the Temple is the first sign of the eschatological woes to come (cf. Mark 13.37–39).

This apocalyptic speech in chapters 24–25 is the fifth and last of Jesus' great discourses in Matthew. Matthew 24.3–8 makes two apocalyptic claims. The first claim is that there will be a terrifying combination of false teaching and natural disaster that are the beginning of the end. The second claim is that all these signs will be *only* the beginning of the end.

In Matthew 24.9–14 Jesus predicts the disasters that will befall the community before the end. Perhaps worst of all for a Gospel that proclaims the fulfilment of the Law (*nomos*), lawlessness (*anomia*) will abound (24.12).

Matthew takes Mark's vision of what must happen before the end and expands it. 'This good news of the kingdom will be proclaimed throughout the world, as a testimony to all the Gentiles; and then the end will come.' Though torn asunder by false prophecy and dissension, Matthew's church is to preach the kingdom to all the Gentiles (cf. 28.17, 19).

The Gospel according to Matthew is driven by apocalyptic hope. Matthew expected a much shorter future for the Church and the world than came to pass. It is an act of hermeneutical hubris to try to link the exact events of the New Testament's apocalyptic passages to particular events in the contemporary world. It is an act of hermeneutical despair to avoid the apocalyptic themes of the New Testament. These claims of Matthew are hard to escape. First, history is from first to last in God's hands. Second, history moves toward a decisive culmination. Third, the decisive figure at the culmination will be Jesus, God's Son. Fourth, the evident sufferings of this present age are nothing compared to the glory that is to be revealed.

Matthew 24.30–35

There are two ways in which Matthew provides a kind of cautionary note against too literal a reading of apocalyptic texts, including this one.

First the reminder of the fig tree (which probably also recalls 21.18–22) calls the reader to attend to metaphoric signs – not to maps or timetables. Matthew quotes Jesus as saying: 'From the fig tree learn this parable' (NRSV: 'lesson').

Like Matthew 13, Matthew 24 is a kind of parable, Let those who have ears, hear.

Second, Matthew, like Mark (or Jesus) provides an example of a reinterpretation of a text in order to adapt it to the needs of a later generation. The earlier tradition of Jesus' words almost surely read: 'This generation will not pass away until these things have come to pass.' By the time Mark, and certainly Matthew, write, most of 'that generation' has passed away, so 'generation' is read allegorically or metaphorically. 'Heaven and earth will pass away, but my words will not pass away.'

The central picture of this portion of Matthew's apocalypse is the depiction of the coming of the Son of Man. Like Mark and Luke, Matthew draws his prediction primarily from Daniel 7.13–14. In Matthew's version of this speech the prophecy from Daniel is introduced by an allusion to Zechariah 12.10, 14. These verses may also have been part of early Christian collections of scriptural testimony to Jesus, but at the very least they provide Matthew with another way to show that his story fulfils prophetic hopes.

The question of who the Son of Man is in Daniel is much discussed, but there is no question at all that in the context of Matthew's Gospel Jesus is himself Son of Man. The props and the settings are less important than two claims. First, the fulfilment of history will be shaped in Christ. Second, at the conclusion of history Christ will gather God's chosen to himself.

Matthew 24.36–44

Matthew, like Mark before him, includes this passage in his book in part to counter the claim that early Christian expectations about Jesus' parousia ('second coming') had been mistaken and that therefore Jesus was a false prophet. In Matthew 24.36 Jesus makes clear that only the Father – not the angels and not Jesus himself – knows the timetable for God's consummation of human history. Matthew underlines the claim by adding the Greek word *monos* – only the Father alone. The verse provides a constant reminder to prognosticators of every generation that it is not given to mortals to know the times and seasons of God's future.

From Q Matthew takes Jesus' interpretation of the story of Noah to provide dramatic underpinning for the claim that the most important thing one can expect about the kingdom is that it will be unexpected (cf. Luke 17.26–37). In Matthew's context the unpredictability of Jesus' return is grounds not for resignation but for attention. 'Keep awake therefore' (24.42).

In 24.40–41 there are clearly grounds for some kind of understanding of a 'rapture' as a subsidiary theme to the great expectation of the coming of the Son of Man. However, for Matthew, it is better to remain than to be taken away, gathered like useless fish (see 13.47–50).

The call to alertness is underscored by the two brief parables that follow. The first parable seems a little paradoxical. If the householder had known what time the thief was coming he would have stayed awake; you have no idea what time Jesus is coming, therefore stay awake. Perhaps the message is: Whether you know, or don't know (and you don't know), stay awake.

The complementary parable in Matthew 24.44–46 (cf. Luke 12.42–46) stresses not only the unexpectedness of the master's return but the responsibility of those entrusted with the master's belongings and the judgement on those who use the excuse of the delayed parousia to slack off (cf. 2 Pet. 3.3–4).

Matthew 25.1–13

The key verb that links the whole section 24.36—25.13 is *gregore-ite*, watch! (see 24.42, 44, 50; 25.13). The three stories of Matthew 25 are Matthew's addition to the apocalyptic sermon, though Luke has his own version of the second parable (see Luke 19.11–27).

For Matthew, the story of the maidens is a further elaboration of the demand that the faithful should always be ready for the consummation of the kingdom. The passage is clearly parabolic and eschatological. This is not a moral homily about how to treat one's needy neighbours but an evangelical call to constant watchfulness. In the life of faith there are many gifts one can give to another, but one's watchfulness, readiness, faith are always one's own.

There is certainly an allegorical element to the story. Both in the synoptic Gospels and elsewhere we find imagery that makes Jesus the bridegroom who brings the eschatological wedding feast (see John 3.9; 1 Cor. 11.2; Rev. 21.9; 22.17). The Old Testament can portray God as Israel's bridegroom, and Christian imagery probably draws on that source (see Isa. 54.5; Jer. 31.32). There is no good reason, however, to read all details of the story allegorically. For instance, there is no evidence that we are to find in the oil a hidden code for some set of Christian virtues.

In the custom of the time the maidens (not really bridesmaids) would be waiting at the groom's house for his return with the bride from her father's house.

The delay of the bridegroom fits Matthew's concern that the foolish will not allow room enough for the delay of the return of the Son of Man (see 24.48).

As with the short parable of the two servants that precedes it, this parable is a story of division. The foolish maidens are not cut in pieces or put with the hypocrites, but the bridegroom does not recognize them. In the Matthean picture of the world and its destiny, that is the worst hell of all.

Matthew 25.14–30

Here we have another eschatological parable with a dire ending for the insufficiently faithful. 25.14 refers back to 25.1, and the comparison is to the kingdom of heaven. Luke 19.11–27 uses the story quite differently.

It is hard not to tilt this parable, too, toward allegory. Jesus says that each slave received a trust 'according to his ability' (25.15; the Greek is *dynamis*, which can also mean 'power'). When this is combined with Matthew's editorial generalization that 'to those who have, more will be given', we see a claim not only to a diversity of gifts but also to a hierarchy of gifts.

So, too, when the one-talent slave says of the master, 'I knew that you were a harsh man, reaping where you did not sow, and gathering where you did not scatter seed', we think not just of a harsh master but of a creative God who brings forth much out of nothing (cf. Rom. 4.17). The slave ought also to bring forth much out of little. The note that the master returns only 'after a long time' reminds us that we deal with a return that is delayed.

It is a fluke of English, not of Greek, that the measure of the money the slaves receive is called a 'talent'. Undaunted by the original language, English-speaking preachers have talked about the differences between five-talent and one-talent people, referring to things that they are good at – not the use to which they put their money. This is not a bad stretch so long as we remember that in the parable itself the only thing we know that makes a five-talented person five-talented is that he or she knows how to make five talents more: to sow well and therefore to reap abundantly. In other words, to invest their resources for maximum returns.

Matthew 25.31–46

This passage is metaphorical but not parabolic: 'When the Son of Man comes in his glory, and all his angels with him'. This (i.e. the judgement scene that Matthew now depicts) *is* what the end will be. Unlike vv. 1–13 and vv. 14–30, vv. 31–46 are not presented as an extended simile.

There is debate whether the 'least of these' in our passage means 'any in need' or whether it is a specific reference to Christians. In either case we note that it is the nations (or the Gentiles) who gather before the judgement throne and it may be as nations, not just as individuals, that sheep will be separated from goats.

If 'the least of these' is a general term for those in need, individuals and nations are judged by their capacity for compassionate action toward the marginalized. If 'the least of these' is a term for Christians – like 'little ones' in Matthew – then the question seems to be how the nations will treat Christian missionaries (see 10.40–42; 11.11; 18.6, 14).

I think the evidence points more toward the second reading of the text, making it a text about the way in which Gentiles treat Christian missionaries. However, the text has also been used as a reminder to Christians to care for the least in our communities and in our society.

Whichever way we read the story it displays an enticing feature of eschatological surprise: 'Lord, when did we see you?' And it retains Matthew's typically unflinching judgement.

If one reads the three narratives of Matthew 25 in order one can see a kind of deepening and expanding of the vision of faithfulness in the light of the coming kingdom. To be sure, like the wise maidens, one cares for the gifts one has received. But taking care does not mean hoarding or hiding, as we see in the story of the talents. And the creative gifts we have been given are used most faithfully when they are used for those with the greatest need.

Matthew 26.14—27.66

Matthew draws heavily on Mark's version of Jesus' arrest, trial and crucifixion. In the story of the betrayal, 26.14–16, Matthew like Mark stresses that the betrayer is one of the twelve. The story serves as a severe warning that even in the closest circle of Jesus' followers there is always the danger of betrayal. Jesus has warned the disciples that they cannot serve both God and mammon (6.24). Judas has chosen mammon. The Greek verb for 'betray', *paradidomi*, can also be used to mean 'hand over'. When Jesus predicts that the Son of Man will be handed over he uses the same verb (17.22; see Isa. 53.6, 12). Judas hands Jesus over; so too does God.

In the story of the preparation for the Last Supper (26.17–20), Matthew follows Mark in showing Jesus entirely in charge of the arrangements for this essential meal. Matthew adds to the story the phrase that the disciples are to use with the stranger: 'The teacher says, "My time is near." ' We recall the message of John the Baptist, of Jesus, and of the disciples: 'The kingdom of heaven has come near' (3.2; 4.17; 10.7).

The scene with Judas in vv. 21–25 follows Mark closely. In both Gospels there is emphasis on Jesus' knowledge of the hearts of his disciples. Matthew, for whom the disciples are forerunners of his own community, makes their question of Jesus even more poignant, not just, 'Is it I?', but 'Is it I, Lord?' In Matthew the query is repeated and revised by Judas, 'Is it I, rabbi?' The use of the term 'rabbi' suggests that even yet Judas does not know the one he betrays.

For both Mark and Matthew the Last Supper establishes the meal where believers celebrate Jesus' new covenant between God and humankind and anticipate the final consummation of God's kingdom. The term 'covenant' reaffirms the way in which Jesus Christ builds on the Law brought by Moses and adds to it his own richer embodiment of God's rule (see Exod. 24.8). Matthew adds a few features to the story. The covenant includes 'forgiveness of sins'. There is a commandment for both bread and cup. There is the promise that when Jesus drinks and eats anew in the kingdom, he will be in the company of the disciples. Hope is communal. Jesus speaks of 'the kingdom of my Father'. Matthew affirms Jesus' special relationship to God, and the Last Supper anticipates an eschatological family feast.

The prediction that follows immediately upon the meal makes clear, however, that discipleship is no guarantee of fidelity and that loyalty requires constant renewal (26.31–35). Peter is again a representative disciple, and he will start bravely but will end badly. The Scripture that must be fulfilled (vv. 51, 52, 54, 56) appears to be Zechariah 13.7.

In the first part of the story of Gethsemane (26.36–46) Matthew tells the story much as Mark does. But for Matthew it is to Peter alone that Jesus addresses the question: 'Peter, are you sleeping?', and he makes the rebuke even more stinging: 'Couldn't you watch with me (even) *one hour*?' (cf. Mark 14.37). The story has both a christological and an ecclesiological point. Christologically, we see Jesus place himself in the hands of his Father and painfully subsume his will to his Father's will. Ecclesiologically, we discover that the test of discipleship is watching and waiting (see 24.36—25.13).

In the arrest (26.47–56) Matthew, like Mark, has Judas again greet Jesus as 'rabbi' (see 26.25). Matthew, unlike Mark, includes Jesus' command to Judas, come to betray him, 'Friend, do what you are here to do.' Jesus is the actor in the fulfilment of God's will, Judas the pawn.

Jesus' response to the disciple who cuts off the soldier's ear resonates with the power of the Sermon on the Mount and the command for non-retaliation. 'Whoever takes the sword by the sword will die' (26.52). Jesus, who has all the best reasons to meet violence with retribution, refuses to do so.

In the dramatic scene that follows, Jesus' steadfastness is contrasted with Peter's cowardice (26.57–75).

The priest not only asks Jesus whether he is the Christ, he adjures Jesus to speak the truth. We remember that Jesus tells the disciples to swear no oaths, and he swears none himself. Where in Mark Jesus confesses that he is the Christ, in Matthew he says to the priest: 'You say so.' Then Jesus goes on to talk about the fulfilment of his mission not as Messiah, but as Son of Man. There is more here than Israel's hope; there is the hope of all the world.

As in Mark, Matthew reports the false witnesses with their talk of the Temple being destroyed and raised up again. Jesus is the true witness, providing a testimony of the coming Son of Man based on Psalm 110.1 and Daniel 7.13.

Peter is the most false witness of all. His denial escalates until finally he takes the kind of oath Jesus has refused and denies the truth that Jesus has affirmed. He will not say who he is.

Two themes emerge from Jesus' very brief dialogue with Pilate (27.11–14). Both are already present in Mark. First, in response to Pilate's query whether Jesus is King of the Jews, Jesus simply answers: 'You say so.' This could mean: 'You've got it!', or 'That's your opinion for what it's worth.' Or, 'Maybe so.' Second, the silence of Jesus before his false accusers surely reminds the readers of Isaiah 53.7, 'He was oppressed, and he was afflicted. Yet he did not open his mouth.'

Though we have no historical evidence of the custom of releasing a prisoner at the festival, the story heightens the responsibility of the people (27.15–26). Though Pilate is far from innocent in all this, it is not he who makes the choice that Jesus be crucified, but the people, urged on by their crafty leaders. The sense of Jewish responsibility for the crucifixion is heightened by a slight change in the form of the verb 'crucify.' In Mark's Gospel the people cry: 'Crucify him!', indicating that crucifixion is Pilate's job. In Matthew's Gospel they cry: 'Let him be crucified.' Pilate is more instrument than instigator. The guilt of the people is heightened by the story of Pilate's wife warning her husband that this execution will be a mistake. In Matthew God uses dreams to inform people of God's truth and intentions.

It is only in Matthew that Pilate washes his hands, becoming the archetype of the powerful person who is able to evade responsibility. The people cry out, again only in Matthew: 'Be his blood on us and on our children.' In Matthew's context this was surely one more salvo in an intra-Jewish fight with contemporary Jewish opponents over who were the true heirs of Moses, but the historical setting does little to redeem the pain this text has caused. That said, it is important to note that Matthew does not treat the people as an authoritative voice in his Gospel (see above, p. 9). Therefore the authoritative voice of Jesus is to be preferred to that of the people, and Matthew has Jesus make clear that the punishment for the people's rejection of him is for one generation alone (23.36) – not on them and on their children.

In 27.27–31 Matthew heightens the drama and the irony by having Jesus hold the hurtful reed like a sceptre. He improves Mark's order by having the soldiers kneel before Jesus at the beginning of the mockery.

The story of the crucifixion in Matthew 27.32–54 follows very closely on Mark's account. Like Mark, it draws heavily on Old Testament images, especially those in Psalm 22. Whatever the historical details of the crucifixion, both Mark and Matthew use the Old Testament to make clear its theological significance. This is the fulfilment of what God has intended all along.

As in Mark a considerable amount of Matthew's account depends on irony. Those who observe the crucifixion tend to say just the wrong thing in such a way that the reader remembers what the right thing is. 'He is the King of Israel, let him come down from the cross now and we will believe in him' (27.42b). Yet true faith is faith in Jesus who stays on the cross until the sacrifice is done. Or they say the right thing for the wrong reason: 'He saved others; he cannot save himself' (27.42a). Yet it is only because he will not save himself that he can save others.

In Matthew as in Mark (but not in Luke or John) Jesus' last cry is, 'My God, my God, why have you forsaken me?' (27.46). In two ways Matthew shifts Mark's story. First, he makes clear that the passion of Jesus is a continuation of his temptation in the wilderness. In Matthew 4.6 Satan says to Jesus: 'If you are the Son of God, throw yourself down (from the Temple).' In Matthew 27.40 the passers-by cry out: 'If you are the Son of God, come down from the cross.'

Second, Matthew adds to Mark's story the eschatological features of earthquake and resurrection of the saints. In Mark, the centurion proclaims Jesus as God's Son because of the way Jesus dies. In Matthew the centurion proclaims Jesus as God's Son because of the miraculous signs that attend his death. Perhaps this is Matthew's way of softening Mark's odd claim that it is precisely as abandoned that Jesus can be recognized as God's Son.

Matthew 27.55–66 prepares the way for the resurrection. The women who stand by, even at a distance, stand there in contrast to the disciples who have fled. But they also witness his real death and then his real burial. This prepares the way for their witness to the resurrection in 28.1–2.

Joseph of Arimathea sticks a big stone over the entrance to the tomb. The soldiers make sure the stone is secure by sealing it. Matthew begins to underline what he will make abundantly clear. Jesus' body was not stolen; sealed in the tomb, he rose from the dead and broke the seal. The story reflects an ongoing controversy with the synagogue about what happened at the tomb. What no one seems to doubt, is that the tomb was empty on the third day.

Matthew 28.1–10

Almost certainly the copy of the Gospel according to Mark that Matthew and Luke used ended with Mark 16.8, since from that point on they diverge in recounting their stories of the risen Lord.

There is a strong apologetic in Matthew's telling of the story of the empty tomb. It takes an angel to move the stone away, so it cannot possibly be the case that the disciples had rolled away the stone and taken the body. The angel is not only God's messenger but also God's surrogate, since the angel sits triumphantly on top of the stone. The fear of the guards is contrasted with the angel's word to the women, 'Fear not!' (28.5). The young man of Mark's account becomes an angel and shines as Jesus shone at the transfiguration. There is an earthquake as there was when the sea was stirred and as there was when Jesus was crucified (see 27.51; 8.24; to translate the latter as 'gale' or 'storm' is misleading and misses the parallels.)

As in Mark the women are the first human witnesses to the resurrection, as they have been witnesses to the burial. They confirm the truth of the story. As in Mark, Luke and John, Matthew holds up a particular role for the women as those who witness and proclaim resurrection.

When Jesus appears he says 'Greetings' but the term also means 'Rejoice', an imperative verbal form of the word for 'joy' found in Matthew 28.8. In this sense he calls the women from joy to deeper joy. When they take hold of his feet and worship him they pay him the homage that he is clearly due. This is narrative Christology; the Gospel moves from following to questioning to worship.

Jesus calls his disciples 'brothers' – an indication that they are family as well as followers is now transmuted into a role as family. In Mark the promised meeting in Galilee lies beyond the narrative.

For Matthew, Jesus makes good his promise within the confines of this Gospel.

Matthew 28.16–20

Matthew shapes his Gospel with great care, and the story ends with a climax that is also a conclusion. Once again as with the great sermon of chapters 5 to 7 and the transfiguration of chapter 17, Jesus goes to a mountain. With astonishing realism or homiletical acuity Matthew announces that even at this time of triumph, 'they saw and worshipped, but some doubted'. (We could also translate the phrase 'they saw and worshipped and some doubted' since worship does not necessarily exclude doubt, nor doubt worship.) It may also be the case that even here at the end Matthew reminds us of the divisions within his own neighbourhood about whether or not Jesus is worthy of worship.

Matthean themes are recapitulated and deepened. The authority with which Jesus taught and performed miracles (7.28–29; 8.9) now becomes the cosmic authority of the risen Christ. Those who have been disciples are now to make disciples.

The baptism the disciples are to practise is different from John's. Believers are baptized not just into repentance but into the threefold name. Matthew does not have a full doctrine of the Trinity but already the threefold name has liturgical and sacramental significance. When Jesus tells the disciples that they are to make disciples of all nations we know that however much the Gospel started out as good news for Israel it has now become good news for Gentiles as well.

Matthew's eschatological expectation is in no way diminished, but the urgency of the mission for the meantime is emphasized and described.

The Gospel according to Matthew comes full circle. The Emmanuel promised to Joseph (1.23) now promises himself to the faithful: 'Look, I am with you always.'

A Gospel that has been full of admonition and exhortation concludes with comfort and encouragement. For the task.

The Gospel according to Mark

MORNA D. HOOKER

Introduction

The shortest of our four canonical Gospels, Mark was almost certainly the first to be written. Heading his work 'the gospel (or "good news") about Jesus Christ', the author appears to have been responsible for creating the genre that we know as 'Gospels'. Nevertheless, since Matthew and Luke contain parallels to almost everything in Mark, it was probably only the tradition that it contained the reminiscences of Peter that saved this Gospel for posterity.

The same tradition (said by the fourth-century historian Eusebius to go back to Papias, whom Eusebius records as having written in the early second century) names Mark (presumably the Mark referred to in 1 Pet. 5.13) as the author. It is usually assumed that this is the 'John Mark' mentioned in Acts 12.12, 25; 15.37, 39) though John Mark seems to have been associated with Paul rather than Peter (see also Col. 4.10; 2 Tim. 4.11), and 'Mark' was a common name in the ancient world. Nothing is known about where the Gospel was written, though tradition places it in Rome, probably because Peter is said to have died there. If the Gospel was used by both Matthew and Luke, it was clearly written before them, and the teaching in chapter 13 suggests that it was written shortly before or – more probably – shortly after the destruction of Jerusalem in AD 70.

The book's structure

Mark's style is simple and unpolished, but nevertheless extremely effective: since books were rare, his Gospel was intended to be read aloud, and though his frequent use of the word 'and' and the phrase 'and immediately' seem crude, they contribute to his story's dramatic power. He uses repetitions, to make sure that his hearers grasp the significance of what he is saying, and summaries, which not only remind us of 'the story so far', but indicate that there are many other similar events which he might have included. Mark was not writing a 'biography' of Jesus, but the good news about what God had done in and through him. His arrangement of the material is designed to convey his understanding of its significance. At the beginning of the story, for example, he relates a series of stories which all convey the amazing authority of Jesus (1.14—3.6); a block of teaching in chapter 4 shows Jesus addressing the crowds, while another in chapter 11 shows him confronting the religious leaders in Jerusalem; a series of miracles in chapters 4–8 confronts us with the question 'Who is this?' The healing of a blind man in 8.22–26 and of another in 10.46–52 frame a section which deals with the nature of Jesus' messiahship and the meaning of discipleship. One of Mark's favourite devices is to interweave related stories, as in 5.21–43; 11.11–24; and 14.53–72.

This means that the only effective way to read Mark is to do so *in toto*! Only in this way can one appreciate the cumulative power of the picture he offers us. Although Lectionary readings allow the congregation to *hear* the Gospel, much as Mark's original hearers did, they inevitably break it into fragments. When consecutive passages are read each week, one may be able to appreciate something of the underlying power of the narrative, but the church year means that we hear some passages out of sequence. Readings from other Gospels frequently replace Mark at the festivals and, most deplorable of all, the Lectionary omits two large sections of the book altogether. Preachers can, of course, treat Lectionary readings as isolated pericopes, but if *Mark's* distinctive voice is to be heard, they need to remember the place each passage has in the whole.

Mark's story begins with a 'prologue', which conveys to readers of the Gospel essential information as to its significance. This section has been compared with the prologue which introduced Greek dramas, in which the author shares with his audience knowledge that is hidden from the participants in the drama. A biblical parallel can also be found in the first two chapters of Job. In the first thirteen verses, Mark alerts us to the fact that what is taking place is the fulfilment of Scripture, that Jesus is Christ, Son of God, and Lord, and that John the Baptist is the one who prepares his way. Although

John himself is apparently unaware that Jesus is the Coming One whom he has announced, the arrangement of the material makes this clear – as does the account of Jesus' baptism, when we overhear words spoken from heaven. We learn, too, that the Holy Spirit of God is at work in Jesus, and that in the power of the Spirit he has confronted Satan in the wilderness, and been tested by him.

With this knowledge, we are in a position to understand the story that follows – a story of events which appear to have bewildered those who witnessed them. The crowds are astonished and perplexed, while the religious authorities demonstrate their obtuseness by dismissing what Jesus does as the work of Satan. Even the disciples are shown to be largely uncomprehending; although they eventually grasp that Jesus is the anointed one promised by the prophets, they fail to understand what this means, either for Jesus himself, or for those who want to be his disciples.

Why did Mark decide to write his 'Gospel'? The answer is by no means obvious. It used to be assumed that he thought it necessary to preserve the tradition about Jesus before the 'eye-witnesses' died out, but he is clearly no mere collector of traditions. Some commentators have argued that his purpose was to attack an interpretation of Jesus as a 'miracle-worker', and present instead his own understanding of Jesus as a suffering Messiah. But while Mark does not regard Jesus as a mere 'miracle worker', he clearly believes his miracles to be part of the inbreaking kingdom of God. Others have suggested that Mark is attacking the church leaders of his day in the guise of 'the twelve'. It seems more likely, however, that the disciples' incomprehension and failure are intended to explain why the truth about Jesus could not be understood until after the resurrection. What we *can* say is that the Gospel is intended to explain who Jesus is and why he died; it also spells out clearly what Jesus demands of his followers. Perhaps Mark – who was himself a preacher, concerned to get across the good news about Jesus to others – felt these to be the most pressing needs in his congregation.

Jesus

Who, then, is Jesus? As we have seen, Mark's response to this question is set out in his opening verses, where we learn that Jesus is both 'Son of God' and 'Christ'. The words 'You are my beloved Son' are spoken from heaven (1.11; 9.7) and can therefore be understood to represent the profoundest truth about Jesus, but it is a truth to which the participants in the drama are almost entirely blind. Until the very end of the story, only the unclean spirits acknowledge him as Son of God (3.11; 5.7); but when the centurion sees how Jesus died, he declares him to be 'Son of God'.

Although Mark's answer can be summed up in a few so-called 'christological titles', he uncovers the *significance* of those titles by the use of narrative. So we learn that being 'Son of God' means that Jesus is well-pleasing to God, and obedient even to the point of death; that he acts and speaks in the power of God, and so is able to defeat evil and to restore men and women to health.

The bald statement that Jesus is 'Christ' (1.1) is also filled out through narrative. First, through Peter's *mis*understanding of the term (8.29–33), and the inappropriate request of John and James, who associate messiahship with glory (10.35–40). Then, by Jesus' actions in Jerusalem when he has entered Jerusalem as king. And finally, when Jesus is anointed for burial, and is condemned, mocked and crucified as 'King of the Jews'. Using narrative, Mark overthrows completely all our natural assumptions about what the Messiah will do and be: Jesus is acknowledged as Son of God and proclaimed King through his death.

Jesus' own distinctive way of referring to himself is 'the Son of Man'. We need not discuss here the vexed question about the origins and meaning of this term, since it is clear that Mark understands Jesus to be using it to refer to himself. In the first half of the Gospel, it occurs only twice, on occasions when Jesus is confronted by opposition from the religious authorities, to affirm his authority to act as he does (2.10, 28). Its rare occurrence is not surprising, since Jesus' message does not concern himself, but the kingdom of God. Only after Caesarea Philippi does he use it regularly, and then always to speak about either his own suffering or his vindication or both (8.31, 38; 9.9, 12, 31; 10.33, 45; 13.26; 14.21, 41, 62). It is significant that what is said about 'the Son of Man' almost always either applies to or has clear implications for his followers; they, too, must learn the necessity to suffer and die; they, too, will be vindicated when the Son of Man enters his glory.

But *why* did Jesus die? To this question Mark gives two very different answers. On the one hand, he is clearly convinced that Jesus could not have been put to death unless this was part of God's plan. God was in control of the world, and what happened must have been his will. So we learn that the Son of Man 'must' suffer and die, and Jesus accepts his coming death as God's will (14.36); Jesus appeals to what the scriptures say about the Son of Man's suffering (9.12; 14.21), though we are not told which scriptures. In 14.27, however, he quotes Zechariah 13.7, and the crucifixion narrative is full of allusions to the psalms.

There is another answer to the question, however, and that is that it was the result of human sin. Jesus dies because of the opposition of the religious leaders, who refuse to recognize his authority and are determined to destroy him (3.6; 14.1). Judas, one of his disciples, betrays him; the priests, elders and scribes condemn him to death; Pilate weakly gives way and orders the sentence to be carried out. All are responsible – and the fact that this is part of God's purpose does not mitigate their guilt (14.21). Mark does not try to reconcile these two very different answers, and indeed they are rooted in a problem that is summed up in 4.11–12: the hearts and minds of Jesus' people are blind and deaf to the truth, but it is God who has made them blind and deaf! Mark baldly states here the paradox of predestination and human responsibility.

Mark also gives another, more positive answer to the question: Jesus dies as a 'ransom' (10.45), and to establish a covenant with 'many' (14.24). Through his death and resurrection, Israel is being recreated.

Following Jesus

Although who Jesus is and why he dies are Mark's chief themes, it is important to note that *Jesus'* message concerns the demands of *God*. It is Mark's arrangement of the material that focuses our attention on Jesus. Inextricably linked with these central themes is another: what it means to be a disciple. It means, basically, not being ashamed of 'the Son of Man', and following him 'in the way' of the Cross. His way of obedience to God and suffering is intended as a pattern for others; if they are to participate in his glory, they must drink his cup of suffering and share his baptism. Here, too, the message is conveyed by means of narrative: remarkably, the people who apparently understand best what is being demanded and who are commended by Jesus are mostly women (5.34; 7.24–30; 12.41–44; 14.3–9; see also 1.31; 15.40, 47; 16.1). In contrast, the twelve continually demonstrate what disciples should *not* do! They fail repeatedly, but readers struggling to be faithful disciples can take courage from this, for the final, enigmatic chapter contains a message of forgiveness, and urges the eleven to try again. Mark's final scene assures us that if we, like the disciples, set out in faith, we too will see Jesus, and will be given the chance to renew our discipleship in spite of our failures.

NB In the notes that follow, references to 'Jesus' should be taken as meaning 'Jesus as Mark presents him', and are not intended as historical judgements.

Commentary on the Sunday readings from Mark

Mark 1.1–8

Mark heads his book 'gospel' (meaning 'good news'), telling us that it concerns Jesus, who is 'Christ', i.e. 'Messiah' (meaning 'anointed'). Although the words 'the Son of God' are missing from some manuscripts, they clearly represent Mark's own understanding of who Jesus is (1.11; 9.7; 15.39). He begins with a quotation (combining phrases from Exod. 23.20; Mal. 3.1 and Isa. 40.3) which he attributes to Isaiah, perhaps because Isaiah was of special importance to him: many of the subsequent quotations come from Isaiah (e.g. 4.12; 7.6f.; 11.17). This good news about Jesus Christ is the fulfilment of God's promises to Israel.

Mark follows the Septuagint (a collection of Greek translations of the Hebrew scriptures) in locating the 'voice' which proclaims the Lord's coming in the wilderness. Isaiah's promise is fulfilled when John appears in the wilderness, 'proclaiming' a baptism. His clothes and food identify him as Elijah (2 Kgs 1.8), who was expected to return before the Day of the Lord (Mal. 4.5). In telling us that 'the whole district of Judaea, together with everyone from Jerusalem' flocked to be baptized, Mark indicates that John has faithfully fulfilled his task.

In contrast to the accounts in Matthew and Luke, John's message here concerns only the one who follows him; although John does not name this Coming One, Mark 1.1 has already alerted us to his identity. Three times John points to the Coming One's superiority. He is 'stronger' than John – a term which will be echoed in the ensuing narrative in references to Jesus' power. John is totally unworthy to undo his sandal – the most menial of tasks; as the identity of Jesus is revealed in the Gospel, we realize why this is true. And whereas John baptizes with water, Jesus will baptize with Holy Spirit. Here we have a third comparison (*not* a contrast): John's baptism with water symbolizes the baptism with Spirit brought by Jesus: it is Jesus who will purge and forgive, bringing renewal and life. This, too, will be unfolded in the story that follows.

Mark 1.4–11

John is something of an enigma: why did he baptize? Though the various ritual washings practised by Jews provide a partial parallel, they were repeated, whereas John's baptism was a 'once only' event. Another partial parallel is seen in proselyte baptism, and though evidence for this is later than John, some such rite of purification must always have been demanded of converts to Judaism. But John was requiring Jews, who were *already* members of God's people, to repent and be baptized. Such a radical demand was nevertheless appropriate when the nation was faced with judgement. The background to John's mission is found in the Old Testament prophets, where water was seen as both a means of cleansing (e.g. Ezek. 36.25–28; Zech. 13.1) and a source of new life (e.g. Isa. 44.3f.). Like his preaching, John's action essentially looks forward: he is a signpost pointing towards the one who follows him, who will baptize with Holy Spirit, bringing the forgiveness and new life which John's baptism symbolizes.

John's announcement of the Coming One is followed by the arrival of Jesus from Galilee. He is baptized by John in the Jordan, so identifying himself with repentant Israel. 'And immediately,' as he came up out of the water, he saw the Spirit descend, and heard the voice from heaven. In Mark's account it is Jesus alone who sees the Spirit and hears the voice. Nevertheless, we should not attempt to speculate about Jesus' own religious experience. For Mark, the Spirit and the voice serve to reveal to *us*, his readers, the true identity of Jesus. There can be no mistake, for Jesus himself sees the Spirit, and the voice speaks from heaven. Since we now know that the Spirit of whom John has spoken has descended on Jesus, we can be sure that whatever he does will be in the power of the Spirit. Furthermore, he has been identified by the divine voice as God's beloved Son. We thus know what is concealed from all the characters in the story, with the exception of Jesus himself.

Mark 1.9–15

The combination of these three short paragraphs in one lection concentrates our attention on Jesus. At his baptism, he is identified as God's beloved Son. In the Old Testament, we find Israel described as 'God's Son' (Exod. 4.22f.; Deut. 1.31; Hos. 11.1), though the term could be used also of the king, as representative of Israel (Pss. 2.7; 89.27) and of righteous individuals (Wisd. 2.13–18; 5.5), who fulfil Israel's calling. The term thus denotes election, privilege – and obedience to God's will. The word 'beloved' is used in the Septuagint to refer to an only son – for example Abraham's son Isaac – and thus indicates that Jesus' relationship to God is unique. The final words, 'with you I am well pleased' imply his obedient response.

This obedience is 'immediately' tested in Jesus' confrontation with Satan. Mark tells us that the Spirit drove Jesus out into the wilderness, reminding us that it is the Spirit of God who is at work in Jesus. Unlike Matthew and Luke, Mark tells us nothing about the content of the testing. His stark treatment of the story concentrates our attention on the few details he gives us. The location – the wilderness – suggests that he is thinking of the testing of Israel, who repeatedly failed; the presence of wild beasts and the reference to angels suggest that he may be thinking of Adam, who succumbed to Satan's temptation, and so lost dominion over wild beasts. Is Mark already hinting here that Jesus is to be seen as 'the Son of Man' – the one who reverses Adam's sin because of his obedience to God, and so exercises the authority which God intended men and women to have?

The last brief paragraph begins the story of the ministry of Jesus. He returns to Galilee, and proclaims 'the good news from God'. He announces that the time is fulfilled, and that the kingdom – or rule – of God has drawn near. In the light of the previous two paragraphs, we realize that it has drawn near in the person of Jesus himself.

Mark 1.14–20

Here we have the opening sentences in the story of Jesus' ministry. Mark begins with a reference to John's arrest (lit. 'handing over'). This is not simply a convenient way to move from John's ministry to that of Jesus, but a warning: the forerunner has been given up into the power of the authorities – what, then, will happen to the one who follows? Mark's narrative begins with an ominous pointer to Jesus' coming death!

Jesus proclaims 'the good news from God' – the good news that the time has arrived for God's rule to be established. Although the

Old Testament affirms that God is King (see especially the Psalms), men and women had continued to disobey him; this led to the hope that one day God would establish his rule on earth. If that time has now arrived, it brings not only salvation but judgement; hence the call to repent.

This brief summary is all that Mark tells us at this point about the content of Jesus' teaching: it concerns only God's kingdom, not himself. Yet because Jesus is the focus of our attention, we realize that the kingdom has drawn near *in him*. Jesus is fully obedient to God (1.11–13), and in him we see the realization of God's rule. By his telling of the story, Mark compels us to recognize that 'the good news from God' is in fact 'the good news *about* Jesus Christ' (1.1).

Although we, Mark's readers, know who Jesus is (having read the 'Prologue'), he is unknown – except as 'Jesus of Nazareth' – to those in Galilee. The authority with which Jesus acts is remarkable, and is seen not only in his preaching but in his call of disciples. There is no indication that any of the four fishermen had seen Jesus before, but when he calls them, they 'immediately' abandon their nets and follow him. Discipleship is a key theme in Mark's Gospel, and means a call to share the ministry of Jesus. Here, the four are summoned to share his task of bringing men and women into the kingdom.

Mark 1.21–28

Once again, the theme of Jesus' teaching is central, even though this time Mark does not report what he said. Mark is concerned here only to stress the authority with which he spoke. On the sabbath, Jesus takes the opportunity to speak in the synagogue. His hearers contrast his teaching with that of the scribes, whose main task is to pass on the traditional interpretation of Scripture, and to quote the teaching of others. Remarkably, Jesus does not quote others, but teaches directly.

Mark links Jesus' authority in teaching with his authority in exorcising unclean spirits. 'Immediately' ('just then', NRSV) a man possessed by an unclean spirit addresses Jesus in the name of all unclean spirits. Why is Jesus interfering with them? Has he come to destroy them? He addresses Jesus by two names: the first, 'Jesus of Nazareth', would be understandable by the bystanders, the second, 'the Holy One of God', would not. The spirit recognizes what is concealed to mortals. God himself is holy, and since Jesus, impelled by God's Spirit, has resisted the testing of Satan, it is understandable if the spirits under Satan's power recognize Jesus as God's Holy One, who is now challenging the whole kingdom of evil. The underlying logic will be spelt out by Jesus in 3.20–30.

Jesus silences the man. Such commands are common in contemporary accounts of exorcisms, but Mark may have seen a deeper significance in Jesus' demand – namely, that the man is being forbidden to reveal Jesus' identity. Certainly, the crowd show no understanding of the man's words.

The exorcism provokes astonishment from all who witness it. Their comment (v. 27) links astonishment at the 'new teaching' they are hearing with amazement at Jesus' power over the spirits. It is not clear whether the phrase 'with authority' should be taken with 'teaching' or 'commands', but Mark clearly believes that Jesus' authority is seen in both. The power of the kingdom of God is demonstrated not only in what Jesus says, but in what he does.

Mark 1.29–39

Mark's favourite phrase 'and immediately' (NRSV 'as soon as') links this section to the preceding one: an example of exorcism is followed by one of healing. The sufferer is identified as Simon's mother-in-law; like the unnecessary reference to Andrew, James and John, this could be 'eye-witness detail'. More importantly, we note how the reference to these four men functions in Mark's narrative. It reminds us that Jesus is accompanied by those whom he called to be disciples. They are about to learn something about what true discipleship means.

Jesus took the woman by the hand – a common feature in his healings – and lifted her up, whereupon the fever left her, and she served them. This final detail may be intended simply to demonstrate the nature of her cure: she had regained her strength, not been left exhausted by the fever's departure. The verb 'to serve' is, however, the one Jesus will use in 10.45 of his own service to others, a service which he expected his disciples to share, though they repeatedly failed to do so. For the first time in Mark – but not the last! – we find a woman grasping what true discipleship means.

The summary in vv. 32–4 assures us that these incidents were by no means unique. 'The whole town' came to the door, and 'all' who were ill or possessed by demons were brought for healing. This time we are told plainly that Jesus forbade the demons to speak 'because they knew him': Jesus' true identity is still unknown to ordinary men and women.

Verse 35 marks an abrupt change: Jesus leaves to pray in a lonely place (the word used earlier for 'wilderness'). He is 'pursued' (not 'followed'!) by his disciples, but their words suggest that they see him as a popular wonder-worker. The word 'came' (v. 38) may signify more than simply 'I came out this morning' (cf. 10.45): Jesus sees his mission as being to 'proclaim the message'. Significantly, Mark understands him to do so not only by preaching but by casting out unclean spirits.

Mark 1.40–45

The word translated 'leprosy' was used in Mark's day of various diseases, some of which were curable – hence the regulations in Leviticus 13–14 for subsequent 'cleansing'. The reaction to this man's cure suggests, however, that it was leprosy proper, then virtually incurable (cf. 2 Kgs 5). Not only was this disease highly contagious, but it rendered the man 'unclean'. The fact that he was expected to avoid all human contact may explain his doubt concerning Jesus' reaction (v. 40).

Although most translations describe Jesus as 'moved with compassion', the alternative Greek reading 'moved with anger' is far more likely to be original. But why should Mark suppose Jesus to have been angry – and with whom? Was it with the leper? If so, was it for approaching him, or for doubting his willingness to respond? It is more likely that his anger was directed against Satan, who would have been seen as ultimately responsible for the man's plight.

Incredibly, Jesus is said to have *touched* the leper. This action should have made him unclean (as well as risking infection); instead of which Jesus said 'Be clean', so dealing with the *cause* of the uncleanness, the leprosy itself. His power was greater than that of the leprosy. Though Mark describes the leprosy as leaving 'immediately', the *signs* of the illness could hardly disappear so abruptly. Jesus does not bypass Moses' teaching: he commands the man to make the prescribed offering and to show himself to the priest. But the man disobeys, so that the priest has no opportunity to see the evidence and pronounce him clean.

The story conveys the amazing power of Jesus to heal. But it conveys an even more profound message. The Torah made provision for declaring people to be clean, but was unable to deal with the underlying cause of uncleanness. Although Jesus loyally observes the teaching of the Torah, his power is even greater than the Torah's. For Mark's community, the priest's declaration seems unnecessary. News of Jesus' far greater power is blazoned far and wide.

Mark 2.1–12

This story introduces the theme of conflict between Jesus and the religious authorities, so linking it closely with the next four stories, where we see increasing tension between Jesus and his opponents. There are obvious links, too, with the previous story. The leper was totally excluded from society, while the paralytic was to a large extent unable to participate in ordinary life: he was dependent on others – hence Mark tells us that Jesus saw '*their* faith'. Both men needed radical treatment. In the case of the paralytic, that meant dealing with the cause of his paralysis. Physical afflictions were generally considered to be the result of sin (cf. John 9.1–3). Jesus once again goes to the root of the problem and does what only God can do, by forgiving the man's sins. The Torah gave priests authority to *pronounce* a person clean, or forgiven, once the cure had been verified and the requisite sacrifices had been made, but only God could remove the disease or forgive the sins.

It is clear that the scribes consider that Jesus' words are empty (v. 7), and his response demonstrates that for him, to speak is to act. He is not making an empty pronouncement, since he has already done the 'more difficult' thing, and the proof is provided in the paralytic's cure, which is once again described as instantaneous.

Jesus' words are remarkable. The scribes are correct in saying that forgiveness is a divine prerogative. Significantly, Jesus is said to have claimed this authority as 'the Son of Man'. The Jewish background to this phrase suggests that Mark understands him to be claiming the authority originally given to Adam to act as God's representative on earth – an authority which Daniel believed would be restored to 'the saints [i.e. holy ones] of the Most High' (Dan. 7.13, 27). Jesus, 'the Holy One of God' (1.24), now claims to have authority on earth to forgive sins. Jesus is not to be seen as a mere wonder-worker, but as one who proclaims and enacts the good news of salvation.

Mark 2.13–22

The call of Levi from his place of work is as abrupt as the call of the fishermen in 1.16–20. Levi is not named in the list of disciples in 3.16–19, which undoubtedly explains why some manuscripts here read 'James' (cf. 3.18; also Matt. 9.9!). Although the man may have had two names (hardly three!), it is probable that Mark himself saw no difficulty in describing the call of disciples who were not included in 'the Twelve' (cf. 8.38; 10.21). Indeed, this would remind his readers that they, too, were called to discipleship. Tax-gatherers were employed by the Roman authorities, and continuous contact with Gentiles meant that they (like the 'sinners' in v. 15) were lax about religious purity; they were also notoriously dishonest. Yet Levi, the outsider, is called to follow Jesus!

It is not clear whether Levi or Jesus is the host at the meal, but if it is Jesus, then his invitation to 'tax-gatherers and sinners' to eat with him symbolizes the fact that he has come to call sinners (v. 17). The final saying reminds us of the purpose of Jesus' mission (cf. 1.24, 38).

From feasting we move to fasting. Even though John is Jesus' fore-runner, he belongs to the old era, like the Pharisees (v. 18), but Jesus has inaugurated the new. In the Old Testament, the image of the bride-groom is used of God (e.g. Isa. 54.4–8; 62.5), whose coming brings joy. The reference to the bridegroom being 'taken away' introduces an alien and sombre note, and is probably an addition to the ori-ginal saying. It is Jesus' disciples who face criticism – a sign that the incident has been shaped by the experience of the early Christian community: it may even reflect a debate as to whether or not Christians should or should not be fasting, now that the bridegroom was no longer present.

The final sayings reflect the tension between old and new. In Jesus' mouth, they would present a challenge to his hearers: the new age was here, and they must respond, or risk losing everything they had. For Mark's generation, the sayings would have suggested that the break between what we now term 'Christianity' and Judaism was inevitable.

Mark 2.23—3.6

Jesus is again challenged about the behaviour of his disciples, who are this time accused of 'doing something that is forbidden on the sabbath'. Reaping and threshing were regarded by the scribes as 'work', and therefore prohibited – reasonable enough, but was plucking a few ears of grain in passing really reaping and threshing? In reply, Jesus reminds the Pharisees of the story of David, who did something forbidden when he and his companions ate the shewbread (1 Sam. 21.1–6). David's action was justified by rabbinic exegetes as necessary because of his hunger: the saving of life took precedence over observing the regulations.

The disciples, however, were clearly not in desperate need. Nevertheless, if the regulations were set aside for David and his companions, they can certainly be set aside for Jesus and his disciples. The Son of Man claims the authority given to Adam at the creation.

Stories about Jesus' conflict with Pharisees would have had special relevance for the early Christian communities, who were continually criticized by their fellow Jews for failing to observe the Law strictly. This story shows signs of adaptation. But Jesus himself certainly clashed with the Pharisees; if he referred to David, he may have been making a claim similar to that expressed in 2.19: something new is happening, and in these circumstances the demands of the gospel are paramount.

Another 'conflict' story follows. Jesus' enemies are waiting for him to make a mistake. But was healing on the sabbath contrary to the Law? This time, Jesus himself reminds his critics that the saving of life took precedence over observing the regulations. His questions contrast doing good and evil, saving life and destroying it: Jesus is *observing* the Law! Certainly he does not 'work' , since he heals with a word alone. The irony is clear: Jesus saves life, and his enemies 'immediately' (on the sabbath!) plot to destroy his. No wonder Jesus is angry! The alliance between Pharisees and Herodians, who were normally totally opposed, is remarkable.

Mark 3.20–35

Mark interleaves two parallel stories. Jesus' family set out to take charge of him, thinking that he must be out of his mind; this probably means that they believe him to be possessed by an unclean spirit. This is certainly the belief of the scribes, who have come from Jerusalem to investigate the rumours about Jesus; tension between Jesus and the religious authorities is becoming more serious. They pronounce him to be possessed by Beelzebul, the prince of demons – i.e. Satan.

Jesus' initial response is blunt: Satan has more sense than to attack himself! To be sure, if his kingdom is seen to be crumbling, that could be because it is divided, since a divided kingdom and a divided house will both totter. But Jesus offers an alternative explanation: Satan's kingdom is falling because it has been invaded; someone has broken into the house, and is plundering his goods. How could this happen? Satan must have been overcome by someone even stronger than himself, who has bound him and is releasing those in his power.

The saying in vv. 28f. spells out the terrible implications of the scribes' charge. They have seen the Holy Spirit at work in Jesus, and have ascribed his achievements to Satan. Their obstinacy is such that it forms an eternal barrier between them and God. In condemning Jesus, they are themselves condemned. Mark's comment in v. 30 is the equivalent of a dig in the ribs: he is anxious lest his readers miss the irony. Jesus, sent by the Holy Spirit who empowers him to battle against Satan, is accused of having an *unclean* spirit!

At this point Jesus' family arrive, and stand 'outside'; believing him to be demented, they distance themselves from those sitting round Jesus, and demand that he comes out to them. Jesus refuses, because his ties with those who do the will of God are closer than those who are related to him by blood. The demands of the kingdom are paramount, and it is those who respond to his message who are his brother, sister and mother. The inclusion of 'sister' in these final words (v. 35) reminds us that women played an important role in the early Christian communities.

Mark 4.26–34

Although Mark has from the very beginning emphasized the teaching of Jesus, it is not until chapter 4 that he spells out its content.

The parable of the sower and its explanation (4.1–20) demonstrate that Mark interpreted Jesus' parables as a challenge to his hearers to respond to his message. The sayings in vv. 21–5, like those in vv. 10–12, remind us that the truth of his teaching is hidden from those who fail to respond.

The last two parables are specifically about the kingdom of God. The first emphasizes the mysterious growth of the seed: human endeavour does not affect its growth, for though the farmer sows the seed, the earth then produces the crop 'by itself'. Jesus' words may well have been meant as a warning to political agitators not to try to force the coming of God's kingdom by armed revolt; as in the parable of the sower, the harvest symbolizes the Day of the Lord.

The second parable is also about growth. This time, the emphasis is on the contrast between the tiny seed, hidden in the ground, and the large plant. Mustard seed was proverbial for its smallness, and the idea of birds roosting in the plant's branches echoes Old Testament imagery for a mighty kingdom (e.g. Ezek. 17.23; Dan. 4.12).

Both parables suggest that although the consummation of the kingdom lies in the future, it is in a sense already present in the person of Jesus; the power of God is at work, and the kingdom's coming is inevitable. For Mark's community, they would have brought reassurance that, though they themselves might be powerless, and though others might be unaware of what was happening, God was in control, and his kingdom would eventually be established.

Mark's final comment shows that he believed Jesus' hearers to be capable of grasping the parables' meaning and of responding to them. It was only obstinacy that led some to be blind and deaf to their meaning (4.10–12).

Mark 4.35–41

This is the first of four 'miracle' stories, which Mark uses to demonstrate the remarkable power of Jesus. It forms a pair with the one that follows in 5.1–20, where we see his authority over a horde of unclean spirits: here it is the powers of nature that are subdued by Jesus' word.

Sudden heavy squalls are by no means unusual on the Lake of Galilee. Since at least four of the disciples were experienced fishermen, their apparent panic is remarkable – even more so, since Jesus sleeps calmly in the stern! The different reactions highlight the contrast between the disciples' lack of faith and Jesus' trust in God.

Jesus reproves the wind, and tells the sea to be silent. The language echoes that used in 1.25, where he reproves and silences an unclean spirit. The coincidence is unsurprising, since the sea was seen as a symbol of chaos and evil, and storms were attributed to rebellious powers. The result is as dramatic as in 1.26: instead of a great storm (v. 37) there is a great calm (v. 39).

Jesus now rebukes the disciples for their cowardice: clearly they have no faith. But now they are even more terrified! Still without faith, they can only ask the question 'Who is he?' Readers of Mark 1.1–13 already know the answer, but the disciples are still groping after the truth.

Later interpreters such as Tertullian explained the boat as representing the Church, battered by persecution and appealing to Christ to come to her aid, apparently in vain. This allegorical interpretation deflected attention from its significance for Mark, which is that it points us to Jesus' true identity. Who is he? Only God is able to control the wind and sea (cf. Ps. 107.23–32; Jonah 1.1–16).

Mark 5.21–43

Two more stories of healing are woven together, so underlining their common themes – Jesus' ability to restore life and the importance of faith (vv. 34, 36).

The woman's complaint is presumably vaginal bleeding; she has been haemorrhaging for twelve years, and is beyond human aid. Moreover, she is 'unclean', and should not be mixing in society, let alone deliberately touching Jesus' garment! As in 1.40–5, however, Jesus' power is stronger. She is healed 'immediately' – and 'immediately' Jesus is aware that the divine power with which he operates has been at work. Jesus does not allow her to treat him as a mere wonder-worker, and demands that she reveal herself. He commends her faith and confirms that the cure is permanent: she has been 'saved' – made whole – and from now on she will be free of her affliction.

The sick child, who is twelve years old, is now reported to be dead. Jesus' comment that she is only asleep is met with laughter, but his words are not a medical diagnosis, but indicate that her death is not irrevocable; since she is to be restored, her death has the nature of sleep. Like Lazarus in John 11 (see especially vv. 4, 11–14), the child is in an interim state from which she is to be awoken. The language used here is clearly appropriate to the Christian hope of resurrection. For Christians, too, death is not final, but a form of 'sleep', and the child's restoration symbolizes our own future resurrection.

Jesus takes the child's hand, addressing her personally, as he did the woman. The effect is 'immediate'. Jesus' command to secrecy is impractical, but it reminds us that who Jesus is and what he is doing cannot be comprehended at this point in the story. For Christians, Jesus is 'the Resurrection and the Life' – but that can be understood only when he himself has been raised from the dead. The woman was not allowed to keep her restoration secret, and the child's must not be reported, but the reason in both cases is the same: these things can be spoken about only in the context of faith.

Mark 6.1–13

The first paragraph (vv. 1–6a) forms the natural climax to the previous three chapters, in which Mark has related various parables and miracles. Now Jesus returns to his home town, and teaches in the synagogue. As in 1.21–28, those who hear him exclaim about his teaching and his works of power – but on this occasion, soon reject the evidence of their ears and eyes. How can a local boy be anything special? Jesus is described as 'the son of Mary', and in Jewish society it would be an insult to refer to the mother alone (the variant reading is probably an attempt to correct this); if Mark was aware of this, it could mean that he knew of a rumour that Jesus was illegitimate. The main point, however, is that the people of Nazareth think they know all there is to know about Jesus and his family, who are still living in the town. Mark's final comment stresses once again the importance of faith: without it, Jesus is *unable* to heal. He is rejected by his own people. Other villages, however, received him (v. 6b).

The Twelve, chosen in 3.13–19 to preach and to have authority over demons, are now sent out. They are sent 'two by two', since the testimony of one would support that of the other, as Jewish law required. They are to travel light, because their errand is urgent. They may accept hospitality when it is offered, but not move around (hoping for something better!). Shaking dust from the feet was a symbolic action performed by Jews on returning home from abroad: foreign dust must not contaminate Jewish territory. Those who truly belong to Israel are those who respond to the disciples' message, and those who do not are cutting themselves off from God's people. We are reminded of the mission of the Baptist, and it is hardly surprising that the disciples set out and demand that people repent.

Mark 6.14–29

The story of the Baptist's death fills the interval between the sending out of the Twelve and their return. For the first and only time in Mark, we have a story that is not specifically about Jesus. As with 1.1–8, however, we are told about John only because what happens to him is relevant to the story of Jesus. John is Jesus' forerunner; already he has been 'handed over' (1.14); now he is put to death by a political ruler who recognizes John's goodness, but is outmanoeuvred by those who demand his death. There are clear parallels with Jesus' own story. The great difference comes only in the final sentence, telling of John's burial, which brings his story to a close.

The passage begins, however, with rumours about his resurrection. These are false, but raise questions as to who Jesus might be. If not John *redivivus*, is he perhaps Elijah, or one of the other prophets? The question is left in suspense. Readers of the Gospel know the answer, but the characters in the story do not.

The story of John's beheading is told with all the dramatic art of a good storyteller. The fact that Herod imprisoned John and then beheaded him is confirmed by the Jewish historian Josephus, though the details of the circumstances differ. Under Roman law, it would have been possible for Herodias to divorce her first husband, but under Jewish law it was not possible. There are interesting parallels with the story of Ahab, Jezebel and Elijah in 1 Kings. Ahab was also a weak man, whose marriage to Jezebel led him into idolatry. Elijah's condemnation of Jezebel and of the worship of Baal led her to plot to kill him. The parallel appears to be picked up in Mark 9.11–13.

Mark 6.30–34, 53–56

The Lectionary omits both of the two accounts of feedings recorded by Mark (6.35–45; 8.1–10), together with the subsequent accounts of the crossing of the lake (6.46–52; 8.11–21), preferring to substitute the Johannine version. This is unfortunate, since it is clear that Mark himself considered the feedings to be of great importance, deliberately including two very similar stories (6.52; 8.17–21). Together, the stories of the feedings and the stilling of the lake lead up to Peter's moment of insight in 8.29.

Our first paragraph concludes the story begun in vv. 7–13. The Twelve are now referred to as 'the apostles', a term meaning literally 'someone sent'. It designates an authorized agent or representative, and denotes function rather than status, since it refers to someone appointed to a particular mission, rather than a permanent post. The 'apostle' was given full authority to act on behalf of the person who had commissioned him. It is an appropriate term for those to whom Jesus had given authority to preach and heal. By the time Mark was writing, however, it had become a technical term for those commissioned by Jesus, though it was not confined to the Twelve.

Jesus' attempt to retreat with his disciples is thwarted by the crowds. The description of the people as having no shepherd implies criticism of the nation's leaders (cf. Num. 27.17; 1 Kgs 22.17; Ezek. 34.5).

The jump to v. 53 is abrupt, and makes little sense. One solution, of course, is to listen to Mark himself, and include the missing verses! Jesus feeds his 'sheep', then again shows his disciples that he is in control of the sea. Verses 53–56 provide a typical Markan summary (cf. 1.32–34; 3.7–12), indicating that the stories Mark records are typical of Jesus' healing ministry.

Mark 7.1–8, 14–15, 21–23

Jesus again comes into conflict with the Jewish religious authorities, and once again it is the behaviour of his disciples that provokes their criticism. The rule that hands must be washed before eating had its origin in the belief that priests eating the sacrifices needed to be 'clean' (Num. 18.8–13). Some of the Pharisees in Jesus' day believed that this rule should be extended to everyday life. This teaching was not in the Torah itself, but was part of 'the tradition of the elders'. Mark's belief that 'all the Jews' followed this rule is untrue.

In response, Jesus attacks his critics: they are so anxious to observe human tradition that they ignore the Torah itself: although they are so concerned about how to honour God, they do not love him with their whole hearts. The quotation from Isaiah 29.13 is closer to the Septuagint than to the Hebrew, which makes it unlikely that it goes back to Jesus himself. This no doubt reflects the fact that stories such as this would have been used by early Christians under attack from their fellow Jews for failing to observe the Torah.

Jesus' teaching to the crowd in vv. 14f. appears to be more radical. Is this, in effect, an attack on the Torah itself? The issue here is not 'unclean hands' but 'unclean food' – i.e. those foods prohibited to the Jews such as pork and shellfish. Jesus appears here to be *contradicting* the Torah! Although Mark interprets it in this way (v. 19), it seems unlikely that this was Jesus' meaning, or the early Church would not have taken so long to implement his teaching. The use of antithesis was common in Hebrew tradition as a way of comparing the relative importance of two commands (cf. Hos. 6.6); if this is the explanation, he is insisting that the Torah's teaching about moral purity is more important than rules about clean and unclean food. This is then spelt out in the saying in vv. 21–23.

Mark 7.24–37

Jesus has moved into Gentile territory, and heals a Gentile; this is the only occasion that Mark specifically mentions a Gentile healing, and it is clearly unusual – indeed, it is presented as an anomaly, and a departure from Jesus' own plans. This story follows on naturally from the previous section, for if good and evil intentions are more important than rules about 'cleanness' and 'uncleanness', then what are we to say when Gentiles have good thoughts and Jews harbour evil ones? Because we assume that Jesus' mission was to all, we find this story puzzling, but the evidence suggests that he confined his mission to Israel. His message was addressed to Jews, and his healing miracles were closely linked with his preaching. Anxious not to be seen as a mere miracle-worker, he was unlikely to respond to the request of a Gentile who would presumably regard him as such.

Jesus' response to her plea is harsh. Gentiles were commonly described as 'dogs' by Jews. Why should the children be deprived of their food for the sake of the dogs? The woman rises to his challenge, and those who have read the story of the feeding in 6.35–44 know that when the children were fed, there were twelve baskets of scraps left over and carefully gathered up. Her faith is rewarded, and her child cured.

In his teaching, Jesus has frequently urged his hearers to hear (4.3, 9; 7.14), and complained that they are apparently unable to do so (4.12). Now he heals someone who is deaf, and as a result is either dumb, or perhaps unable to speak clearly. The healing is performed in private (cf. 5.35–43), perhaps because it signifies the true 'hearing' – with understanding – of Jesus' message, which will happen only with his death and resurrection. Jesus orders the witnesses to tell no one what has happened – an instruction that is, as usual, ignored, even though they do not understand the significance of what has occurred.

Mark 8.27–38

Once again, the Lectionary makes a most unfortunate jump. Not only is the second feeding narrative omitted, but so is the subsequent demand by the Pharisees for signs, and the conversation in the boat, where Jesus rebukes the disciples for their failure to see and hear the truth. These scenes pave the way for what happens at Caesarea Philippi. Even more unfortunate is the omission of the story of the healing of a blind man. Like the healing of the deaf mute, with which it makes a pair, this miracle, which is unique to Mark (though cf. John 9) has symbolic meaning; the blind man's eyes are gradually opened, and he begins to see, at first only dimly. Mark intends us to read 8.22–6 and 8.27–33 together.

Caesarea Philippi marks an important turning-point in Mark's narrative. In this scene the disciples' eyes begin to open to the truth about Jesus. In contrast to the general public, who think of Jesus as a figure from the past – the Baptist, Elijah, or one of the prophets – Peter grasps that he is God's anointed one. What that means, however, he is still far from understanding. Jesus insists on silence: his messiahship must not be spoken of until it is fully understood, and that cannot happen until the Son of Man has suffered, died and been raised.

The disciples do not yet comprehend that Jesus' messiahship involves suffering and humiliation, as Peter quickly demonstrates by attempting to 'rebuke' Jesus. Jesus rebukes him in return; Satan is using him to try to tempt Jesus from the path of obedience.

If this is what Jesus understands 'messiahship' to involve, what does it mean to be his disciple? Verses 34–38 spell out the implications. Those who wish to follow Jesus should not seek power or glory; they must abandon self-interest and personal desires, and follow in Jesus' footsteps – if necessary to a shameful death. Such teaching can be grasped only in the light of the resurrection.

Mark 8.31–38

Verses 31–33 are the first of Mark's three so-called 'passion predictions', which are such important elements in the story between Peter's confession and the end of chapter 10. 'So-called', because they affirm Jesus' final vindication, as well as his suffering. Jesus refers to himself as 'the Son of Man'; in Mark, this phrase suggests the role of one who is obedient to God and is given authority to act as God's representative. In Old Testament thought, such obedience might well mean suffering, but those who were faithful to God's will would be rewarded. The disciples have just acknowledged Jesus to be God's Messiah, the chosen representative of Israel, and we can expect him to embody what Israel should have been.

Although Jesus speaks 'plainly', not in parables, the disciples are unable – or unwilling – to hear. Each of the predictions is followed by a scene in which the disciples demonstrate their inability to accept Jesus' teaching. The teaching horrifies them, because it has implications for them. They are looking for glory, but they must be prepared to follow the same path as Jesus.

The call to 'take up the cross' would have shocked those who first heard it. Who would willingly embrace a gruesome death involving both shame and agony? The saying may well have been shaped *after* Jesus' own death, since in Jesus' mouth it could have been misunderstood as a call to risk the consequences of armed rebellion against Rome. Its impact on Mark's hearers would have been dramatic: this was what discipleship involved! The saying in vv. 34–37 plays on the double meaning of the word translated 'life'; it is not mere existence that is important, but *quality* of life. Jesus' words imply an eschatological recompense. Following Jesus was not easy; but if they were ashamed of him, and were reluctant to embrace his way of suffering, the Son of Man would be ashamed of them when he came in glory.

Mark 9.2–9

Mark's opening phrase points us back to what precedes: the disciples have had their eyes partially opened, and now three of them are allowed to glimpse his glory; but it points back, too, to what he said about suffering, death and resurrection (8.31–33), as v. 9 reminds us. In concluding the reading at v. 9, however, the Lectionary does what the disciples do, and plays down this essential link between glory and suffering!

There are clear echoes of the story of Moses' ascent of Sinai (Exod. 24.1f., 15–18): the reference to 'six days' (replacing Mark's normal 'immediately'), the cloud, the voice, the glory. Moses himself appears, together with Elijah; commentators offer various suggestions about these figures' significance for Mark: each suffered persecution, and each experienced a theophany. It seems most likely that they appear here, however, as witnesses to Jesus' true identity. In 9.13 Elijah is identified with the Baptist, who announced Jesus' coming; Moses was the first and greatest of the prophets, whose name was inextricably linked with Scripture. Mark's readers had already listened to the witness of John the Baptist – and Isaiah – to Jesus; now, as they tried to understand his death and resurrection, they found themselves being directed to 'what is written'.

Peter's comment again demonstrates his lack of understanding: he imagines he is honouring Jesus by putting him on a par with Moses and Elijah. But Jesus is unique: he is the beloved Son, and they are to hear *him*. The three disciples have been given a glimpse of Jesus' true glory – a glory that belongs to him because he is God's beloved (and obedient) Son; their subsequent behaviour will demonstrate how far they are from comprehending what they have seen! It is only after the resurrection that they will grasp its meaning.

The logic in vv. 10–12 is clear, even if the details are obscure: Elijah has returned to prepare the way and been rejected: the fate of the Son of Man is sealed.

Mark 9.30–37

From Caesarea Philippi onwards, Mark's story concentrates our attention on what lies ahead. Jesus is making his way through Galilee; but his public ministry there is over: his task now is to teach the disciples about the meaning of his own calling, and of theirs. The goal of the journey soon becomes apparent.

The prediction of suffering and vindication is the simplest of the three. Most translations translate the Greek *paradidomi* – used already of the Baptist in 1.14 – by 'betrayed', but the verb is ambiguous, and may mean simply 'delivered', or 'handed over'. Here is the paradox: the Son of Man, who should be exercising authority over others, is delivered into their hands.

The disciples did not understand Jesus' teaching and were afraid to ask – not surprising, we may think, after Peter's rebuff in 8.33. But for Mark, incomprehension and fear typify human reaction to what is taking place. The disciples now demonstrate their inability to understand, by arguing about their own status while on 'the way' – a term which for Mark seems to mean the way to Jerusalem (cf. 10.32, 52) – though their silence in v. 34 suggests that at least they are beginning to recognize how inappropriate this is!

Jesus' response is surprising. The child is an appropriate symbol of humility, but why does he talk about *receiving* those who are humble, when the issue is the disciples' own lack of humility? The saying in 10.16 seems far more relevant here – and vv. 36f. seem much more relevant to the incident in 10.13–16! Have the two incidents been confused at some stage?

We, however, have to make sense of what Mark has given us. The disciples' attention – and ours! – is turned away from preoccupation with power and status to the needs of a child, who symbolizes weakness and humility; in receiving the child, they will receive Jesus himself – and they are reminded again of Jesus' own example, who identifies himself with the lowly.

Mark 9.38–50

The common theme here is that of discipleship. In v. 38, John, speaking in the name of all the disciples, addresses Jesus as 'Teacher', which is not the address we expect of a disciple after 8.27—9.8 – but neither is his attitude! His comment demonstrates the disciples' cliquishness: they are not worried about whether the exorcist believes in Jesus, or is simply using his name as a magic formula (cf. Acts 19.13–17), but about whether or not he belongs to the right party. The use of 'us' (v. 38) rather than 'you' suggests that the story perhaps originated in the life of the early Church, where such disputes may well have been common. How did one recognize true Christians?

Jesus' answer is a positive one – contrast Matthew 12.30//Luke 11.23 – and is reminiscent of Numbers 11.26–30. If the man is working in Jesus' name and demons obey him, he clearly recognizes the authority of Jesus, and that is sufficient; cf. 1 Corinthians 12.3. Jesus is prepared to recognize him as a disciple.

The saying in v. 37 stressed the importance of attitudes towards Jesus' – unexpected – representatives: there, he spoke of receiving a child in his name, while in vv. 38–40 he recognized those acting in his name. Verses 41f. continue this theme: those who offer the disciples a cup of water because they belong to Jesus will be rewarded, while those who cause the least of believers to stumble will be punished.

Although the sayings in vv. 41–50 seem to have been put together on the basis of common catchwords, they do have a common theme: reward and punishment. Verses 43–48 spell out the cost of obtaining life, reminding us of 8.34–38. The reward – entering God's kingdom – is such that any sacrifice is worthwhile. The alternative is to be thrown into the rubbish-pit, Gehenna. The enigmatic saying in v. 49 probably refers to purification, while v. 50 suggests that disciples who do not show the essential characteristics of disciples are useless; they must 'share salt' – live in harmony with one another.

Mark 10.2–16

Approaching Jerusalem (v. 1), Jesus is confronted by Pharisees, intent on tripping him up. Their question is surprising, since divorce was clearly permitted in the Mosaic law. Contemporary debate concerned the grounds on which it could be allowed: the school of Rabbi Hillel permitted it on trivial grounds, that of Shammai for adultery alone.

Jesus is far stricter. Pointing first to what Moses said in Deuteronomy 24.1, he does not dispute the validity of Moses' teaching in permitting a man to divorce his wife, but argues that the legislation was necessary because of the hardness of human hearts. He then turns from what the Law *allows* to what God *intends*, and quotes from Genesis 1.27 and 2.24, which set out God's purpose at creation. If a man and a woman have been joined by God, the man should not divide them by divorcing his wife.

Jesus' teaching appears uncompromising. Nevertheless, he recognizes the necessity of the Mosaic provision – and since hearts continue to be 'hard', the provision must remain. But Jesus reminds us of what God intended 'from the beginning of creation', and of what remains the ideal.

Verses 10–12 explain the teaching to the disciples 'indoors'; this is Mark's typical way of spelling out what he thinks are the implications of Jesus' teaching. If a man *does* divorce his wife and marries another, he commits adultery against her. On the basis of v. 9, this seems logical – except that in Jewish law, adultery could be committed only against the husband: this saying implies that the wife has equal rights! Verse 11 applies the same rule to a woman who divorces her husband. This, too, is impossible in Jewish law, and the saying indicates the way Jesus' teaching was interpreted in Roman society. These verses may reflect debates in the early Christian community: if divorce *is* permitted, is remarriage possible?

In vv. 13–16 the disciples are again rebuked for their exclusive and authoritarian attitude – a warning to all church leaders! The kingdom is a gift, to be received with humility. Though used from early times to support infant baptism, this is not mentioned here.

Mark 10.17–31

Once again, we are confronted by the demands of discipleship. Jesus himself sets out on a 'journey', which we know to be the 'way' leading to Jerusalem. Concerning the man who approaches him, Mark tells us only that he is very wealthy (v. 22). Jesus' response to his greeting is difficult (cf. Matt. 19.16f.) – and so likely to be authentic. It is typical of Mark's Jesus, however, that he deflects attention from himself to God. It is *God* who is good, and what the questioner must do is ask what God demands of him. Jesus' message concerns only the kingdom (rule) of God, and how we may serve him. It is also typical of Mark, however, that the test of this man's obedience is whether or not he is prepared to follow Jesus.

Jesus again appeals to the Torah, and quotes the last six commandments, all of which concern 'love of neighbour'. The man's claim to have kept them is apparently not arrogant, since he is anxious to do something more. Jesus' answer is radical: he must give away everything, and follow him. Instead of worrying about how to earn his own salvation, he must be prepared to fling everything away (cf. 8.34–38).

The comment in v. 23 draws the moral – one that astonishes the disciples, who probably regard wealth as a sign of God's favour. Riches are in fact a handicap, since they make entering God's kingdom even more difficult.

The saying in v. 25 may be proverbial; commentators have not always appreciated its wry humour, and have attempted to enlarge the eye in the needle to a gate or to reduce the camel to a rope! Jesus deliberately presents his hearers with an absurd picture. The disciples, however, are once again unable to comprehend his teaching.

Nevertheless, the disciples have done what the rich man could not do; they have left everything and followed Jesus. Peter's words will have been echoed by many of Mark's readers. Discipleship is not easy: but there is reward. Jesus himself left his mother, brothers and sisters, claiming that those who did the will of God were now his family (3.31–34); his followers will be similarly rewarded, as well as gaining the eternal life sought by the rich man.

Mark 10.35–45

This incident follows the third, and most detailed, of the predictions of Jesus' death and resurrection (vv. 32–34). For the third time, the disciples demonstrate their total inability to grasp the meaning of Jesus' teaching, either for him, or for themselves. Approaching Jerusalem (v. 32), James and John have their eyes set on the glory ahead, and they want as much of it as possible. Once again, they address Jesus as 'Teacher' (cf. 9.38), an indication that they do not know what they are asking; those familiar with the end of the story *do* know, realizing that the places at Jesus' right and left hand have been prepared for two robbers. The images Jesus himself uses are ambiguous: 'cup' and 'baptism' can refer to salvation and life. But the cup Jesus drinks is the cup of suffering (14.36), and his baptism will engulf him in death: only because he accepts both do they become the means of salvation.

The indignation of the remaining disciples is probably caused by the fact that the brothers had put their request in first, rather than any awareness of its inappropriateness. Jesus needs to address them *all*. The disciples expect to be given authority; they must learn, then, that greatness is expressed in service. The saying in vv. 43f. echoes teaching found in 8.35; 9.35 and 10.31, but now the link between what is said in the three 'passion predictions' and the sayings about discipleship is spelt out. The Son of Man himself is presented as the supreme example of service to others, and for the first time we are told *why* the Son of Man must die.

The idea that the Son of Man should serve others rather than be served is paradoxical. This service culminates in his death as a ransom – language that reminds us of God's redemption – or 'ransoming' – of Israel from Egypt. Jesus' death will benefit 'many'; this does not imply that others are *not* included, but refers to the new community of God's people which comes about because the Son of Man is prepared to give his life up for them.

Mark 10.46–52

This is the final healing miracle in the Gospel; as with the story in 8.22–26, the blind man's recovery of sight symbolizes his grow-ing ability to see the truth, in contrast to those around him, who remain blind. The two stories mark the beginning and end of a sec-tion that has been particularly concerned with understanding what it means to be Jesus' disciple.

Unusually, Mark names both the place and the man. Jericho was only 15 miles from Jerusalem, so we realize at once that Jesus is near-ing the end of his journey. Bartimaeus is perhaps named because at the end of the story he becomes a disciple, following Jesus 'on the way'.

Bartimaeus addresses Jesus as 'Son of David', recognizing him as the promised descendant of David; apart from Peter at Caesarea Philippi and those possessed by unclean spirits, he is the only person to give Jesus a 'messianic' title of any kind in Mark's Gospel. The blind man sees more than those with sight! It is true that 'Son of David' is for Mark an inadequate title (12.35–37), but it conveys something of the truth, and will be echoed by the crowds when Jesus enters Jerusalem. The Son of David can be proclaimed king only through his death. The blind man shows more understanding than those around him, and this time it is they, not Jesus, who try to silence him. Jesus recognizes his faith, and summons him, as he did the woman with a haemorrhage.

In his eagerness to respond, the man abandons what may have been his only possession, his cloak. Acknowledging his personal commitment, he addresses Jesus now as 'My rabbi', and having recovered his sight, he follows Jesus. He does what disciples are required to do: leaving everything, he follows on the road to Jerusalem.

Mark 11.1–11

Following 10.48, we cannot miss the significance of this story. Pilgrims to the festivals *walked* into Jerusalem; Jesus, who has hitherto walked everywhere, now deliberately rides. Although the Septuagint version of Zechariah 9.9 leads us to associate the ass with humility, Mark makes no reference to that verse, and the ass was an appropriate mount for kings (cf. 1 Kgs 1.33), especially since this one has been ridden by no one else. The description of the way in which the animal was procured indicates that Jesus himself was believed to have planned the event. As he enters into Jerusalem, this dramatic action proclaims his identity – a remarkable change from previous demands for secrecy.

The instructions regarding the foal imply that Jesus has the authority to commandeer the animal. 'The Lord has need of it', and that is enough. By spreading garments on the animal, his followers turn its back into a throne. Spreading garments on the ground is appropriate for a king (cf. 2 Kgs 9.13), though spreading them before his mount seems an extravagant gesture.

The word 'Hosanna' means literally 'Save now', though Mark seems to understand it as a shout of praise. The word occurs in Psalm 118.25; and Mark 11.9b, which is taken from Psalm 118.26, was the welcome given to pilgrims arriving for the festival. For Mark, however, it was an appropriate greeting for the one who came 'in the name of the Lord'. Verse 10 expresses the Jewish hope for the messianic kingdom, though the wording is unfamiliar in Jewish texts. The scene is typical of Mark's irony. The crowds sing psalms and welcome one another as they enter Jerusalem, unaware of the deeper significance of their words. To the readers of the Gospel, however, the meaning is plain (cf. John 12.16).

The final verse sets the scene for the next section, vv. 12–19: the Lord has come to the Temple, inspected it, and found its worship hollow.

Mark 12.28–34

In the church year, we move straight from 10.46–52 to this encounter with a scribe, so continuing the theme of what Jesus demands of his followers. The Lectionary omits altogether 11.12—12.27, but this section is of vital importance for understanding the development of Mark's drama.

In 11.12–25, Mark interweaves the stories of the fig tree and the Temple. Having already inspected the Temple, Jesus searches the fig tree for fruit, but finds none, so curses it. It was not the season for figs, comments Mark! Nevertheless, the tree should have borne fruit when the Lord came to Jerusalem. His actions in the Temple signify condemnation of what is happening there: like the fig tree, the Temple is failing to fulfil its purpose, for it is not a house of prayer, but a den of robbers. Mark interprets Jesus' action as a sign of coming destruction, and the swift withering of the tree suggests that this destruction is inevitable.

Questioned about his authority to act in this way, Jesus confronts his opponents with a similar question about John's baptism. If they can answer that, they will answer their own question, since John's baptism pointed forward to Jesus' ministry: the authority of both is from heaven.

In the Temple, Jesus teaches in parables, though Mark records only one – the story of the vineyard, based on Isaiah 5. In contrast to the hopeful parable of the Sower (Mark 4), which described a bumper harvest as well as some failures, this parable continues the theme of 11.11–25: the leaders of Israel have failed to deliver the harvest. The climax of the story is the tenants' rejection and murder of the owner's beloved son, and their own consequent punishment. Mark sees a clear link between Jesus' rejection and death, and the future judgement of his opponents.

The very leaders whom Jesus has attacked now try to entrap him. First, Pharisees and Herodians combine to ask about the payment of tax; then Sadducees ask about the resurrection. Jesus' answers are not merely clever; he points behind the casuistry of his opponents to the deeper questions and to the implications of their actions. By using Roman money, the Pharisees and Herodians show their dependence on and obligation to Rome; are they also giving God what they owe him, or are they – like the vineyard tenants – with-olding it? The Sadducees deny what they think is 'new' teaching about resurrection, but also ignore the implications of the scriptures and the power of God to give life.

Returning to today's lection, we find a third question. Unusually, the scribe who poses it is presented in a sympathetic light (contrast Matt. 22.35/Luke 10.25). The task of the scribes was to expound the Torah, and one question they debated was which commandment was the first, meaning not which was most important (since all were important), but which was the basic principle from which the rest could be derived. In response to the man's question Jesus again quotes the Torah, beginning with words from the *Shema* (Deut. 6), recited daily by all pious Jews.

Asked for one commandment, Jesus gives two, but they belong together. Here we see the essential unity of faith and ethics in the Old Testament. To love God means to love one's neighbour, and if one fails to love one's neighbour, any claim to love God is empty. Similar statements are attributed to rabbis such as Hillel (first century AD) and Akiba (second century). The saying could, however, be interpreted in very different ways: as meaning either that the 613 commands in the Torah spell out how to love God and neighbour, and so must all be rigorously oberved, or that to love God and one's neighbour is to fulfil the whole purpose of the Law (cf. Rom. 13.8–10; Gal. 5.14).

The scribe concurs: right attitudes are more important than religious observance. His words echo those of the prophets (e.g. Jer. 7.22f.; Hos. 6.6). The incident is set in the Temple, between Jesus' condemnation of worship there, and his prophecy of its destruction (see also 12.38–44).

As a teacher, the scribe assumes that he is entitled to approve Jesus' teaching; in fact, Jesus' authority is greater – so he in turn commends the scribe! The man's honest desire to love God and his neighbour means that he is close to the kingdom. As usual, the authority of Jesus' teaching silences others.

Mark 13.1–8

In 11.11—12.44, Mark described Jesus' dramatic action in the Temple, and his subsequent teaching there. With rare exceptions (12.28–34 and 41–44), Jesus has condemned what he has seen, and encountered only opposition. Not surprisingly, he now speaks of judgement for the Temple. His prophecy of its destruction is in the prophetic tradition (cf. Jer. 7.4, 14).

The magnificence and size of Herod's Temple were famous. Josephus gives precise measurements for some of the stones, and they were indeed enormous. The dimensions and splendour of the marble and gold building would have overwhelmed visitors, and the disciples' reaction is natural.

From the Mount of Olives, one has a panoramic view of Jerusalem. It was an appropriate setting for Jesus' words, since Zechariah 14 speaks of the Lord standing on the Mount of Olives following the destruction of Jerusalem, in order to inaugurate his reign. The teaching is given privately to four disciples only: only later will its significance be understood.

The disciples' question 'When?' is never really answered, except for a 'Not yet', and their request for a sign introduces the first section of the discourse, which warns them against assuming that various disasters are signs of the approaching End. The wording of this passage may well reflect the situation in Mark's own time, when the emergence of false Messiahs, together with 'wars and rumours of wars', were leading many to suppose that the Day of the Lord was imminent. War, earthquake and famine were frequently referred to by prophets and apocalyptic writers when attempting to describe the Day of the Lord. These things were, however, only the beginning of future sufferings. Mark's readers must not suppose that they are the sign that the End has arrived. In spite of this clear warning, reiterated in the following verses, Christians down the ages have persisted in trying to calculate the time of its coming!

Mark 13.24–37

This long discourse in Mark 13 now comes to its climax, in words taken from Isaiah 13.10 and 34.4, passages which describe the wrath that overtakes the world on the Day of the Lord. The darkening of sun and moon indicates that creation itself is in disarray: judgement is now imminent.

In contrast to what the disciples may expect to see (vv. 5, 9, 14), it is an unspecified 'they' who will see the Son of Man coming in clouds, normally associated with God himself. The imagery is that of Daniel 7.13, but the one like a Son of Man is no longer simply a representative of Israel, but Jesus himself. Exercising the power and authority given to him by God, he will gather the elect, the members of the kingdom, acknowledging them as his own (contrast 8.38).

Are the darkening of sun and moon, then, the sign that the end of all things is at hand? The parable in vv. 28–31 suggests that this is so. The deciduous fig-tree was the obvious harbinger of summer, and in Jewish thought it symbolized the joys of the messianic age. When it sprouts, 'he' will be at the very door. But now comes a warning that the end can be expected within a generation. Jesus' followers must be prepared. The day and hour are unknown – even to the Son – so the servants left in charge of the house must keep watch.

Previous sections of the discourse have warned against assuming that the end is imminent: the disciples must beware of undue eschatological excitement. These parables deliver a rather different message: the fact that these signs have not yet occurred does not mean that they can relax their vigilance! They must be alert. Both warnings were necessary in the early Church, where Christians were sometimes carried away by a fervour of eschatological expectation (e.g. 2 Thess. 2), and at other times needed to be reminded of the eschatological hope and warned to be ready for the Lord's coming.

Mark 14.1–72

The religious authorities, who have long wished to destroy Jesus (cf. 3.6; 11.18; 12.12), now hesitate to do so during the festival; somewhat suprisingly, Mark then describes them arresting Jesus on Passover night! Since there are grave historical problems with the idea that any kind of hearing could have been held then, vv. 1f. lend support to the alternative Johannine dating, where Jesus dies *before* the Passover was eaten.

The unnamed woman turns an ordinary act of courtesy into an extravagant gesture: demonstrating her total commitment (like the widow in 12.41–44), she breaks the jar and pours out ointment worth 300 denarii (a year's wages); her action contrasts with the indignation of the onlookers. Jesus commends her: not because the needs of the poor are unimportant, but because times are urgent, and response to him is more important than the religious duty of almsgiving. Her action is a prophetic sign of his coming burial; it is also the 'anointing' of Jesus as Messiah. For a woman to do this rather than the high priest is, of course, an absurd anomaly – though anomalies are typical of Mark's story. She will be remembered, not because of who she is (her name is forgotten!), but because her action proclaims not only the gospel of Jesus' death and resurrection, but her own response.

Mark gives no hint of Judas' motive in agreeing to betray Jesus; he stresses only that he is one of the Twelve. The promise to pay Judas for his treachery stands in contrast to the generosity we have just witnessed.

In v. 12, Mark identifies the Last Supper as a Passover meal. This had to be eaten in Jerusalem, and the instructions given to the disciples are reminiscent of 11.1–6. Once again, Jesus is shown to be in control of the situation: this time he demands not an animal, but what he describes as 'my room'.

Returning to the theme of betrayal, Mark indicates that Jesus was fully aware of what was about to happen. Since it 'is written', it is part of the divine plan. Nevertheless, this does not relieve Judas of responsibility.

The description of the meal is brief, and probably reflects the wording used at celebrations of the Eucharist attended by Mark himself. The Passover was the celebration of Israel's redemption from Egypt, and the various elements at the meal were interpreted of that event; now the bread and cup are given new interpretations. The four verbs used in v. 22 – took, blessed (i.e. praised God), broke, gave – describe what took place at any Jewish meal, but the explanations are distinctive. Mark does not include the instructions to 'eat' and 'drink' found in Matthew, and the emphasis therefore falls on these four actions. 'Body' can mean 'physical body' (*not* 'flesh'!), but also 'self'; taken with his action in breaking and sharing the bread, Jesus' words suggest that in breaking the bread he is sharing something of his own personality with them, as well as handing over authority and mission (cf. 1 Kgs 19.19). Paul's comment in 1 Corinthians 10.17 is relevant: to share the one loaf means to share in his 'body', to be members of the community.

The common cup was also a sign of fellowship: Jesus again took, blessed God, and gave; 'broke' is inappropriate this time, but the emphasis on sharing is conveyed by the statement that 'they all drank from it'. The words 'This is my blood' are very difficult, since Jews regarded drinking blood with horror: significantly, the blood is then said to be poured out. The blood of the covenant was poured out (not drunk!) on Sinai (Exod. 24.8): Jesus' blood will be poured out for 'many', to ratify God's (new) covenant with his people. His death points forward to the time when God's kingdom is established, when his people will feast at the messianic banquet (v. 25).

Christian tradition has tended to focus on the bread and wine themselves, but Mark emphasizes Jesus' *actions* (breaking and pouring), which – like other prophetic actions – signify the meaning of what is happening; Jesus hands over to his disciples – but will continue to be with them (cf. John 14–17); through his death and resurrection, a new people of God is being brought into being.

It was traditional to sing Psalms 114–18 at the end of the Passover meal. The Mount of Olives was part of greater Jerusalem, so accessible on Passover night. Jesus' prediction of the disciples' coming failure is supported by Zechariah 13.7. The promise in v. 28 will be picked up in 16.7. To 'go before' is ambiguous – it could mean 'precede', but following the reference to Jesus as a shepherd, probably means 'lead'. The shepherd will be raised, and the flock brought together. Typically, Peter protests – only to be told that he will deny Jesus three times. Mark stresses Jesus' accurate foreknowledge of events: it will happen that very night. The disciples protest their loyalty, but they are not yet ready to follow in his footsteps (cf. 8.34).

In Gethsemane, Jesus himself shrinks from the cup. This conflicts with what Mark says elsewhere about Jesus accepting his coming sufferings as inevitable. Now he is distressed and overwhelmed with grief, and prays that the cup may be removed (cf. Heb. 5.7). This scene cannot have been invented! (Contrast John 12.27, where Jesus contemplates death serenely.) Jesus here faces the horror of imminent pain and humiliation, though obedient to God's will, whatever that may be. Only Peter, James and John are invited to share his vigil – the three disciples who have most adamantly declared their willingness to share his suffering. They must keep awake, since this is the time of testing (cf. Mark 13.35, 37). To fail will mean that they escape suffering.

Jesus addresses God as 'Abba', and though calling God 'Father' was by no means unique, it appears to have been a distinctive element of Jesus' prayers. This and other phrases echo the Lord's Prayer (though Mark does not record it): note the acceptance of God's will, and the instruction to the disciples to pray lest they fall into temptation. But they fall asleep three times: their failure is comprehensive.

The mood now changes again. Jesus announces the arrival of the hour from which he has just prayed to be delivered (vv. 35, 41), together with the approach of his betrayer. His words are instantly fulfilled: what is happening is the fulfilment of Scripture (v. 49). Judas' greeting stresses his treachery; the remaining disciples flee. The bystander who attempts to resist arrest is not identified, and neither is the young man who flees naked; why Mark includes this brief incident (vv. 51f.) is a total mystery – unless it is to contrast this unnamed disciple, who follows Jesus (albeit briefly!), with the Twelve, who have all deserted him.

Jesus' interrogation by the high priest bristles with historical problems, but the theological impact is clear. The accusation against Jesus is 'false', as the failure of witnesses to agree demonstrates: Jesus has indeed spoken of the Temple's coming destruction, but he has not threatened to destroy it himself. Part of the Jewish eschatological hope was that God himself would rebuild the Temple and live with his people. Mark's first readers may perhaps have seen the accusation as a garbled version of their belief that their own community was a spiritual 'temple' (cf. 1 Cor. 3.16f.; 2 Cor. 6.16; John 4.21). Jesus is innocent, so remains silent.

Faced with a direct challenge from the high priest, however, Jesus for the first time acknowledges openly that he is indeed the Messiah, and the Son of the Blessed. As at Caesarea Philippi, however, he speaks immediately of the Son of Man – this time to affirm his vindication. Jesus' enemies will see him at God's right hand, and coming with clouds – i.e. as judge (cf. Dan. 7.13f.). The irony is that Jesus' judges thereupon condemn him – so condemning themselves.

In contrast to this story, Mark interweaves with it his account of Peter's denial (vv. 54, 66–72). Peter's courage collapses when challenged by a servant-girl! The charge becomes more specific, and Peter's response more adamant. While Jesus is announcing the coming of the Son of Man in glory, Peter denies his discipleship (cf. 8.38). The crowing of the cock reminds us that Jesus' words have been fulfilled.

Mark 15.1–39 (40–47)

Mark's account of the hearing before Pilate raises further historical problems. Pilate is unlikely to have given in to this kind of pressure, and there is no evidence elsewhere for the Passover amnesty (v. 6). The story reflects Mark's view that the Jews were responsible for Jesus' death and used the Romans to carry out the sentence they had already passed on him (14.64). It brings to a climax the opposition to Jesus that Mark has traced throughout his narrative, and was no doubt influenced by the continuing opposition of many Jews to the gospel in Mark's own day.

Throughout this chapter Mark stresses that Jesus dies as King of the Jews (vv. 2, 9, 12, 18, 26, 32). The story is suffused with irony. Jesus' answer to the charge – 'You say so' – throws the responsibility back onto Pilate; like the high priest (14.61), he has unwittingly spoken the truth. The idea that Pilate would offer the crowd a choice between a convicted murderer and someone whom he never finds guilty is implausible, as is his release of someone who had taken part in an uprising. He would have had no hesitation in executing anyone he considered guilty of sedition, whether Jesus or Barabbas. This incident serves two purposes: for Mark's first readers, it would have emphasized the guilt of the Jews; but it also hints at a theological truth, since Jesus' coming death has already brought freedom and life to another.

Jesus is then mocked by the soldiers, who give him the trappings of monarchy and hail him as 'King of the Jews'. The irony of the scene is plain: the one they mock is in fact the King, but he is King only because he is prepared to die.

101

Criminals were normally forced to carry their own crosses; Mark does not explain why Jesus did not do so. In carrying the cross, Simon is compelled to do what Jesus had demanded of his followers (8.34); Alexander and Rufus were presumably known to Mark's first readers. Jesus would have been stripped naked; the division of clothes and casting of lots is reminiscent of Psalm 22.18.

The 'charge' nailed to the cross is extraordinary: not what Jesus was alleged to have claimed, but what, to Mark, was the simple truth. Jesus is enthroned on the cross, proclaimed King in death. To grasp the absurdity of the scene we have to remember the barbaric nature of crucifixion, a punishment which inflicted an agonizing death on its victims, as well as exposing them to shame and ridicule. Two bandits are crucified on his right hand and his left; the phrase reminds us of 10.37, 40, so hinting at the idea spelt out in the Fourth Gospel that Jesus' death is his glorification. The quotation from Isaiah 53.12 (v. 28) is missing from the earliest and best manuscripts; it appears to have been added in order to emphasize that what happened was part of the divine plan.

The taunts of passers-by echo earlier accusations of blasphemy (2.7; 14.64); in fact, it is they who blaspheme (3.28–30). They repeat the accusation of 14.58; if he can destroy and rebuild the Temple, he can surely save himself! The chief priests and scribes echo the charge that he claimed – falsely! – to be God's Messiah (14.61); like the Pharisees in 8.11, they demand a sign, so that they may believe. The one who saved others can surely save himself. But for Mark and his readers, it is precisely because Jesus does *not* save himself that he is able to save others. Even those crucified with Jesus taunt him. Once again, we have Mark's familiar triple pattern: *everyone* turns against him.

Jesus is totally alone: the disciples have fled, and everyone on Golgotha has taunted him. No wonder, then, that Mark says that darkness falls over the whole land for three hours: it is pointless to look for some natural explanation of this darkness: for Mark, it is a sign of judgement on those who have rejected Jesus (cf. Amos 8.9). Mark reports only one saying from the cross – the opening words of Psalm 22, quoted in Aramaic. The suggestion that we are meant to think of later verses, which express the psalmist's hope of deliverance, avoid the problem, and miss the profundity of the words. This is what Jesus' oneness with humanity means: he shares human despair and isolation to the full. At this moment he feels that he has been abandoned even by God. This is what Paul means in Galatians 3.13 and 2 Corinthians 5.21. Jesus is tested to the full, and is completely obedient.

Jesus is then offered sour wine; though presumably a humane gesture, it was probably seen by Mark as a fulfilment of Psalm 69.21, where David complains that his enemies give him vinegar to drink. There was a tradition that Elijah would come to the aid of the righteous when they were in trouble. The suggestion that he might come to help seems to be intended as another taunt. Readers know it to be absurd, since Elijah (who has been identified with the Baptist, 9.13) has himself been put to death.

Jesus dies with a loud cry; no explanation is given, but Mark may well think of this as the 'unanswered' cry of Psalm 22.2. Contrast Luke 23.46 and John 19.30! The curtain that is torn is probably the one separating the Holy of Holies from the rest of the Temple. Is this a sign of judgement? Jesus' death makes the destruction of the Temple inevitable. Or is Mark thinking that men and women now have free access into God's presence (Heb. 9.11f., 24–28)? That would include Gentiles, and it is a Gentile – Jesus' executioner! – who now declares him to be God's Son. This confession is specifically linked to Jesus' death: Jesus is finally acknowledged to be Son of God – and it is because of the way he died! This is the truth the disciples failed to grasp.

At this point we realize that followers *have* been present throughout, though at a distance: the women are mentioned now as witnesses of his death (v. 41) and of his burial (vv. 46f.). This is undertaken hurriedly by Joseph of Arimathea, though whether because he was sympathetic to Jesus' cause or anxious that his body should be buried (cf. Deut. 21.23) Mark does not say. Jesus had died quickly – was he really dead? Verses 44f. are intended to scotch any rumours to the contrary. There is apparently no time to anoint the body – but we already know that this is unnecessary (14.8; 16.1–8).

Mark 16.1–8

The women come to anoint Jesus' body, though they are too late – not because it had begun to decay (as should have been the case), but because it is not there. Their question about the stone underlines the fact that the tomb had been firmly sealed. Now the huge stone has been moved. The young man is dressed in white, indicating that he is an angel, and he tells the women that Jesus has been raised, then gives them a message for the disciples. Since Peter has denied that he is a disciple he is mentioned by name, and the words 'and Peter' convey an assurance of forgiveness; he had been ashamed of Jesus (8.38), but is now summoned to follow him once more. The message echoes Jesus' words in 14.28: he is leading his disciples back to Galilee, where they can begin again to learn what discipleship means, though it is only if they obey and follow that they will see him.

We expect Mark to follow this with an account of an appearance of Jesus to his disciples. Instead, he tells us only that the women fled in terror – and silence! – from the tomb. Mark's ending is abrupt, and Matthew and Luke felt it necessary to add more, as did those who made additions to Mark itself (vv. 9–20, and the 'shorter ending', neither of which is Markan in style or vocabulary). The fear and disobedience are, however, typical of Mark; confronted with the greatest of all miracles, it is not surprising if even the women – hitherto depicted as faithful – are overcome by terror and say nothing.

Commentators have often assumed that Mark intended to write more, and was prevented, or that the ending has been lost. His story seems incomplete, but there are parallels – notably in the ending of Acts, written by a skilled literary author. The fact that in Mark's story women are the only people to be given the news of Jesus' resurrection must have stunned his readers! Mark's ending is, however, theologically profound. Instead of recording that the disciples saw Jesus and believed, he ends with a promise that if they believe they will see. He challenges us to do the same: if we believe Jesus' word and follow him, we too will see him. Mark insists that we must finish the story for ourselves, by setting out on the way of discipleship.

The Gospel according to Luke

ANDREW F. GREGORY

Introduction

Luke is the longest of the Gospels. Together with Acts (the second part of its author's two-volume work; see Luke 1.1–4; Acts 1.1–2) it accounts for a quarter of the New Testament. We know very little of its author – tradition identifies him with Luke, a companion of Paul on some of his travels (cf. Col. 4.14; 2 Tim. 4.11) – but he wrote more of the New Testament than any other of its contributors.

It is unclear from his own writings whether Luke was a Jew or a Gentile. Certainly he writes in the knowledge that churches of his day contained followers of Jesus from each background, and that relationships between them have not always been – and perhaps often still are not – straightforward. If Luke is to be identified with the beloved physician of Colossians 4.14, he was a Gentile, but one with a good knowledge of the Jewish scriptures. If a companion of Paul, Luke is unlikely to have lived beyond the 90s of the first century, so this would provide an upper limit to the period during which he may have written his two volumes; if Luke was not a companion of Paul, the date may be later still. Most scholars believe that Luke used Mark; if so, he cannot have written earlier than whatever date is assigned to that Gospel – usually around AD 70, the date at which the Romans destroyed Jerusalem. Nothing in Luke or in Acts either supports or undermines his traditional identification as a doctor.

Luke begins his two volumes with a formal preface (Luke 1.1–4; cf. Acts 1.1–2). It follows conventions that can be paralleled with those in other prefaces in approximately contemporary texts written in Greek. However its closest affinities appear to be with prefaces found in what we might think of as academic, technical or professional writings from the ancient world, not with genres such as history that were considered more 'high brow'. It is perhaps best thought of as literate rather than literary. Although a finely balanced and carefully structured periodic composition, the meaning of the preface is not always as clear as we might like. Nevertheless, it merits close attention. If we are to approach Luke in the way that he invites his reader or hearer to approach his work – or at least, to understand how he invited them to do so – it is important to pay attention to the keys that he gives us as we begin to unlock his text. A number of points may be noted.

First, Luke dedicates his work to an otherwise unknown Theophilus. It is a common name, so while it may be interpreted as symbolic – the adjective *theophilēs* may mean beloved of God – it seems unnecessary to do so. Theophilus is addressed as 'most excellent', so perhaps he is a person of some status and wealth. More important is the point that it is unlikely that Theophilus is coming to much of the information in this text for the first time, for Luke goes on to say that he writes so that Theophilus may know the truth or reliability of the things concerning which he has already been instructed (v. 4). This suggests that Theophilus is a Christian, and makes clear that Luke's narrative is intended not merely to convey information but to convince Theophilus (and others who read it or hear it read) that they may rely on what they have been taught.

Second, and closely related to Luke's statement of purpose, are his reference to the *many* predecessors who have undertaken to write similar accounts (v. 1), and his comments about the way in which he has received traditions handed down by 'those who from the beginning were eyewitnesses and servants of the word' (v. 2; cf. 1 Cor. 11.2, 23; 15.3). Luke's reference to many predecessors is certainly conventional (cf. Acts 24.10; Heb. 1.1), but this need not mean that it is without substance. As noted already, most scholars agree that Mark was among Luke's written sources. Many of them also believe that he had access to another source known also to Matthew, usually referred to as Q. If other material recorded only by Luke is also ascribed to a written source or sources, this would bring the number of such predecessors to at least three. Some scholars have also included either Matthew or John among the sources known to Luke, but these are minority positions.

A certain amount of dissatisfaction at the work of those who wrote any of the written sources on which Luke drew may be implied in his reference to what they *undertook* to do (v. 1). When *we* read the Gospels in their canonical context, we are invited and encouraged to see them as complementary works: one gospel, but according to four complementary perspectives. Yet this may not be what Luke intended (or indeed Matthew, nor perhaps even John; nor does it seem likely that Mark envisaged such a scenario). The very strong likelihood that Luke used so much of Mark tends to suggest that he wished to preserve its basic outline and content, but the way in which he edited and added to what he used suggests that Luke will have considered Mark redundant after his own account was written. Why read Mark when instead you can read the fuller account by Luke? The earlier Gospel is not so much supplemented as supplanted.

Luke does not seem to believe that Theophilus already had access to an orderly account that would be sufficient for him to know the truth concerning the things about which he has been instructed, so to this extent at least Luke's precedents do not match up to his requirements of what this sort of narrative account should be. Theophilus can rely on what Luke writes – even if it differs on points of detail from what he has heard already. Luke has drawn on a living tradition from those who were eyewitnesses to the events that he narrates (v. 2), and has used their testimony with care (v. 3). Like all subsequent readers and hearers of his Gospel, neither Luke nor Theophilus had the opportunity to meet Jesus for themselves, but they may rely on the faithful testimony that comes from those who were with him from the beginning of his ministry to his resurrection from the dead (Acts 1.21–22; 2.32; 10.34–43). Theophilus may be assured that he does not need to see the risen Jesus to know that he is alive; he needs rather to understand the scriptures, to remember what Jesus taught and to participate in the breaking of the bread (Luke 24.25–35).

Third, we may note Luke's description of his own work as an 'orderly account' (v. 1). The way in which Luke orders his account is an important tool with which to understand what it contains. This can be seen not only in the way in which different incidents and teachings help to illuminate each other (see, for example, on 7.11–17, and on 8.22–25 and 8.26–39 in the following commentary), but also in the overall arrangement of his two-volume work. The narrative of the Gospel begins and ends in the Temple in Jerusalem, and it may be divided into four main parts: the infancy and child-hood of Jesus (1.5—2.52); his ministry in Galilee (3.1—9.50); his journey to Jerusalem (9.51—19.44 (or 27)) and his ministry, passion and resurrection in that city (19.45 (or 28)—24.53).

Fourth, we may note Luke's summary of the content of his orderly account: 'the events that have been fulfilled among us'. Luke goes to great lengths throughout his two volumes to emphasize that the story of Jesus and those who follow him is not a series of random events but the outworking of God's plan as laid out in Jewish scripture and fulfilled in the events that have brought him and Theophilus together. The story that follows does not begin in 'the fifteenth year of the reign of the Emperor Tiberius' (3.1), in the days of Augustus (2.1) or even 'in the days of King Herod of Judaea' (1.5). It takes place in the contemporary world, but has its beginnings in God's purposes for the whole world (3.23–38) as set out in all the scriptures (3.4–6; 4.17–21; 24.25–27, 45, etc.). The cross was a necessary point on Jesus' journey, neither a terrible mistake nor an end in itself (24.46–49). Just as Luke depicts Jesus' resolute and costly decision to travel the way that he should (9.51; 22.42), so he depicts the disciples who travel with him to the cross (23.49) and invites his readers and hearers to do the same (9.23–24).

Only Luke has all Jesus' acquaintances at the foot of the cross (23.49), not just the faithful women whose important role he accentuates more than any other of the canonical evangelists (8.1–3; 24.6–10, on which see below). His gentler and more positive depiction of the disciples than that of Mark or Matthew, his continued emphasis on the importance of women as well as men in the purposes of God, his emphasis on the inclusion of those on the margins, and his portrayal of the compassion and mercy of a God who longs to forgive, and the declaration of joy in heaven at the repentance of a sinner, are among the features that contribute to the accessibility and popularity of the third Gospel today. They help to explain why many Western Christians find Luke's presentation of Jesus more congenial than that of Matthew and more gentle and less breathless than that of Mark. Mark gives hardly any of Jesus' teaching at all, though he often refers to him as a teacher. Matthew concentrates it in five heavy sermons, but Luke conveys movement and a lightness of touch by presenting much of Jesus' teaching in the course of his journey to Jerusalem.

If any parable from Matthew were to sum up the teaching of Jesus as Matthew presents him, it might be the parable of the sheep and the goats. In Luke it is more likely to be the good Samaritan or the prodigal son. Almost half the third Gospel consists of these parables and other material recorded only by Luke: not just many parables but powerful and life-giving encounters with individuals such as Zacchaeus, or the penitent thief on the cross. Only in Luke do we find the narrative basis for the festivals of Candlemas, the Ascension and Pentecost. Only in Luke (at least in Acts) have we the scriptural basis for a 40-day observation of Easter. Only in Luke have we much of the material that is important in the celebration of Christmas and the development of Marian devotions and belief. Only in Luke is there a narrative account of the life of Jesus that begins with the virginal conception and ends with a visible and explicitly narrated ascension. So of the canonical evangelists it is Luke alone who provides the full sweep of the christological content of the Apostles' Creed.

Luke's contribution to the Christian understanding of Jesus and his continuing significance is not restricted to material peculiar to his account, however. It is found also in those parts of his narrative that he shares with the other Gospels, though often in his presentation of such material he gives more attention to themes and motifs that are less prominent in parallel accounts. These distinctive emphases will be given particular attention in the commentary that follows, but not, I hope, to the detriment of the Gospel as a whole – or at least as it is read in the Lectionary.

Commentary on the Sunday readings from Luke

Luke 1.26–38

The prophecy of Jesus' birth is the second annunciation scene in Luke (cf. 1.5–24). The angel's appearance to Mary is in the sixth month after John was conceived (v. 26), so the prophecy here is explicitly linked to the earlier prophecy to Zechariah and its fulfilment.

Each account is part of a larger sequence in which Luke emphasizes both the importance of John and his subordination to Jesus. John's mother was elderly and barren, yet God caused her to conceive; now by his Spirit he will cause a virgin to conceive, for nothing is impossible for God (vv. 35–37). Elizabeth's child will be great in the sight of the Lord; but Mary's will be called the Son of the Most High, and God will give to him the throne of his ancestor David (vv. 13–15, 30–32). John will make a people prepared for the Lord; Jesus will reign over the house of Jacob for ever (vv. 16–17, 33). John's father questioned his angelic visitor, and is deprived of speech as a result; Mary believes, and commits herself to the purposes of God (vv. 18–20, 38). Mary is young, poor, vulnerable – and a woman. Yet not only does she accept that God has chosen her, she responds enthusiastically as one who will co-operate actively with God and his plan of salvation.

Luke's interest in Mary is typical of his interest in women, yet his concerns here remain primarily christological. The focus of the passage is not on Mary but on Jesus, whose identity the angel announces. Luke is emphatic about Jesus' Davidic descent (vv. 27, 32; cf. 2.4, 11; 3.31; 18.38–39) but also clear that Jesus is greater than David (20.41–44; Acts 2.25–36). Jesus is the promised Davidic Messiah (v. 32; cf. 2 Sam. 7.12–13), but he is also more than that. He is also Son of God, in whose conception and birth the Holy Spirit and the power of the Most High (a favourite Lukan expression for God; vv. 32, 35, 76; 8.28; Acts 7.48; 16.17) are at work.

Luke 1.39–45 (46–55)

There is a cartoon-like quality to the episodes in Luke's infancy narrative, and its immediacy and vitality may be lost if we move too quickly to view it as a documentary. Elizabeth and Mary are presented as larger than life characters in the one vivid encounter that

Luke portrays at the beginning of Mary's three-month stay with Elizabeth. The episode is steeped in the atmosphere of the Jewish scriptures. This gives a certain 'once upon a time' (cf. 'in those days', v. 39) ambience to the narrative, and it serves to show the continuity between the story of Israel and its God and the story that Luke will unfold of the ministries of John and Jesus. Yet this account does not only look backwards to the older story of which it is now a part. It also includes distinctive Lukan interests that foreshadow and anticipate elements that will be prominent in the main part of his two-volume narrative. This episode, like the rest of the infancy narrative, is an overture that introduces themes yet to be developed.

Elizabeth and John are each filled with the Holy Spirit, a recurring Lukan interest. We are told this explicitly of Elizabeth, but it is implied of John when he too recognizes Jesus (1.41, 44, cf. 1.15). Thus Luke also shows how prophecy and therefore God's design is being fulfilled in the events that he relates (cf. 1.45). Luke stresses the importance of Elizabeth and John in God's purposes, but already it is clear that John is subordinate to Jesus and Elizabeth to Mary: each older figure recognizes the greater importance of his or her younger counterpart (vv. 42, 44).

Elizabeth underlines the importance of Mary's accepting belief of God's word to her (1.45, cf. 1.38), yet Mary is not merely passive. She rushes to visit Elizabeth, presumably because the angel has told her of Elizabeth's part in God's unfolding drama (1.39, cf. 1.36). Mary is no wilting violet, and on her lips we hear the prophetic message of the radical and revolutionary nature of the rule of the God whose son she carries.

Luke may have taken an existing hymn that he adapted to this context by the insertion of v. 48, but we cannot be sure. It is modelled on Hannah's song (1 Sam. 2), but it offers comfort for all who are lowly/humiliated/poor/dependent on God and not proud of their own resources and independence. God will continue to act in conformity with his action in the past – the implicit message of the echoes of Jewish Scripture, and the explicit point of vv. 54–55 – and he will do so in practical and material ways. These words of warning to those who are wealthy and powerful should not be robbed of their economic and political force. Nor should we minimize or obscure Luke's words of solace and hope to those whose poverty and oppression sustains the wealth and comfort that we enjoy – for now, at least. A hard edge is present in this hymn of praise.

The importance of the way in which individuals and communities use and share their material resources is a recurring theme in Luke and in the early part of Acts. Here Luke presents his hearers with a reminder of the revolutionary nature of God's rule – past (vv. 50–55), present – for Mary (vv. 48–49), and future (vv. 48b, 50).

Luke 2.1–14 (15–21)

Luke's account of the census allows him to explain why Jesus was born in Bethlehem (with its Davidic connections, v. 4; cf. Micah 5.2, and above on 1.26–38), not in Nazareth in Galilee, where he grew up and began his public ministry. (Matthew shares Luke's concern to place Jesus' birth in Bethlehem, not Nazareth, but presents it as his family's home prior to their flight to Egypt.) An interest in placing Jesus' ministry in the context of the wider political landscape in which he lived is characteristic of Luke (1.5; 3.1–2; 23.6–12; Acts 18.2, 12), but the reference to an empire-wide census under Augustus while Quirinius was governor (v. 2) and Herod was king (1.5) raises considerable historical difficulties that commentators continue to debate.

Luke's brief description of Jesus' birth is matter-of-fact, but its significance is made clear by the angel's words to the shepherds (vv. 10–12). Luke focuses on the identity of the child (v. 11) to whose origin (1.35) and destiny (1.32–33) he has already alerted the hearers of his Gospel. Jesus' Jewishness is underlined by the report of his circumcision (v. 21), a practice that Greeks and Romans – perhaps a significant part of Luke's intended audience – found abhorrent. The giving of a name announced by an angel points to the heavenly dimension of his origin.

There may be an element of political subversion in what the angels announce. Roman emperors were hailed as saviours and benefactors whose birth, accession or return to good health was 'good news' or 'gospel' for the peoples whom they ruled (cf. v. 10). Augustus in particular (v. 1) was praised for making wars to cease and ushering in a new age of peace (cf. v. 14; 19.38). What others proclaimed of Roman emperors who came and went, the angels proclaim of Christ – of whose kingdom there will be no end (1.33). Augustus is no more than the unwitting agent of God through whose census prophecies concerning the birth of the Messiah in Bethlehem are fulfilled. The realization that this is the case is more important for a full appreciation of Luke's work as a narrator than the question of whether he is factually accurate in every detail of his account.

The sign to the shepherds (v. 12) is that what they are told they will find proves to be true (v. 16). Luke often records prophecies that are then fulfilled in his narrative, thus demonstrating the dependability of God and his messengers (cf. 1.20, fulfilled in 1.22; 1.13, fulfilled in 1.24, 57, 60; 1.15–17, 76–79, fulfilled in 3.1–18; 1.31, fulfilled in 2.21; 9.22, fulfilled in chapters 22–24; 24.49 and Acts 1.8, fulfilled in Acts 2; etc.).

Those who see most fully the significance of Jesus' birth come from and return to heaven (vv. 13, 15). The shepherds are sufficiently receptive to praise God (a recurrent theme in Luke–Acts, often presented as the appropriate response to what God has done: see below on 7.11–17) and to tell others what has been made known to them. Their forthrightness is in contrast with the reaction of Mary, told for the first time that her son will be a Saviour. Her reaction is similar to that of those who heard the news about John (1.66), and is depicted as part of a continuing process (2.51) in which she tries to grasp the significance of what she sees and hears.

Luke 2.22–40

Luke's Gospel begins and ends in the Temple. Here Luke presents the first of two accounts of Jesus' being brought to the Temple as a child, perhaps echoing stories of the presentation and childhood of Samuel (1 Sam. 1–2). Only mothers needed to be purified after childbirth (Lev. 12.2–5), so some scribes changed their manuscripts to read 'her' instead of 'their' (v. 22). Luke's point is to emphasize the faithful law-observant piety of Jesus' parents (vv. 22, 23, 24, 27, 39). As in his reference to the census (above, 2.1–14), it is more important to note what Luke does with his material than to quibble over the accuracy of its details. Luke depicts Jesus' parents as doing everything that he thought was required after the birth of a child.

That they offer only birds as a sacrifice, not also a lamb (Lev. 12), is a sign of their material poverty.

Simeon and Anna are one of a number of pairs of men and women found in Luke's infancy narratives and elsewhere in his Gospel. (Others include Zechariah and Mary, 1.5–37; Naaman and the widow of Zarephath, 4.25–27; the centurion's servant and the widow's son, 7.1–17, cf. Jairus' daughter, 8.40–56; Peter and the women at the tomb, 24.1–12. In each case, the pairing seems deliberate and serves to emphasize the prominent position and active role of women as well as men in the ministry of Jesus.) Both are recognizable as the sort of prophetic figures found in the Jewish scriptures, as seen most notably in the description of Simeon, a Spirit-led man looking forward to God acting on behalf of his people (vv. 25–27). The description of Anna (vv. 36–38) reinforces the atmosphere of Jewish piety that Luke has already established in his depiction of Mary, Joseph and Simeon. It gives depth to the picture, but adds little in the way of specific detail. Yet this underlines rather than diminishes the importance of Luke including a woman as well as a man in his account.

Simeon and Anna help to root the story of Jesus in the story of what God has done already, as recorded in the Jewish scriptures which Luke echoes repeatedly throughout his first two chapters, each of which would sit naturally with stories found in those earlier texts. But Simeon and Anna also point to the future. Anna speaks about the child 'to all who were looking for the redemption of Jerusalem' (v. 38), and Simeon speaks of both the extent and cost that such redemption will entail. Thus he speaks of salvation for all peoples and a light for revelation to the Gentiles and for the glory of Israel (vv. 30–32, a prophecy that anticipates the story that Luke will tell in Acts) but also the division that Jesus will bring (vv. 34–35). This is the first hint of a divided Jewish response to Jesus. This theme will be picked up again from the beginning of Jesus' public ministry (cf. 4.28, where the change in the people's response is a direct reaction to Jesus' teaching about God's provision for Gentiles). Simeon's words foreshadow in sorrow both the political cost to the nation as whole that will follow from their divided re-action to Jesus (19.41–44) and also the personal cost to Mary as his mother.

Luke 2.33–35

See above, on 2.22–40.

Luke 2.41–52

Luke shares with Matthew an interest in Jesus' birth, but Luke is alone among the canonical evangelists in his attempt to fill in some of the details of Jesus' life between his infancy and the beginning of his public ministry. Such details are further elaborated in later Gospels that were not included in the canon. Luke's summarizing introduction (v. 41) is typical of the way in which he adds depth to his narrative – he tells one story in detail, but implies that it may be typical of other incidents in Jesus' life (cf. 2.40; 3.18; 4.15, 44, etc.). Thus Luke notes that each year Jesus' parents would go to Jerusalem for the Passover (a further sign of their piety; cf. on 2.22–40, above).

As a boy, Jesus is in the Temple among the teachers (v. 46). Teaching is a prominent activity in Luke's account of his public ministry, and 'teacher' a common title or form of address (7.40; 8.49; 9.38, etc.), not least when Jesus returns to the Temple in the period before his passion (20.21, 28, 39; 21.37; 22.11). Here we hear Jesus' own voice for the first time, when he speaks to his earthly parents of his identity as the obedient son of a heavenly Father. This is in line with Gabriel's words to Mary (1.36), but the enormity of the boy Jesus' claim (and perhaps the incongruity of it upon his own lips) is emphasized by the uncomprehending reaction of Mary and Joseph. Luke implies increasing understanding on the part of Mary (v. 51; cf. 2.19) but is explicit about Jesus' increase in wisdom, years and favour, a further example of the way in which he uses summaries to progress his narrative and to move from the specific to the general.

Luke's main point is christological, and the gravity of Jesus' claim to be God's obedient Son is underlined by its setting in the Temple, the place where Yahweh dwells. Some readers have seen an anticipation of the resurrection in Jesus being lost and then found 'after three days' (v. 46).

Luke 3.1–6

Luke's narrative might easily begin with these verses, and perhaps once did if there was an early version to which he had not yet added the infancy narratives. He certainly identifies it as the beginning of the Gospel proper when he refers back to it in his second volume (Acts 10.37; cf. Acts 1.22). From here on Luke appears to have used Mark as a source, which explains why he seems to introduce John as if for a second time. Luke's use of named political leaders to date the ministry of John reminds us that his story is set in the realities of the Roman empire and its means of imperial administration, and is a recurrent emphasis in his text (cf. 1.5; 2.1). Pilate and Herod will feature prominently later in Luke's account (see below on 23.6–12), but for now the focus is on John.

John is introduced as a prophet – one to whom the word of God came (v. 2; cf. Jer. 1.2; Ezek. 1.3; Jonah 1.1; Zeph. 1.1; Zech. 1.1; etc.). His importance is made clear, but his own words emphasize that his role is one of preparation for another. This is in line with Luke's dual emphasis on the importance of John and his subordination to Jesus (cf. above, on 1.39–45; below, on 3.7–18).

Mark and Matthew both record John as quoting Isaiah 40.3. Luke extends the quotation through to v. 5, to which he appends Isaiah 52.10. The language of radical reversal (v. 5, quoting Isaiah 40.4) echoes Mary's song of praise (1.51b–53). The announcement of God's salvation (v. 6, quoting Isa. 52.10) introduces another of Luke's distinctive emphases (cf. 1.69, 71, 77; 2.30; 3.6; 17.19, which is translated literally 'your faith has saved you'; 19.9–10; 23.35, 37, 39).

Luke 3.7–18, 21–22

Luke provides the fullest account of John the Baptist in the New Testament. He gives the impression that his ministry continued for some time (v. 18; cf. Acts 19.3), even though he notes John's arrest before the adult Jesus appears on the scene (vv. 19–20). He takes care both to subordinate John to Jesus and to note the continuity be-tween them (v. 16), apparently emphasizing common concerns when he describes John's proclamation, like that of Jesus, as good news (v. 18; cf. 4.18). Such good news consists of John's announcement of God's coming wrath (vv. 7, 9) and the consequent need for repen-tance that leads to practical action. John is a prophetic figure who emphasizes the moral consequences appropriate to conversion (v. 8a). Repentance is a recurring Lukan motif, as also is the motif that the use of one's possessions symbolizes one's response to the call of God (vv. 10–11).

John's baptism appears to be the outward sign of repentance. Those baptized respond to God by realigning themselves with God's purpose. A new Abrahamic people is being formed, but it is based on the response of lives lived in a manner appropriate to God's call, not on the basis of inherited descent. Such repentance looks to the future and the imminent reality of God's judgement, but it manifests itself in the mundane details of everyday life in the present.

John's vision takes in both personal responsibilities and relationships (v. 11) as well as the need for the responsible and unselfinterested exercise of political, economic and military might (vv. 12–14). God will include even tax-collectors (v. 12) and soldiers among the children of Abraham: they must behave justly, but they are not called to renounce their occupations. Luke blends social conservatism with a radical ethic; the status quo that John questions is on the level of individual conduct rather than larger structures. Luke's concern for the possibility of salvation outside Israel emerges once again (cf. 2.32), but the suggestion that not all who claim Abrahamic descent will escape the wrath to come makes salvation universally available but not universally enacted. Abraham's children are those who live appropriately.

Perhaps John's questioning of, and challenge to, a merely genealogical understanding of God's covenant with Abraham, the Isaianic new Exodus context of his baptism (3.3–6: NIV and NRSV omit the 'therefore' that links vv. 6–7) and the eschatological wrath of which he speaks cause those who come to John to ask if he is Messiah. Again Luke subordinates John to Jesus, and now John points to the greater figure to come. He will baptize with Holy Spirit, and with fire. Luke later picks up the promise of baptism with Holy Spirit and appears to see it fulfilled at Pentecost and subsequently (Acts 1.5; 11.16). The reference to fire is more puzzling and is much debated. It is unclear whether Jesus will offer one baptism consisting of both Holy Spirit and fire, or two baptisms for different groups, one of blessing and another of judgement. Certainly John has judgement in mind in his image of the wheat and the chaff. John has separated them in his ministry: another will assign them to their respective places. This good news is not a blank cheque.

It is difficult to speak of the baptism of Jesus in the third Gospel. Mark's account of John's baptism of Jesus is brief and matter-of-fact (Mark 1.11–12). Matthew betrays a certain embarrassment, as seen in the dialogue between Jesus and John which explains why this baptism takes place (Matt. 3.14–15). Luke appears to share his concern that misunderstandings might arise as to why Jesus was baptized by John, so he removes him from the scene (schematically at least) before he notes that Jesus was baptized. Thus Luke removes the link, present in Mark and in Matthew, between Jesus' baptism by John and the declaration of his Sonship that follows.

Prayer is among Luke's distinctive emphases (5.16; 6.12; 18.1; 22.39–46; Acts 2.4, etc.), so it is characteristic of his account that Jesus is praying when the Spirit comes on him. Thus the visible descent of the Spirit (it is in bodily form like a dove; cf. his depiction of physical manifestations of the descent of the Spirit at Pentecost, Acts 2.3–4) and the heavenly voice (v. 22; cf. 9.35–36) are a response to Jesus' prayer, not to the ministry of John. Whether Luke thought that bystanders heard the voice, or he as omniscient narrator is sharing with his readers Jesus' experience of prayer, is unclear. Luke's focus is on Jesus' identity, his divine Sonship, which is also the climax (3.38) of the genealogy that follows.

Luke 3.15–17, 21–22

See above, on 3.7–18, 21–22.

Luke 4.1–13

Luke's account of the temptation of Jesus is a bridge between earlier chapters which establish Jesus' identity and later chapters which relate his public ministry. It is primarily christological in focus. (Only secondarily, if at all, is Jesus presented as a model for the believer facing temptation. Jesus' overcoming of temptation is unique, an integral part of who he is and what he is called to do.) Jesus' obedience under trial, established before his public ministry begins, will undo the disobedience of Adam, and his faithful sojourn in the wilderness will undo the disobedience of Israel. Israel sought to put God to the test; Jesus submits to be tested himself (v. 12; cf. Deut. 6.16). Jesus' Sonship will emerge as one of simple but faithful obedience.

Luke's narrative links with his preceding account of Jesus' identity. He is full of the Holy Spirit (a distinctively Lukan phrase), as befits one who is conceived by the Spirit (1.35), anticipated as the one who will baptize with the Holy Spirit (3.16), and publicly and visibly given the Spirit when endorsed as God's Son (3.22). Yet the Spirit of whom Jesus is full, is the Spirit by whom he is led into the wilderness. It is God who leads Jesus into this period of trial, not the devil. The specific temptations narrated are only part of a longer (v. 2) and comprehensive (v. 13) trial.

If it is not clear to those who heard God's voice (3.22) that Jesus is God's Son in a way that others are not, then this seems clear from the genealogy. Jesus is not descended from Joseph (3.23). Rather, like Adam (3.38), his life comes directly from God. Thus it is the nature rather than the fact of Jesus' identity as God's Son that the devil sets out to challenge, seeking to cause Jesus to reinterpret and pervert his role by exploiting it for personal gain. This is the question underlying each of the devil's tests: will Jesus be a faithful and obedient son, unlike Adam, God's first disobedient son?

The link with Israel, also God's son (Exod. 4.2–23) and his trial/testing in the wilderness (v. 1, cf. Deut. 8.2; Exod. 16.4) for 40 days (v. 2) adds a further dimension to the implicit comparison with Adam. Jesus will be tested to see not only if he will adhere to the God-given constraints of his position (v. 3; cf. Gen. 2.16–17), but also if he will keep God's commands and understand that one does not live by bread alone, but by every word that comes from the mouth of the Lord (v. 4; cf. Deut. 8.3).

Three times the devil tests Jesus by asking him to seize power to be used for his own personal benefit. Three times Jesus chooses to serve not self but God. Luke places the Jerusalem temptation in the third and climactic position. Jerusalem is Jesus' goal in the third Gospel (9.51; 19.28; etc.), but Jesus will be exalted there and enter his glory (24.46) not by forcing God's hand now (vv. 9–11), but by conforming to God's will (22.42). He will go the way of the cross.

Luke 4.14–21

Luke introduces Jesus' public ministry with a summarizing statement which presents him as a Spirit-filled prophet (v. 14; cf. v. 18; 1.35; 3.22; 4.1) and popular teacher (v. 15). This prepares the way for his appearance in the synagogue at Nazareth, used by Luke as an opportunity to present a programmatic prophecy which explains what sort of Messiah Jesus will be and anticipates and explains the rejection by his own people that will lead to his death on the cross. Luke knows that Jesus has already been active elsewhere in Galilee (4.23), so he places this story at the beginning of his account of Jesus' public ministry in order to encapsulate the ministry as a whole and the different reactions to which it will lead.

Jesus reads from the prophet Isaiah (Isa. 61.1–2; 58.6) and applies his words to his own ministry, just as John had done before him (3.4–6, quoting Isa. 40.3–5; 52.10; see above, on 3.1–6). Luke's readers know already that Jesus' birth was good news (2.10); now Jesus explains what that good news will mean to the poor, those who rely on God for the sustenance that they need (6.20; 7.22; 14.13, 21; 16.22, etc.). The good news that the prophet announced to a people in exile, Jesus says is fulfilled in him. This will be seen both in specific incidents that Luke records, as well as in claims that Jesus makes (6.20; 7.22).

'Today' is emphatic, and typical of Luke's stress on the immediacy of both the demands and rewards of the gospel (cf. 2.11; 5.26; 19.5, 9; 22.34, 61; 23.43).

Luke 4.21–30

At first everything goes well, for Jesus' audience are pleased with what they hear. The question of whether Jesus is Joseph's son may imply some unwillingness of Jesus' audience to accept his claims, but the change in their reaction that follows is violent and abrupt. Readers and hearers of Luke's Gospel know that the scope of Jesus' ministry will reach to Gentiles as well as to Israel (2.34), but this is unwelcome news to the people of Nazareth. They are the first to reject God's prophet, as Simeon had prophesied that some in Israel would do (2.34).

Jesus' appeal to the stories of the widow of Zarephath (1 Kgs 17) and of Naaman the Syrian (2 Kgs 5) makes clear that his prophetic mission to the Gentile stands full square with what God had done in the past through Elijah, but his message is no more palatable for that. It is ironic that those who are convinced that they are the covenant people of God wish to restrict the privileges of the covenant to themselves, and in so doing fail to recognize God at work in reaching out to others as well.

The attempted lynching in Nazareth anticipates his rejection in Jerusalem, so already Jesus begins on the way that will lead him to death (v. 30; cf. 9.51; 19.28).

Luke 5.1–11

Luke reserves his accounts of the calling of the disciples until Jesus' own ministry of teaching and healing has been established. Jesus' preceding ministry was conducted alone; now he calls on others to follow him and to join in his work.

Simon's response to Jesus offers a model for others to follow: first those who were with him on the lake, then those who will read or hear Luke's account. Simon does what Jesus asks, even though he might question the wisdom of his command (vv. 4–5). He appears to recognize the presence of God manifested in the miraculous catch of fish and realizes that it points to the authority of Jesus. Simon's call or commission can thus be compared to that of Isaiah of Jerusalem (Isa. 6.1–10). Simon is fearful and conscious of his own sinfulness in response to an epiphany of God, but is reassured and commissioned to go to others under the authority of the one who sends him.

Jesus' command to make fishers of men is addressed to Simon alone, but others who have sailed with him also obey. Luke thus introduces the prominent members of the Twelve: Simon, James and John. They have participated in a catch of fish under the authority of Jesus that perhaps anticipates and represents the expansion of the Church through the outreach of those who will later preach under the authority of Jesus, even when he has gone.

Luke's statement that those who followed Jesus left everything (v. 11) is an example of Luke's insistence that their disposition towards possessions is symbolic of their response to God's call on their lives. The place of possessions in the life of those who follow Jesus is a recurring Lukan emphasis: the disciple's attitude to her possessions is an expression of her faith in practice, even if there is no uniformity in the way in which this faith is to be expressed (cf. 10.33–35; 12.13–21, 33–34; 14.28–33; 16.1–15, 19–25; 18.18–30; 19.1–27; Acts 2.42, etc.). Possessions and wealth – and boat-owners may be thought of as running their own business – need not be evil, but Luke leaves no room for the Christian to be neutral about them.

Here the emphasis is on the centrality of putting God before wealth and material security. Simon, James and John see beyond the short-term gain of the marvellous catch to the one who has brought it about. Elsewhere Luke shows how this works in practice for a variety of individuals in a variety of circumstances.

Luke 6.17–26

Luke's 'sermon on the plain' (which takes its name from the 'level place', v. 17, on which Jesus stands) is less well known than Matthew's longer 'sermon on the mount'. But the pattern of differences and similarities between them shows how each evangelist has reshaped the material on which he drew according to the purposes – and perhaps his understanding of the audience – for which he wrote. The context for Luke's presentation of Jesus' teaching is important. Jesus, who has spent the previous night in prayer (an important Lukan emphasis; see above on 3.7–18, 21–22) before choosing his disciples, now addresses the twelve apostles, but in the hearing of a great crowd that has gathered (6.12–19; cf. 7.1). The boundary between the groups appears not to be absolute, and Luke makes clear that Jesus' teaching is addressed to all who hear his gospel (6.27), not just those who heard Jesus in the flesh.

Luke's use of the second person ('blessed are you') underlines the immediacy of Jesus' address to those who hear him. His presentation of four woes parallel to the beatitudes underscores the contrast between each group addressed. Luke speaks of the poor both literally and metaphorically, and his meaning varies from context to context. Here those whom Jesus addresses in the first three beatitudes as poor, hungry and weeping appear to be literally so, unlike those whose poverty is spiritualized in Matthew 5.3f. The promise that they shall experience a change in their fortunes picks up the theme of radical reversal introduced both in the Magnificat (1.51–53) and in Jesus' sermon at Nazareth (4.18–19). That this reversal may be to the physical cost of other disciples who are currently rich, well-fed and happy may perhaps be implied by the first three woes, apparently addressed primarily also to disciples and other would-be followers of Jesus. It seems that Luke envisages an audience in which rich and poor Christians come together, but do not enjoy the same level of material comfort (cf. 1 Cor. 11.21). His challenge to this situation emphasizes the nature and content of Jesus' teaching, and the conduct that it demands of disciples in the present (note the recurring 'now' in vv. 21 and 25).

The fourth beatitude and woe are parallel to each other, but stand apart from those that precede them. They address reactions to disciples from outsiders, not a state in which they may find themselves. The reference to opposition (hatred, exclusion – perhaps from synagogues – mocking and defamation) may reflect the experience of Luke's contemporaries, and is narrated at length in Acts. That such things happen should be no surprise to these who hear Jesus' teaching here, or the similar warning before his arrest (21.12–17). That Jesus presents such opposition as a cause for rejoicing heightens further the reversal of values that he proclaims, embodies and lays before those who would follow him.

Luke 6.20–31

See above, on 6.17–26; below, on 6.27–38.

Luke 6.27–38

Though radical in the extreme, Jesus' command that we love our enemies (vv. 27, 35) is both practical and paradoxical. Practical, in that he gives demanding yet achievable ways in which such love may be shown (do good . . . bless . . . curse . . . lend, vv. 27–28, 35). Paradoxical, in that behaving in this way towards another begins to challenge our perception of them as enemies in the first place and begins a process that may turn enemies into friends.

Intertwined with the specific command to love our enemies is a subversion of conventional understandings of doing what one is required to (but no more) and of giving in order to receive in return. Loving our enemies – those from whom we might expect nothing in return – is a striking example of what such selfless giving to others will mean. But whether it is more radical or more demanding than the command to give to everyone who asks, and not to seek the return of what is ours but has been taken from us, is unclear.

Two positive motivations for such behaviour are offered in addition to the rejection of giving in order to receive. The first is the 'golden rule', which in this context suggests that we should treat others in the way that we hope that they would behave, not on the basis of how they act or have acted. The second is the character of God, whose kindness extends already to those who do not deserve it (cf. Rom. 5.6–8). Those who follow God should be like God, but Luke seems careful not to present God's approval as a third motivation to justify behaving in this way.

Yet there is a warning for those who do not act as God acts. Christians should be merciful and compassionate (v. 36; the word used may be translated either way), not judgemental and fault-finding, forgiving (v. 37) and generous (v. 38). But if we refuse to do so, God will apply to us the standards that we ourselves have applied to others. None of us could survive the scrutiny of God should justice be strictly applied; who are we to expect such standards of others? (On which see further below, on 6.39–49.)

Luke 6.39–49

Luke's reference to Jesus telling a parable introduces a series of teachings that are less straightforward than those that precede them. This last section of Jesus' first address to his disciples after he has appointed the apostles may be divided into three parts.

The first, vv. 39–42, both emphasizes the need for appropriate teaching and guidance from those qualified to offer it (vv. 39–40), and also picks up on his earlier words about non-judgement (vv. 41–42; cf. v. 37). If the insertion of the parable of one blind person leading another and of the saying about a disciple and his teacher in between warnings against inappropriate judgement and fault-finding determine their interpretation, then perhaps Jesus warns his disciples against false teachers whose message differs from his on these points. But it is not easy to see a clear thread of thought connecting these verses. The statement that anyone who is fully qualified will be like the teacher who has taught them (v. 40) perhaps echoes the earlier statement that those who behave as he does are children of the Most High (v. 35) and may suggest that the relationship between Jesus and his disciples is analogous to that between God and his children.

The second block, vv. 43–45, takes up the relationship between character and behaviour. Matthew twice uses similar material, in each case presenting it in a context in which judgement is the dominant theme (Matt. 7.16–20; 12.33–35). Luke emphasizes rather the principle that one's true inner self is revealed in one's words and deeds. Thus one's attitude towards one's enemies and to others is a measure of the true disposition of one's heart. Luke regularly makes a similar point in relation to the way in which individuals use their wealth and resources.

Luke closes the sermon with an emphasis on the need for disciples to do what Jesus teaches, vv. 46–49. In the narrative so far, only Peter and the leper have called Jesus 'Lord' (5.8, 12). Thus Jesus' warning is addressed not to characters in the Gospel but to succeeding generations of Christians who call Jesus Lord but settle for a way of life less demanding than the one that Jesus demands. Luke's shaping of the materials with which he works is designed to present Jesus' demands clearly and forcefully to those who read and hear his carefully ordered account.

Luke 7.1–10

Jesus' healing of the centurion's servant is the first of two similar prophetic wonders (cf. below, on 7.11–17). The story of a Gentile soldier seeking help from an Israelite prophet seems a clear echo of the story of Naaman and Elisha (2 Kgs 5.1–4; Luke 4.27), as the story of the widow whose son has died evokes the story of Elijah and the widow of Zarephath (1 Kgs 17.20; Luke 4.25–26). The centurion is probably to be thought of as a God-fearer, like Cornelius (Acts 10.2) – sympathetic to Judaism, but not circumcised himself.

Luke has made clear that the impact of Jesus' ministry will be to bring Gentiles as well as Jews into the people of God (2.32; 4.25–27), but here he distances Jesus from any direct contact with Gentiles (vv. 3–4, 6). It is his followers, not Jesus himself, who will bring his teaching and significance to the end of the earth, as narrated in Acts. The fact that Luke wrote two volumes allows him to maintain a historical perspective in a way that the other evangelists did not always do. Peter goes further than Jesus did when he went to Cornelius' house (Acts 10), but he was only carrying to its logical conclusion what God had already begun in Jesus and in other prophets before him.

Luke gives no account of how the servant was healed or of what Jesus said to bring it about. The focus of the story is rather the dialogue between the centurion's friends and Jesus (vv. 6–9). The climax comes with Jesus' praise for the centurion's faith which consists in his understanding of the power and authority with which Jesus acts. Jesus' response singles out the centurion for praise and contrasts the strength of this outsider's faith with what he has found in Israel. Jesus' words challenge the hearers of Luke's Gospel to respond to him in the same way that the centurion did.

Luke 7.11–17

The raising of the widow's son is the second of two complementary prophetic wonders (see above, on 7.1–10). The juxtaposition of a man (the centurion) and a woman (the widow) is typical of Luke's composition (see above on 2.22–40). That each story is to be read in the light of the other is implied in the temporal line between them ('soon afterwards', or 'next day', v. 11).

In the previous story, Jesus' miraculous healing of the centurion's servant was occasioned by the centurion's faith in him. Here Jesus raises the widow's son on account of the compassion that he feels for her plight. As before, his word alone is effective (vv. 14–15). Elijah had prostrated himself over the body of the widow of Zarephath's son (1 Kgs 17.21); Jesus simply commands the young man to rise.

Those who see what Jesus has done glorify God, a phrase that Luke uses to denote a positive and appropriate response to Jesus' work (v. 16; cf. 2.20; 4.15; 5.25, 26; 18.43). They recognize Jesus as a prophet (v. 16; cf. 24.19; Acts 3.22) through whom God has visited (v. 16; NRSV 'looked favourably upon') his people. Those in Galilee see in Jesus what those in Jerusalem do not (v. 16; 19.44). Thus Jesus fulfils what Zechariah had prophesied (1.68). Both incidents, narrated in some detail, provide specific examples of the wider ministry that Luke summarizes at 7.22–23, a fulfilment of what Jesus had proclaimed in the synagogue at Nazareth. In each instance he draws on Isaiah.

Luke 7.36—8.3

Luke again makes use of the pairing of a man (Simon, a Pharisee) and a woman (unnamed, but identified as a sinner) to present the point that he wishes to make. Her generous and lavish response to

Jesus is mirrored by that of the other named women whose financial support plays a vital part in Jesus' continuing ministry in Galilee (8.1–3).

The narrative makes most sense if we may assume that this woman is already aware of Jesus and the forgiveness that he brings, perhaps through the ministry of John, whose role was to prepare for Jesus (7.24–28). If so, her response to John and to Jesus is typical of that of the people (7.29) whereas Simon's rudeness to Jesus typifies the Pharisees' rejection of John and the one who had sent him (7.30; note how Simon is identified four times as a Pharisee in vv. 36–39). She is lavish and unstinting in generosity towards Jesus, the appropriate response of someone who knows that her sins have been forgiven; Simon fails to provide even the basic hospitality that he owed to Jesus as a guest in his home (vv. 38–47). The parable of the debtors and the context in which it is set serve to interpret each other.

Various Lukan themes are prominent: the inclusion of someone from the margins; the use of possessions as an indicator of someone's inner disposition; the forgiveness of sins; faith that leads to salvation.

Three points about Luke's presentation of Jesus may be noted. First, that he is a prophet. Simon questions that this is so, for he believes that Jesus cannot read the heart of this woman as a prophet should be able to do. But the dramatic irony lies in the fact that Jesus can read his heart as well as hers (vv. 39–43). Thus the prophecy of Simeon (2.35) continues to be fulfilled. Second, Jesus continues to bring good news to the poor and marginalized – in this case, an outcast woman – both in word and in deed (cf. 4.18–19; 7.22). Third, he has power to declare sins forgiven (vv. 48–49), though this is not a point that Luke develops here (cf. 5.20–26). His emphasis falls rather on the saving faith of the woman (v. 50; cf. 8.12, 48; 17.19; 18.42; Acts 15.11).

Luke 8.22–25

Luke now opens a new section of the Galilean ministry with the first of a series of three miracles. Each emphasizes the power of Jesus. Jesus has just spoken of the need to do the word of God (v. 21); now by his word he stills the winds and waves and brings to safety his disciples. The miracle depends not on the faith of the disciples (which is absent) but on the authority of Jesus.

Luke's focus is christological. Although the disciples call Jesus master, their amazement at his mastery of nature and their question as to who he really is reveals that they still have much to learn. Fear and amazement has not yet given way to faith. Perhaps Luke's concern is to show them and those who encounter Jesus through the eyes and ears of the first disciples that Jesus has the same dominion over the seas and waters as Yahweh: cf. Psalms 18.16; 29.3–4; 65.7; 89.9; 104.6–7; 106.9; 107.23–32. If so, then Jesus' control over the waters may also symbolize his control over the forces of evil.

Certainly Jesus' rebuke of the waters (v. 24) recalls his earlier exorcisms (4.35, 41), and the stilling of the storm is followed immediately by the account of the exorcism of the demoniac called Legion. Thus each story helps to interpret the other: Jesus overcomes chaotic forces through a spoken command leading to the return of calm and a sense of fear and wonder among those who have witnessed his power. Sudden storms on the Sea of Galilee are well known; the ferocity of this storm, enough to terrify even seasoned sailors, serves as a foil to the extent of Jesus' majestic power, as do the huge number of the demons expelled from Legion and destroyed with the Gadarene swine.

Luke indicates that Jesus, like Yahweh, is to be known to his disciples as their Saviour and deliverer no matter what the circumstances: no opposing power can resist his word of command.

Luke 8.26–39

Luke shares the story of the healing of the Gerasene demoniac with Mark and with Matthew, but it is only in Luke's version that it is read in the Lectionary. The healing develops further some of the motifs found in the account of Jesus' stilling of the storm which immediately precedes it (see above).

This healing is a miracle story that bristles with difficulties. It brings home forcefully the differences between the worldviews of first-century Jews and Christians and those of many Christians today, particularly in the West. Even putting to one side questions about how we are to understand demon-possession and exorcism, the apparently senseless cruelty to animals and the likely devastating economic consequences for their owners will raise questions for many. Elsewhere Luke narrates exorcisms in a way that is much more matter-of-fact (4.33–35); here some of the additional material that he includes has led to more heat than light in attempts to understand this passage. Nevertheless, Luke's central point seems clear: demons obey Jesus' commands, as do winds and water (v. 31; cf. 8.25).

Luke links this incident to Jesus' Galilean ministry (v. 26) and does not mention the Decapolis, a pagan region where Mark says that the demoniac proclaimed what Jesus had done (Mark 5.20). Yet the demoniac still appears to be a Gentile – the only one whom Jesus will meet – so in this exorcism Jesus foreshadows the way in which his followers will move out into the Gentile world (Acts 1.8).

Luke 9.28b–36 (37–43)

Jesus' true identity has not yet been fully understood by those in Luke's narrative, and Luke seeks now to heighten the christological understanding of his audience. The focus is on Jesus' identity and his place in the purpose of God. Peter has just declared Jesus to be the Messiah (9.20), but this incident reveals that he does not yet appreciate what this means.

Luke's account of the transfiguration is closely related to what has gone before. Jesus has just spoken of glory to come (9.26), and such glory is manifested now on the mountain (9.31–32). If the decision to remove from this reading the strong and specific connective at v. 28a – 'about eight days after these sayings' – is intended to obscure this link, it would appear to be perverse. Luke seems insistent that glory will come only through the cross. Jesus' glory is revealed only after he has spoken of the costly way of the cross, the way that he will take and which he calls his disciples to follow. Conversely, it is in the context of glory that Moses and Elijah speak of Jesus' impending exodus at Jerusalem (v. 31; the decision of the NRSV and other translations to translate this as 'departure' weakens the force of the allusion). Thus Luke provides his audience with a framework in which to understand the narrative of his journey to Jerusalem and death. God is in control, and Jesus is to fulfil his will (v. 31; cf. 9.51; 24.44).

Prayer is a key Lukan interest, and Jesus' own private prayer often precedes significant events (cf. above, on 3.7–18, 21–22). The mountain (v. 28b) is a place of prayer, somewhere Jesus goes for communion with his father (cf. 6.12; 22.39–40). Just as prayer preceded another heavenly voice when God addressed Jesus as his Son (3.21–22), so prayer now precedes the words of acclamation addressed to the disciples (vv. 34–35). The disciples hear who Jesus is – for they are told explicitly – in case (or because) they have not understood what they have seen.

These words are also an implicit rebuke to Peter. His wish to build three tents may represent misunderstanding on a number of levels. The offer of three tents may suggest that he sees Jesus, Moses and Elijah as on a par; but Moses and Elijah speak of Jesus, and God tells Peter to listen to his Son. Jesus' pre-eminence is thus asserted. Peter may also wish to capture and domesticate the presence of God's glory as if it could be contained in a dwelling (cf. Acts 7.48–50). Perhaps most importantly, his offer may indicate a failure to understand the necessity of Jesus' journey to Jerusalem. Peter wishes to linger at the place where God's presence has been experienced, but Moses and Elijah indicate that Jesus must go to Jerusalem, where he will accomplish his departure (v. 31; cf. 9.51; 19.28). Peter offers an obstacle to the divine purpose that Jesus is to fulfil.

What has been revealed to the disciples is not yet for public consumption (v. 36). But when Jesus descends from the mountain, back to the level of human suffering, God's majesty is nevertheless apparent in his compassion for a father and his only child (vv. 37–43).

Luke 9.51–62

Luke 9.51 marks the beginning of Jesus' journey to Jerusalem. It is a significant turning-point in Luke's narrative, anticipated already in 9.31. The NRSV translation 'when the days drew near' (v. 51) masks the force of Luke's statement, which might be translated 'it happened that the days were fulfilled for his being taken up'. This move towards a more literal translation is clumsy, but it preserves the way in which Luke emphasizes that Jesus is acting according to the pre-determined plan of God, now fulfilled through him. Luke uses the same verb at Acts 2.1, another key transitional point in his orderly account.

Jesus has been a traveller on the move ever since 4.42, but now he sets his face to go to Jerusalem (v. 51; note the resolution on Jesus' part to which Luke draws attention), for it is a matter of divine necessity that the prophet perish in that city (13.33). Luke gives great emphasis to this journey, but it does not originate with him. The motif of a journey from Galilee to Jerusalem is present already in Mark, where the account of the journey comes in chapter 10. Thus Luke does not invent the motif, but he does make much more of it than did Mark; Luke's account of this journey amounts to about one-third of his first volume. The contents of the section are very varied. Very little is shared with Mark, and very little has any intrinsic connection with a journey. Rather, Luke introduces a number of references to a journey (9.51, 52, 56, 57; 13.22, 33; 17.11; 18.31; 19.11, 28) and uses them as pegs on which to hang a great deal of Jesus' teaching. This allows Luke to provide a sense of movement and progress, in contrast to Matthew whose five blocks of Jesus' teaching might be thought to slow the pace of his narrative. Luke takes care to note Jesus' audience at each point, and the different ways in which they respond to what he says.

Jesus travels with Jerusalem, the place of his death, resurrection and exaltation, in mind. As Jesus is single-minded in 'going along the way' (v. 57), so would-be followers must be equally determined and single-minded.

Luke 10.1–11, 16–20

All three synoptic Gospels have an account of Jesus sending out the twelve apostles (Luke 9.1–6; Mark 6.6–11; Matthew 10.5–15). Only Luke also presents Jesus sending out these seventy (or seventy-two; the manuscript evidence is very finely balanced) others. This doubling-up of similar material suggests that it may be important. Luke generally avoids including such 'doublets', so it seems likely that he saw the mission-charge and journey depicted here as of particular significance.

Those sent out go from Jesus and return to Jesus, and it is their status as representatives of Jesus and the One who sent him (v. 16) that is of more importance than any geographical details of their journey, which Luke passes over in silence. Some scholars have questioned whether such a journey goes back to the ministry of Jesus, or if Luke uses it to emphasize the continuity between the mission of the Church and the Lord in whose name it speaks. But the latter alternative can stand whether or not the former is true. Luke shows that Jesus wants others besides the twelve apostles to be his witnesses, as he will show again in Acts where the role of the twelve diminishes as the Church continues to advance in space and in time. The fact that these seventy(-two) are not called apostles or given any other title (Luke refers to them only as 'others') may serve to underline this implicit challenge to all who hear Luke's Gospel, that they too must speak in his name.

The message to be proclaimed is clear: 'the kingdom of God has come near' (v. 9; cf. 4.43). This underlines the urgency of the message entrusted to those whom Jesus sends, as does the fact that the harvest is plentiful. If enough workers do not collect it in time, the crop will be ruined. Those whom God calls to collaborate with him must both work and pray (vv. 2–3) if his harvest is to be reaped. There is much to do, but Jesus assures those who follow him that God will not be thwarted, either by human hostility and uncooperativeness (vv. 3–11), or by Satan and the evil associated with him (vv. 19–20). This is cause for confidence – but much more important is that God has placed in the book of life the names of those who work with him (v. 20; cf. Exod. 32.32–33; Ps. 69.28; Dan. 12.1; Phil. 4.3; Heb. 12.23; Rev. 3.5; etc.).

Luke 10.25–37

Previously Jesus has compared his disciples to infants, and has contrasted the way in which God has revealed to them what he has withheld from the wise and the intelligent (10.21–22). Now Luke introduces a lawyer, presumably one of those thought of as wise and intelligent, and makes clear that his purpose is to test Jesus, not to learn from him (v. 25).

Luke's account of the 'golden rule' differs in two significant ways from the presentation of similar material in Mark and in Matthew (Mark 12.28–31; Matthew 22.34–40). First, whereas Mark and Matthew present two distinct commands, Luke collapses them into one – 'love the Lord your God . . . and your neighbour . . .' (v. 27). Perhaps this emphasizes the close relationship between loving God and loving one's neighbour. The one who would have eternal life must do (vv. 25, 28) both these things. Second, Luke has Jesus elicit these words from the lawyer seeking to test him, whereas Mark and

Matthew present Jesus himself saying these (or similar) words in reply to a question that a scribe (so Mark) or a lawyer (so Matthew) has put to him. Matthew and Mark leave open the question whether Jesus was the first to combine these laws. Since Luke puts the words in the mouth of the lawyer, he perhaps suggests that the combination was already known.

It is Jesus, not the lawyer, who points to the Law as the source of teaching that must be obeyed in order to inherit eternal life (v. 26) or to live (v. 28). This is the first reference to the Jewish law since its observance played such an important part in Luke's account of the birth and childhood of Jesus. The first command singled out makes clear the need for the absolute love of God in a total response on the part of each individual; Deuteronomy 6.5, on which the lawyer draws, speaks of loving God with heart, soul and strength. Luke (like Matthew, to whom he is closer than Mark) includes mind as well. The second is just as all-encompassing in its command that those who love God should also love their neighbours as themselves, a quotation from Leviticus 19.18.

'Do this and you will live', says Jesus. But rather than do what he knows that he should, the lawyer comes back with a further query, the often neglected question that gives the parable of the Good Samaritan its socially – and politically – charged theological point. In Leviticus, the neighbours whom the Israelites were commanded to love were fellow-Israelites or those who dwelt with them in their land. Jesus does not quite answer the question that the lawyer puts, but describes as a neighbour a Samaritan, a despised non-Israelite, who shows more mercy and compassion for an injured Israelite than do other privileged members of his own race. Implicit in his answer is a question more fundamental than that of the lawyer: who are the true people of God?

Luke 10.38–42

This story of Jesus' encounter with Martha and Mary is found only in Luke, and exemplifies his interest in the role of women in the ministry of Jesus. A brief reference to Jesus' continuing journey to Jerusalem (v. 38) provides a transition from the preceding parable of the good Samaritan, but it is unclear whether there is anything intrinsic to these two stories that has led Luke to place them in succession. Some commentators draw attention to the contrast between the reactions of Martha and Mary to Jesus and compare it to the different reactions of the priest, Levite and Samaritan to the injured man whom they found by the road. Others suggest that whereas the parable illustrates the need to love one's neighbour, the example of Mary illustrates the need to love God (10.27), as seen in the way in which she sits at Jesus' feet – the posture of a disciple (v. 39; cf. 8.35, 41; 17.16; Acts 22.3) – listening to the word that he brings.

Other interpreters have allegorized the passage as a commendation of the contemplative over the active life, but this is difficult to sustain if the passage is read in its wider context. The unnamed woman who offers Jesus lavish generosity is commended (7.44–46), and other women play a vital role in sustaining Jesus' ministry (8.1–3). Martha's hospitable instincts and generous use of what she possesses are not themselves at fault, but good intentions and important responsibilities can distract (cf. 8.14; 12.22, 25, 26; 21.34) from the one thing that matters most – whole-hearted attention to the word that Jesus brings (v. 39). This is the one thing necessary; this is the one thing that will last (v. 42).

Luke 11.1–13

Luke shows a distinctive interest in prayer throughout his two-volume work (see above, on 3.7–18, 21–22). This passage is the first of two blocks of teaching on prayer that he includes in the travel narrative (the other is 18.1–14). Jesus' example as one who prays leads the disciples to ask to be taught how to pray (v. 1; cf. 10.21–22). Jesus' answer is in three parts. First, an example of prayer (vv. 2–4); second, a parable teaching the need for persistence in prayer (vv. 5–8); and, third, sayings on the efficacy of prayer, climaxing in a prophecy about the Father's gift of the Holy Spirit to those who ask him (vv. 9–13).

Luke's form of the Lord's Prayer is shorter than Matthew's, and much less well known. It is possible that it reflects more closely than does Matthew's the form of the prayer that may have been found in a postulated source, usually referred to as Q, that Matthew and Luke may have used for material that they share with each other but not with Mark (see above, p. 4). This may mean that it brings us closer to the words of Jesus than does the version recorded in Matthew.

Jesus tells the disciples to call God Father, which is what he does himself (10.21; 22.42). This form of address implies intimacy, as does Jesus' comparison of God's wish to give the Holy Spirit to a human father's wish to give good things to his children. Thus Christians are to pray expectantly because they can be confident of the goodness and generosity of God. Humans may give even to friends only because they are asked persistently; God is more reliable than that (vv. 5–8). Human parents give more readily to their children than friends give to each other, but God is a Father more generous than any earthly counterpart, for he will give the Holy Spirit (v. 13; cf. 24.49; Acts 2.33). Thus Luke roots the gift of the Spirit to the contemporary Church in the ministry of Jesus by means of this promise that his readers know has been already fulfilled.

Luke 12.13–21

Jesus (probably echoing Moses; cf. Exod. 2.14) refuses to be distracted by a family dispute (vv. 13–14; cf. 10.40), but responds to the question with teaching of his own. Jesus' pithy warning against greed points to the dangers of inappropriate reliance on possessions, thus addressing obliquely the underlying concerns that prompted the person in the crowd to ask Jesus to arbitrate in the question of his inheritance.

The parable that follows illustrates Jesus' teaching that 'one's life does not consist in the abundance of possessions' (v. 15). Here as elsewhere Luke underlines how a person's attitude towards material possessions serves as a symbol of his or her inner disposition and his or her attitudes to God and to others. The foolish farmer is not untypical of those who believe that their riches allow them to control the course of their lives, but is no less short-sighted and misguided for that. He cannot guarantee his life, even if he has accumulated wealth and possessions for many years to come. His riches give him a false sense of security, such that he forgets that material possessions are no less a gift than is his life itself, and that either might be lost at any time.

Perhaps too there is a hint that riches isolate and distance oneself from others. Though living in a society where tight-knit communities mattered, this landowner has no-one but himself to talk to when he considers what to do with his crops (vv. 17, 19). There is no-one else with whom he can dialogue. It is as if Jesus paints a picture of his isolation, of the kind of prison that wealth can build. This man has the money to buy a vacuum and to live in it. Life in the vacuum creates its own realities, and out of this warped perspective he plans for his future without regard to the needs of others in the present and without any acknowledgement of God (v. 21). He thinks only of himself, but fails to realize that even his life is not his own.

Similar themes are developed in 12.22–30, on which see below.

Luke 12.22–30

This passage stands parallel with and develops the teaching found in 12.13–21 (on which see above). There Jesus spoke to the crowd; here he addresses his disciples (v. 22). His words to the disciples build on those previously addressed to a more general audience, and may be seen either as intensification or as a practical application of the parable of the rich fool and its call to be rich towards God (12.21). Similar teaching about not worrying about everyday needs is found in Matthew's sermon on the mount; there it builds on Jesus' warning that it is not possible to serve both God and Wealth (Matt. 6.24–32).

Luke makes clear the link between these exhortations and the preceding parable by inserting the statement that worry cannot lengthen life (v. 26) into material that he shares with Matthew, and by adding the command to sell possessions, give alms and secure lasting treasure in heaven (v. 33; cf. Matt. 6.19–20).

Jesus' teaching about wealth is easy to understand, if difficult to follow, not least because we know that ravens die if they go without the food and other resources that they need (v. 24). Yet Luke actually guards against the sentimental way in which we might be tempted to hear these words. He acknowledges that plants and flowers do not last for ever (vv. 27–28), despite the glory that they have at their best. This is a message that those of us too prone to forget our mortality need to hear; we neglect it at our peril, just like the rich fool before us (v. 26; 12.19–21).

Being rich to God and laying up treasure that will last both depend on the same thing – the realization that God wishes to give his followers the kingdom even more than human parents wish to give good things to their children (12.32; cf. 11.5–13, on which see above); and the resolve to get priorities right, even when striving for God's kingdom is at variance with the ways of the world (vv. 30–31; cf. 16.13).

Luke 12.32–40

Luke's presentation of Jesus' teaching about the need to store treasure not on earth but in heaven (vv. 32–34; on which see above, on 12.13–21 and 12.22–30) leads naturally to teaching about the disciples' need to be ready for his return at an unexpected time. (It is perhaps not until 12.54 that Jesus addresses the crowds.) Sitting lightly to earthly goods and being alert to heavenly realities are two sides of one coin for those whose awareness of the transience of earthly wealth and confidence in a future heavenly life actually makes a difference to the way that they live in the present.

The common theme of the need for alert and expectant watchfulness links together the parable about servants waiting for the master to return (vv. 35–38, found only in Luke), and the saying about the owner of the house (v. 39) and the application to which it leads (v. 40). This is the dominant theme of these parables; that of reward is only secondary, though the image of the master serving his servants is striking (v. 37; cf. 22.27). Thus the focus of the parables is on the present, not the future. Disciples must always be ready for the coming of the Son of Man, and will best express this readiness through continual availability for practical service or other action whenever it may be required (vv. 35–36, 39).

Most of the earlier Son of Man sayings in Luke have referred to Jesus' ministry (5.24; 6.5, 22, etc.) or to his suffering (9.22, 26, 44). From now on, most refer to the future coming of the Son of Man as judge (17.22, 24, 26, 30; 18.8; 21.27, 36; 22.69).

Luke 12.49–56

Previously Jesus has been reluctant to adjudicate between siblings (10.40–41; 12.13); now he reveals the extent to which he will divide households, presumably on the basis of their response to him. As was already the case in the previous parable in which he builds on his saying about the coming of the Son of Man (12.40–48), Jesus' teaching is now concerned explicitly with judgement. Jesus the prophet pronounces for himself what the prophet Simeon foresaw – that he would bring division to Israel (vv. 52–53; 2.35).

Jesus' first saying (v. 49) is found nowhere else in the canonical Gospels (although there is a partial parallel in the Gospel of Thomas, perhaps derived from Luke). His second saying (v. 50) may be compared to Mark 10.38. Elsewhere Luke associates fire with the Holy Spirit (3.16–17; Acts 2.3), but in each instance the idea of judgement is also present. John speaks of Jesus gathering the wheat but burning the chaff, and there is a divided response to the manifestations of the Spirit seen at Pentecost. Previously Jesus rebuked his disciples for wanting to call down fire on a Samaritan village that would not receive him (9.54). Now he expresses a similar wish himself. Perhaps Luke is drawing further parallels between Jesus and Elijah (1 Kgs 18.36–40; 2 Kgs 1.10, 12, 14; see above on 4.21–30; 7.1–10).

If fire means judgement, then baptism might refer to Jesus' death, as it does in Mark 10.38. It is possible that Luke brings these sayings together to show that Jesus himself must face the fiery ordeal with which he will baptize others (cf. 3.17). However, this is not altogether obvious either in the immediate context or in the context of Luke's Gospel as a whole.

Luke 13.1–9

Parables and sayings of eschatological judgement (12.35–59) provide the context 'at that very time' (13.1) when Jesus is told of the death of the Galileans killed by Pilate and warns his hearers to repent (vv. 3, 5).

Apparently implicit in the report of the death of the Galileans is the suggestion that they were sinners who had met the sort of end of which Jesus has just spoken. Perhaps there is an element of Jerusalemite snobbery in pointing to Galileans as sinners. If so, Jesus deflects it with a counter-example of the sudden and unexpected death of dwellers in Jerusalem. But this report of a Roman official putting to death Galilean pilgrims in Jerusalem may in fact anticipate the sudden and cruel death that will be the fate of another Galilean pilgrim at the hands of Pilate. Luke foreshadows what is to happen to Jesus, and Jesus' denial that either these Galileans or Jerusalemites were punished as sinners perhaps anticipates and refutes any charge that his own appalling death at the hands of Pilate was the result of the judgement of God upon him.

Modern readers, at least in the affluent West where death is kept usually at a comfortable distance, may naturally see in this discussion a debate about the problem of evil, suffering and injustice. Luke's ancient audience may have been more matter-of-fact about death, aware that it was an ever-present part of everyday life. Jesus challenges the belief that present misfortunes are punishment for past sins, and urges his readers to look not at others but at themselves (vv. 3, 5). There is still time to produce good fruit, but it will not last for ever. Thus Jesus suggests that it is on account of the patient mercy and forbearance of God that so far they have escaped his judgement, not any relative sanctity that they may claim for themselves.

The parable of the fig tree therefore offers a mixture of judgement and hope, and the fate of those killed by a brutal dictator or a collapsing building sheds little light on questions of theodicy. Such questions are not unimportant, but their answers may be beyond our reach. Yet each of us has the chance to take responsibility for our own sinfulness and to repent in the period in which God withholds his judgement. That time may end at a time and in a manner that we do not expect; Luke warns us to examine not others but ourselves.

Luke 13.10–17

Jesus' continuing journey brings him to an unspecified village on a sabbath, where he heals a crippled woman. Jesus' miraculous healing reveals the division in Israel of which he has recently spoken. He is opposed by the leader of the synagogue (to whom Jesus replies with a saying about hypocrites, plural, v. 15) but welcomed by the whole crowd, whom Luke distinguishes from Jesus' opponents (v. 17).

Jesus' willingness to heal on the sabbath (in this instance a woman; elsewhere a man, 14.1–6 – part of Luke's recurrent presentation of complementary pairs of men and women) demonstrates his status as Lord of the sabbath (6.1–11, esp. v. 5), and shows his prioritization of compassion for needy people over religious obligations. The decision to heal is Jesus' initiative, not a response to the

139

woman's request. He sees that she is in bondage, and speaks to set her free. Faced with such need, it is necessary (v. 16; the NRSV translates 'ought') to heal on the sabbath. Jesus has seen Satan fall (10.18), so allows him no dominion (v. 16); it is his mission to set free those who are oppressed (4.18; cf. 7.22). The theme of radical reversal is again prominent, and provides a thread through much of what follows in 13.10—14.34.

Luke's apparent association of Satan with an evil spirit (vv. 16, 11) and a link between the evil spirit and the woman's condition is taken as read and presented in a manner that is matter-of-fact. Something that will trouble many modern Western readers of the Gospel is no more than a detail in Luke's account to which he seems to draw no particular attention.

To glorify God is the appropriate response to the miracle that Jesus has done (v. 13; cf. 2.20; 5.25–26; 7.16); her individual response parallels that of the crowd (v. 17).

Luke 13.31–35

These verses offer a succinct summary of the central section of Luke's Gospel, his account of Jesus' journey to Jerusalem (cf. 9.51; 13.22; 19.28, 41). This journey gives Luke an opportunity to present a great deal of Jesus' teaching, much of it found only in this Gospel. The journey also underlines the importance of Jerusalem in Luke–Acts. Luke conveys a sense of continuing and inexorable movement, for Jesus' journey is rooted not in his own desires but in the purpose of God. It is necessary for him to go to Jerusalem (v. 33).

It is unclear and probably unimportant whether these Pharisees are friendly or hostile. Their message allows Jesus to reflect on his destiny, and his reply to Herod makes clear that he journeys to Jerusalem to fulfil the will of God, not to escape any human plot. Jesus is not concerned to avoid his death at the hands of Herod: he is under a higher authority, which means that he must continue on his journey.

The reference to the third day (v. 32) cannot but resonate with a Christian audience. We are reminded that Jesus' goal is resurrection (cf. 9.22, perhaps also 2.46). This is the accomplishment of his course, the end for which he strives, the goal of all his work. Yet it is closely related to his exorcisms and healings, the substance of his ministry (together with his teaching, although that is not here made explicit) in Galilee and on his way to Jerusalem.

Luke's first volume begins and ends in Jerusalem. But the portrait of the city here is not a flattering one. Jesus shows compassion for the city, echoing feminine images of God as a bird who shelters her young under her wings (v. 34; cf. Deut. 32.11; Ps. 91.4). The characterization of the city as one that rejects repeatedly those whom God sends to it does not preclude Jesus' compassion for Jerusalem, and his apparent prediction of her demise (v. 35a) is clearly made in sorrow rather than in anger. The fact that Jesus will be killed not only in Jerusalem but also through Jerusalem adds further poignancy to his lament for the city.

These words, probably an allusion to Jeremiah 22.5, are ambiguous in the present context. It is unclear whether the 'house' of v. 35 is the city, the Temple or the people (household) of Jerusalem, nor whether it is rejected/abandoned/forsaken or merely left. Jesus will be acclaimed as the one who comes in the name of the Lord (19.38) – but it will be by the whole multitude of the disciples (19.37), not by the people of Jerusalem (cf. 23.13, 18, 27–31). Jerusalem's judgement is therefore inevitable, the consequence of its failure to see who Jesus is and to respond to him accordingly. This hard message may not be conducive to modern ears, but it should come as no surprise in the unfolding development of Luke's narrative. John's message was one of wrath to come, and the very hour at which Jesus spoke of Jerusalem's fate (v. 31) was one in which he had spoken of many who would fail to enter the narrow door (13.24) and many who would be thrown out of the kingdom of God (13.28).

Luke 14.1, 7–14

Participating in shared meals appears to have been an important role in Jesus' ministry, whose practice was radically inclusive. This may be seen throughout the synoptic Gospels, but is particularly prominent in the writings of Luke, who gives more attention to matters of table etiquette, table fellowship and the households on which meals were written than any of the other evangelists. Here, in material found only in his Gospel, Luke presents Jesus at table, where he takes the opportunity to comment on what he sees around him. His teaching is in two parts. The first is addressed to fellow guests (vv. 7–11); the second to his host (vv. 12–14).

Jesus' host and his fellow Pharisees have invited Jesus with hostile intent, and watch closely how he will behave (v. 1). But Jesus watches them (v. 7), and turns on its head their understanding of social order and honour. They chose the best places for themselves, therefore exposing themselves to the shame of being moved lower. True honour comes from being asked to move higher by one's host (vv. 10–11). The point is clear enough to be appreciated by those to whom it is addressed; how much more clear to the hearers of Luke's Gospel, who know that this is how God will act (1.52–53; 6.20–21, 24–25).

In speaking to his host, Jesus is equally revolutionary in calling for him to ignore social conventions of recipricocity according to which invitations are given to those of equal social standing who will then be obligated to repay them in return. Jesus' radical inclusiveness, which gives without thought of receiving in return, calls into question the social mores of his day (cf. above, on 6.27–38). His advice is not only rude and insulting (for a guest should not tell a host how to behave) but also profoundly shocking. But to give to those who cannot give back is to do as God does (14.15–24). It also shows what it means to be rich to God (cf. 12.21) and therefore to be acknowledged as such by him (v. 14).

Luke 14.25–33

As Jesus' journey continues, he addresses the crowds about what true discipleship entails. All might be invited to the great dinner, but now we learn that the cost to the guest who accepts the invitation will be high. Three uncompromising demands are made of the would-be disciple, followed by a call for sober and serious prior evaluation about what the cost of following Jesus will be.

Jesus' words about the relativization of family ties may be compared to his earlier response to a would-be follower who wished first to fulfil their obligations to their families (9.59–62). The call to hate one's parents is stronger than in the similar saying in Matthew 10.37. Its force should not be diminished, even if it is not intended to be taken literally. God must come before anyone else, even a parent or a spouse (9.59–62; 14.20). The possibility that this may lead to family strife seems real (cf. 12.52–53). Jesus' words bring an uncomfortable challenge to any naive endorsement on the basis of Christian faith of so-called family values and the commitments – or entanglements? – that they bring.

The demand that one should also hate one's life is equally stark and uncompromising, and prepares the way for the life-threatening possibilities entailed in the demand for the disciple to take up his or her cross. Luke's emphasis is on carrying the cross continually, as seen also in Jesus' earlier demand that disciples take up the cross *daily* (9.23). No true disciple can be completely involved with other people, with possessions or with his or her own preoccupations. Jesus' teaching here offers little by way of comfort to those who would accompany him on his way (v. 25).

Luke 15.1–10, 11–32

As the longest and most detailed of all the parables in the Gospels, the so-called parable of the prodigal son is often removed from its context and read by itself. But Luke presents it as the third of three parables each concerned to express the joy experienced by a person who recovers something that he or she (note Luke's concern to pair a man and a woman, vv. 3–10) has lost. Thus the language of losing (vv. 4, 6, 8, 9, 24, 32), finding (vv. 5, 6, 8, 9, 24, 32) and joy (vv. 5, 6, 7, 9, 10, 32) occurs in all three parables and their application.

All three parables are presented as a justification of Jesus' behaviour in response to the grumbling of the Pharisees and the scribes. Jesus has come to seek out and to save the lost (19.10), and the repentance that he elicits (vv. 7, 10) is a cause of heavenly (and thus of God's) joy; God rejoices at what Jesus does. Together these parables encapsulate Luke's interest in God's love and mercy for sinful human beings and Jesus' call for repentance (vv. 7, 10, 21; cf. 10.13; 11.32; 13.3, 5; 16.30; 17.3–4; 19.8) and conversion. So distinctive are they of Luke's portrayal of Jesus and his teaching that they may be considered, as one commentator has observed, the heart of the third Gospel.

Some differences may be observed between the longer third parable and the two that precede it. The focus is on the breakdown and restoration of relationships, not on the recovery of lost possessions. The central character (analogous to the shepherd and the woman in the parables that precede) is the father, but although he takes the initiative to restore fully their relationship when the son who was lost reappears on the horizon, he welcomes rather than sets out to look for him. He experiences in different ways the alienation and loss of both his sons, only one of whom is fully restored to him. Each son fails to treat his father as he should, albeit in different ways: the younger by ignoring responsibilities and leaving home, vv. 12–13; the older by referring to himself as a slave, not a son – the NRSV lessens the impact of his words, which may be translated 'being a slave' rather than 'working like a slave' – and denying kinship with his brother, vv. 29–30. Each son distances himself from the father, even if one continues to live on his land, yet the father shows compassion and concern for them both.

Given the setting in which the parables are spoken, it seems difficult not to conclude that the elder son who exaggerates the sin of his brother (v. 30) and refuses to join the rejoicing at his return (vv. 25–28) stands in some way for the Pharisees and the scribes who grumbled at Jesus eating with sinners (vv. 1–3) or those who refused to attend the banquet to which they were invited (14.16–18).

Luke 15.1–10

See above, 15.1–10, 11–32.

Luke 15.1–3, 11b–32

See above, 15.1–10, 11–32.

Luke 16.1–13

Having just told three parables concerned with joy at finding what was lost (see above on 15.1–10, 11b–32), Jesus turns next to the subject of material wealth and how disciples (v. 1) should use it – an important and recurring theme in Luke (see on 1.39–45 (46–55); 3.7–18, 21–22; 6.39–49; 12.13–21, 22–30, etc.).

The parable of the dishonest manager, recorded only by Luke, has puzzled many readers. The likelihood that such bewilderment goes back to a very early stage in its transmission may be seen in the way that Luke appends three possible applications, the precise relationship between each of which is unclear. There is also a problem in knowing exactly when the parable proper finishes. If (as seems like-

144

ly) it includes v. 8a, the master's commendation of the dishonest manager, the applications are vv. 8b–9, 10–12 and 13 (which is paralleled at Matthew 6.24). The original emphasis of the parable may have been eschatological, warning disciples of the need to prepare for the return of their master (v. 9), but this appears blunted somewhat by the moralizing force of these applications.

What causes most problems for interpreters is the parable's apparent endorsement of dishonesty. But to focus on this issue is to miss the main point that the parable makes. The manager is a model for the disciples not because of any dishonesty on his part but because of his prudence. Faced with a crisis, he dealt with it wisely, using material resources well. It is because he responds appropriately to the circumstances that he is praised, not because of the morality (or otherwise) of his actions. His wise use of possessions is in contrast with that of the rich man in the parable that follows in 16.19–31.

Luke 16.19–31

Luke's juxtaposition of a rich man (v. 19) and a poor man (v. 20) and the contrast between them recalls the first of his beatitudes and woes (6.20, 24). Here in this parable – again, like many in the travel narrative, found only in Luke – we find enacted the radical reversal of which Jesus spoke. Luke continues to present Jesus' teaching on the theme of the use and abuse of riches, the thread that runs throughout chapter 16, but also introduces the theme of resurrection – both of individuals to judgement or to reward, and also that of Jesus.

Lazarus is the only character in a parable who is named; the parallel to another Lazarus whom John records Jesus as having raised from the dead is striking (John 11), although it is difficult to know what conclusions, if any, to draw.

Yet the focus of the parable is not on Lazarus but on the rich man outside whose house he sat. The parable begins by drawing attention to his conspicuous consumption (v. 19) and presents his experience in Hades (vv. 23–31). He was a rich fool who did not use his resources wisely, and now he will pay the price (12.15–21). Themes of radical reversal and post-mortem judgement are both present, but the climax and the focus of the parable concerns a warning to those who are alive, not an emphasis on the fate of those already dead. This is a cautionary tale in which Luke's readers and hearers are invited to learn from the disaster experienced by the rich man in the parable. We should use our resources well, not squander them in self-indulgence when the greater need of others is close at hand. The message could hardly be clearer – but nor could the teaching of Scripture and the resurrection of Jesus from the dead, yet many fail to respond to them as well.

Luke 17.5–10

The disciples' request for faith and Jesus' answer (vv. 5–6) follows stern teaching from Jesus about the need not to cause others to stumble (17.1–2) and always to forgive those who repent (17.3–4). There is no obvious substantive link between these three blocks of teaching, nor any with the parable that follows (vv. 7–10), although each is in some way concerned with the demands of discipleship. Perhaps Luke is keen to present as much of Jesus' teaching as he can before he concludes his journey to Jerusalem.

The apostles' request for faith is abrupt and unexpected. It could mean 'give us more faith in addition to the faith that we already have', or 'give us faith in addition to the other gifts that we have'. Jesus appears not to answer directly, but suggests that even faith as small as a mustard seed can do great things, provided only (he appears to imply) that it is real. The strange but striking picture of a tree being planted in the sea suggests the limitless bounds of what faith can achieve.

Just as challenging is Jesus' depiction of what a master should expect of and owe to his slave, and therefore what he should expect others to owe to him in return for doing what he himself was ordered to do. Slaves exist for their masters as disciples exist to serve God, so neither may demand any reward or special recognition for doing only what is required of them. This austere warning needs to be heard within, but not overwhelmed by, the wider context of Luke's teaching about God as generous, merciful and compassionate, giving more than his children ask for (11.9–13) and rushing out to meet us when we come home (15.20). This is how God treats *us* because of who *God* is. But we should not presume upon his goodness, nor should we expect it as our due.

Luke 17.11–19

Luke reminds his audience that Jesus is still on his way to Jerusalem, but a glance at a map shows the difficulty in understanding what he means when he describes Jesus as going through the region between Samaria and Galilee (v. 11). As elsewhere, it is more important to grasp the point that Luke is making than to dwell on details of geography or chronology. Jesus remains *en route* to Jerusalem, but a reference to Samaria prepares the way for this encounter with a Samaritan leper. Luke's focus is on Jesus' journey and the proper response of gratitude to those who encounter and receive from him on the way.

Luke alone records this miracle; it may be compared with a similar healing at 5.12–16, with parallels in Mark and Matthew. Luke's account of the healing is matter-of-fact, and does not dominate the passage. The Samaritan's healing is associated with faith (v. 19; cf. 7.50; 8.48; 18.42), as presumably is that of the Jewish lepers who were also healed. What sets him apart from them is the gratitude with which he responds. Once again it is an outsider, a foreigner (v. 18), a Samaritan and not a Jew, who offers an example to follow (cf. 10.29–37). Disciples should not expect gratitude *from* God (19.7–10), but it is incumbent upon them to give it. Here it is only the thankful Samaritan who glorifies God (vv. 15–16), acknowledging that Jesus acts on his behalf.

Jesus' frustration at the lack of an appropriate response by the others (v. 18) may be compared with his frustration at the generation of which they are a part (9.41; cf. 19.44).

Luke 18.1–8

This is the second of two parables that concern the coming of the Son of Man (v. 8; see also 17.20–37, the first of the two, but omitted from the Lectionary). The widow's cry for vindication and deliverance may pick up on the suffering predicted for disciples in 17.22, 25, in which case the role of the Son of Man in this passage looks back to his role in 17.22–37. But Luke's introduction to the parable (v. 1) makes clear that its central emphasis is on the need for persistence in prayer, not just on endurance in tribulation, and there are stronger links forward to the second parable on prayer in

19.9–14 than to Jesus' teaching on the coming of the kingdom in 17.20–34. The first, directed to disciples (v. 1; cf. 17.22) offers encouragement to persist in prayer; the second, directed to outsiders (v. 9) is a story of their own rejection.

As in earlier teaching on the need for persistence in prayer (cf. 11.5–13), God is to be contrasted with a human judge (or neighbour) who accedes to requests for help only out of self-interest. God's justice and readiness to help his chosen ones who call on him is not to be doubted; the only question is whether they will persist in prayer until the Son of Man comes (vv. 7–8).

Luke 18.9–14

This second parable on prayer (cf. above, on 18.1–8) is a warning of rejection for those who do not pray in the spirit that they should. Thus intertwined with its warning of how not to pray and its illustration of how one should come before God (v. 13; cf. 17.7–10) is a further illustration of God's willingness to show mercy to sinners who repent (cf. 3.7–18, 21–22; 15.1–10, 11–32). Its addressees, whom Luke characterizes as those who trust themselves as righteous and consider others with contempt, presumably include at least some Pharisees (cf. 16.14–15), but Jesus' warning should not be restricted to them. Jesus not only reminds his audience what God is like, but also continues to defend his attitude towards Pharisees and others who are too confident of earning favour from God (vv. 11–12; cf. 17.7–10), and towards tax-collectors and others on the margins of society (5.29–32; 7.36–50; 19.1–10).

Luke shows a particular interest both in prayer and in God's inclusion of the outcast, and his Gospel begins and ends with people worshipping in the Temple (1.5–10; 24.52–53), so this is a fitting finale to the main part of the distinctively Lukan material that he has presented in his extended account of Jesus' journey to Jerusalem (cf. above, on 9.51–62).

From 18.15 onwards, Luke's travel account is closer to the shorter journey narrated by Mark. Three significant differences may be noted. First, Luke adds the story of Zacchaeus (19.1–10). Second, he presents a parable found also in Matthew, but in a distinctively Lukan way (19.11–27, esp. 11). Third, Luke offers an account of Jesus' poignant prophecy on the fate that will befall the city because it did not recognize the time of his visitation (19.39–44; the NRSV's addition to v. 44 of the words 'from God' seems unwarranted).

Luke 19.1–10

The Lectionary jumps from 18.14 to 19.1, omitting material mostly shared with Mark and/or Matthew (see above, on 18.9–14). Jesus shares with Mark and with Matthew the story of the healing of Bartimaeus in Jericho (18.35–43; cf. Mark 10.46–52; Matt. 20.29–34) but uses reference to that city as an appropriate place at which to add the story of Zacchaeus. Thus Luke returns to the theme of God's love and mercy for sinners (cf. above on 15.1–10, 11–32).

Whether Jesus needs to call Zacchaeus to repentance is unclear. Most modern translations put Zacchaeus' words to Jesus in v. 8 in the future tense, thus implying that he pledges to do something new in response to Jesus' coming to his house. The Greek present tense verbs that Zacchaeus uses may be translated in this way, but they can just as easily – or perhaps even better – be translated in the present, indicating a practice that is already Zacchaeus' custom. If so, Zacchaeus defends himself to Jesus against the charge that he is simply a sinner (v. 7). Unlike the Pharisee of Jesus' parable (18.9–12) he does not boast of his righteousness, but he is not sufficiently reticent to let a public slur go unanswered. Thus this tax-collector can be recognized as a son of Abraham (v. 9), because Jesus includes tax-collectors among God's people even if others do not (5.27–30; 7.29–34; 15.1–2; 18.13–14). Zacchaeus does not knowingly extort, as John had said tax-collectors should not (3.12–13), and when he takes what is not his, he repays it fourfold as required by the most stringent of the Mosaic stipulations about restitution (Exod. 22.1; cf. Lev. 6.5, Num. 5.6–7). He also gives regularly to the poor, which in Luke is a sure sign of a proper disposition to God (6.30–31, 38; 11.41; 12.33; 16.9; 18.22, 29).

Luke's description of Zacchaeus as a chief tax-collector may be significant. The word is not found elsewhere in the New Testament, but the prefix 'chief' translates a Greek word that is related to the word that is translated as 'ruler' in 18.18. That rich man could not give away his wealth, and Jesus' teaching about the difficulty of discipleship for those who are wealthy led his disciples to ask who could be saved (18.26). This other rich man (Zacchaeus) neither gives away all that he has nor reduces himself to poverty, but because he shares his resources with others Jesus can exclaim that salvation has come to his house (19.9). Jesus vindicates Zacchaeus in the face of his neighbours' slurs because of his concern for the poor and the way in which he conducts his life. 'He too is a son of Abraham' – Jesus addresses not Zacchaeus but the crowd.

Luke 19.28–40

Luke continues to draw attention to Jesus' journey to Jerusalem (vv. 28, 37; cf. 19.11, a very Lukan introduction to a parable that the Lectionary omits from Luke, instead including it in the version in which it occurs in Matthew).

His account of Jesus' entry into Jerusalem follows closely that of Mark, but he omits any reference to palm branches (an interesting observation on Palm Sunday of Year C?).

Several distinctive Lukan touches may be noted. First, the disciples find the colt 'just as Jesus had told them' (v. 32), a characteristically Lukan fulfilment of prophecy (cf. 2.20 etc., on which see above on 2.1–14 (15–21)). Second, he distinguishes Jesus' disciples, now a whole multitude (v. 37; cf. the smaller number with which he had begun at 8.1–3) from the people as a whole, and depicts them as joyfully praising God for all the deeds of power that they had seen (v. 37; cf. 4.14, 36; 5.17; 6.19; 8.46; 9.1; 10.13, 19; Acts 2.22). Thus the greeting of the crowd reminds Luke's readers and hearers of what Jesus has done. Third, Jesus' exchange with the Pharisees is distinctive to Luke, and his words about stones are the first of a number of such sayings (19.44; 20.17, 18; 21.5–6; 24.2; cf. 3.8). Also peculiar to Luke is 19.41–42, where Jesus speaks of the devastation that will come as a result of the people's divided response to him (cf. 2.34).

Finally, Luke's insertion of a parable about the return to his citizens (19.14) of a nobleman with royal (i.e. kingly) power (19.12, 15) immediately prior to Jesus' entry into Jerusalem makes clearer still what is implicit in Mark and in Matthew. Jesus' entry into the city is the return of its king.

Luke 20.27–38

The Lectionary moves from Luke 19.40 to 20.27, passing over several incidents recorded also in Mark, and a small number of verses found only in Luke (19.41–44). Previously Jesus has answered a trick but very practical question in an unexpected way; now the question is hypothetical, but put by Jews who do not believe in the resurrection of the dead. (This is the first and only appearance of the Sadducees in the third Gospel, as is also the case with the parallel account in Mark; they will appear again in Acts as opponents of the followers of Jesus.) Luke appears to draw heavily on Mark, but offers his own conclusion (vv. 38b–40) and places a different answer on Jesus' lips (vv. 34–36) than the response found in Mark and in Matthew.

The Sadducees seek to make belief in the resurrection look ridiculous (vv. 28–33); Jesus' answer shows that their problem is that they are unable to see beyond the categories of this present but finite life (vv. 34–35a). Luke omits his accusation (found in Mark and in Matthew) that the Sadducees know neither the scriptures nor the power of God, and concentrates instead on Jesus' teaching about differences between life in this age and life in the next. Once death no longer exists, the need for procreation and therefore for marriage is gone (vv. 35b–36).

Jesus' more general teaching on the resurrection suggests that a belief in resurrection may be found even in the books of Moses (v. 37), which is one of the things that the Sadducees denied. His statement that all are alive to God (v. 38), presented here as an explanation of the preceding statement that the Lord is God not of the dead but the living, is recorded only by Luke. This may be an allusion to 4 Maccabees 7.19. It appears to suggest belief in some sort of a continuing life-after-death prior to the resurrection of the dead (cf. 16.19–31; 23.42–43).

Luke 21.5–19

Jesus' prophecy of the destruction of the Temple causes some of those present to ask when this will be, and how they will know that it is about to begin. His account of what it will be like when Jerusalem falls (21.20–24) is omitted by the Lectionary. There (v. 24) Luke has Jesus make clear that the fall of Jerusalem is not the end of the world, for the time of the Gentiles must be fulfilled (v. 24). In the present reading Luke shows a similar concern to ensure that Jesus' teaching distinguishes between things that will happen in the future and those that will be associated with the end of the world. The persecution of his followers as well as wars and insurrections will take place long before signs of the end, not as part of them (vv. 12, 9b) so those who come in Jesus' name and claim that the end-time is near are not to be believed (v. 8). Jesus rejects warnings of an imminent end.

Jesus' words about the persecution of his followers (and probably also the destruction of Jerusalem) will be in the past for those who first heard Luke's Gospel, as they are for those who read and hear it today. Thus Luke shows that Jesus' prophetic words can be seen to have come true already. This gives confidence to those suffering in his name, whose story is outlined in Acts where named individuals such as Paul find themselves tried by synagogues, put in prison and brought before kings and governors (vv. 12–13), just as Jesus was himself (23.1–12). Thus Luke builds bridges between the story of Jesus in his first volume and that of the Church in his second. His hearers know already what it is to face opposition, and that they have received words and wisdom through the gift of the Holy Spirit (v. 15; cf. 24.49; Acts 2.1–4, 33).

Luke 21.25–36

Luke's account of Jesus' eschatological discourse continues to emphasize the need to prepare for the coming of the Son of Man at a time *after* the imminent fate of Jerusalem (cf. 21.2–24). The references to heavenly signs (v. 25; cf. 21.27; also Acts 2.19 where Luke puts signs on the earth below) mark the transition from teaching concerning Jerusalem to teaching concerning last days yet to come. This period of crisis and drama will involve more than the fate of Jerusalem. Jesus speaks now of what is coming on all the world (vv. 26, 35).

Jesus' prediction of the coming of the Son of Man (vv. 25–28) is followed by the parable of the fig tree (vv. 29–31). As sure and as visibly as the plant comes into season, so the kingdom of God will come. Each passage prepares the way for warnings to be ready to stand before the Son of Man (vv. 35–36). Luke's audience will know that Jesus' predictions concerning Jerusalem have already been fulfilled. This will engender confidence in his predictions for the future, and it underlines the enduring permanence and validity of Jesus' words to which he refers explicitly (v. 33).

Luke hints at the connection between the Son of Man (v. 27) and the kingdom of God (v. 31). His reference to the coming of the Son of Man picks up Daniel 7.14. It is not unexpected, for Luke has prepared carefully for this climactic announcement as his narrative has unfolded (cf. 9.26; 11.30; 12.8, 40; 17.22, 24, 26, 30; 18.8). The one cloud (Luke's reference to a single cloud is in striking contrast to the plural clouds of Mark 13.26; Matthew 24.30; and Daniel 7.14) may suggest the divine glory which indicates God's presence but hides God from human view (cf. Luke 9.34). Alternatively (or also) it may point forward to Luke's account of the ascension at Acts 1.9–11. The passage in Acts certainly refers to Jesus' second coming, but there is debate as to whether there is any reference to the second coming here in Luke 21. It seems more likely that here Luke portrays the Son of Man (i.e. the risen and ascended Jesus) coming before God's throne in heaven, not coming to earth for a second time.

The Son of Man comes as judge, but Christians may look up in hope rather than down in fear because he comes to bring them deliverance (v. 28). It is in this context of assurance that the disciples are actively to stand fast and to pray that they will have strength to stand before the Son of Man. Luke seems to see redemption for the believer, and the coming of the Son of Man and the kingship of God that he establishes, as each partially present. There is a tension between the already and the not-yet, and it is within this tension that disciples are to live.

Luke shows no interest in providing a timetable to allow others to chart the outworking of God's purpose. The reference to 'this generation' (v. 32) may have little temporal application. This is Luke's expression for those who resist or turn their backs on God and his prophets (cf. 7.31; 9.41; 11.29–32, 50, 51; 16.8; 17.25). Signs will be self-evident, and Luke's focus is on the need for disciples to live now in a state of constant readiness for what they can be assured is to come.

The place of prayer in the Christian life (v. 36) is a recurring Lukan theme (10.2; 11.5–13; 18.6; Acts 1.14; 2.42; 6.4; etc.). See also on 3.7–18, 21–22.

Luke 22.14—23.56

Luke differs from Mark much more in his passion narrative than he does in many other parts of his narrative that are parallel to

Mark. This has led some scholars to argue that he may have drawn on another lengthy passion narrative as an additional or alternative source to the passion narrative of Mark. Other scholars who reject this suggestion argue that Luke's differences from Mark are more likely the result of the author adapting Mark according to his own theological and literary motives, for these chapters show considerable theological and literary harmony with the rest of his orderly account. This view does not rule out the possibility that Luke had access to sources or traditions of which he alone of the canonical evangelists makes use, but it does emphasize his own original contribution.

A further corollary of this view is the proposal that one of Luke's motivations for writing his Gospel was to rewrite Mark in such a way as to alter subtly the image of Jesus that he presents, especially his understanding of his passion. This is possible, but it is important not to lose sight of the many similarities between Mark and Luke even in these chapters. If Luke modifies Mark here, he may not be doing anything dramatically different from what he has done in other places where Mark may have been available as a model and a source. His debt to Mark can hardly be exaggerated, even if he feels free to modify and therefore implicitly to criticize or to correct aspects of his presentation of Jesus and his continuing significance. Thus in the following commentary I shall consider Luke's passion narrative as a whole, but with particular reference to passages that are distinctive to the passion according to Luke. These include some of Jesus' sayings at supper (22.15–38), the involvement of Herod in his trial (23.6–16), Jesus' words to the women of Jerusalem (23.27–31), his conversation with the penitent thief (23.40–43), his last words (23.46) and the centurion's description of Jesus as innocent/righteous (23.47).

The Lectionary picks up Luke's passion narrative at the beginning of Jesus' final meal with his disciples. Judas has already agreed to betray Jesus – a decision that Luke is the only synoptic evangelist to attribute explicitly to Satan (22.3; cf. John 13.2, 27). Luke makes clear that human opposition to Jesus is part of a larger cosmic battle in which God and Satan are at war (22.53). Jesus has long been in conflict with Satan's forces (10.17–19; 11.14–22); now Satan resumes the

154

personal attack on Jesus at the opportune time for which he had waited (4.13).

If Luke implies in his reference to Satan entering Judas that a decisive moment has been reached, he says so explicitly in his introduction to the supper. It is 'when the hour came' that Jesus takes his place at the table (v. 14; cf. v. 53; John 13.1).

Luke clearly identifies the meal as a Passover (v. 15; 22.13), so it is in this light that we should seek to understand the scene that he depicts. His presentation of two blessings over a cup, one before and one after the bread (vv. 17–20) is one of a number of differences between his account and that of Mark and Matthew; at various points he is closer to Paul's accounts of Jesus' words (1 Cor. 11.23–26) than to those of the other Gospel writers. These differences, together with John's presentation of Jesus' final meal with his disciples on the previous day, the day of preparation for the Passover rather than the day itself (John 13.1–4, 21–30), have led to significant and still unresolved debates about the historical events behind these theologically laden accounts of this meal. Such issues cannot be addressed here, save to underline the point that Luke shapes his narrative in accordance with the theological points that he wishes to make.

One way in which Luke's account may be read is to take vv. 15–18 as Jesus' celebration of the Passover meal, and vv. 19–20 as his reinterpretation of that meal and hence his institution of the Lord's Supper. (Textual variants have led some commentators to ask whether vv. 19b–20 formed part of the original text of Luke, but most scholars now agree that they did.) Thus Luke has Jesus celebrate the deliverance that God has already brought in the past, and relate it closely to the deliverance that he will bring in the future – through him. Luke's introduction of the word 'given' (v. 19) and the repeated 'for you' (vv. 19, 20; cf. 1 Cor. 11.24) is important. Broken bread and a cup poured out symbolize Jesus' sacrificial and vicarious death for the disciples, and its continued practice in remembrance of him will not only remind his followers of what he has done but will serve also as a way of making known his presence after he has been raised from the dead (24.35, on which see 24.13–35 below).

Jesus' words about Judas' betrayal are deferred until afterwards. Thus during the meal itself the unity symbolized by the disciples dividing bread among themselves (no hierarchy is maintained) and drinking one cup is preserved. Division comes only later; first in Judas' departure, and second in the remaining disciples' squabble among themselves. Participation in the Lord's Supper (Luke implies) precludes neither the subsequent betrayal of Jesus (v. 22, cf. v. 48) nor a continuing failure to grasp the nature of true discipleship (v. 24). Thus whereas Mark and Matthew end the meal with a hymn and shift the scene to the Mount of Olives, Luke (like John) presents a farewell discourse to the disciples (vv. 24–38). Jesus' words that he is among the disciples as one who serves (v. 27) may be compared with John 13.3–16.

Jesus' words in vv. 25–26 have a parallel in Mark 10.42–44, which previously Luke has omitted. Many commentators have drawn attention to Luke's apparent omission of anything parallel to Mark 10.45, for such words would seem apposite in the present context. Arguments from silence are precarious by their very nature, but the presence of similar teaching in Luke 19.10 and 22.20 goes some way to lessening any inferences that might be drawn from this apparent omission.

Luke does not whitewash the disciples, as seen in his account of their dispute and Jesus' subsequent warning against abuses of power among those to whom he gives authority (vv. 24–30) and in his warning to Peter, tempered as it is with the promise of forgiveness and restitution after he has turned back from his denial of Jesus (vv. 31–34). Yet when Jesus brings the disciples to the Mount of Olives there is no prediction that they will run away, for Luke does not present them as fleeing when Jesus is arrested (see vv. 39–54). Indeed they appear to be present at the foot of the cross (23.49).

Luke's account of Jesus' prayer on the Mount of Olives is much shorter than the parallel account in Mark, and consistent with his own interest in prayer. Luke focuses on Jesus' prayer, not on the failings of his disciples. Jesus not only prays himself, but twice he also commands his disciples to do so (vv. 40, 46). Luke tells us the content of his prayer, and records the presence of an angel who strengthens Jesus in the struggle that he undergoes. The authenticity of vv. 43–44 has been questioned, but a proper understanding of Jesus undergoing a great struggle or trial (not agony, despite the similarity of the English word to the Greek *agōnia*, which can mean struggle, trial or contest) supports their inclusion as an integral part of Luke's composition. Having come through this trial, Jesus is now in control. The disciples are sorrowful, but he is not (v. 45; cf. Mark 14.34; Matt. 26.38).

Jesus takes steps to prepare the disciples for the future (v. 46), takes the initiative in addressing Judas (v. 48) and continues his ministry of healing (v. 51; cf. 6.18–19; 7.22; etc.). There is irony and mockery in his question to those who would arrest him as a robber (v. 52), not least because he has recently prophesied that he would be counted among the lawless (v. 37; cf. 23.32–33, and Isa. 53.12). The prophet's words are being fulfilled, and it is with prophetic insight that he knows that even his heavily armed opponents are not truly in control of the situation (22.53).

Luke presents his account of Peter's denial of Jesus as taking place prior to Jesus' trial before the Sanhedrin. Mark puts them in the opposite order. Only Luke notes how Jesus turned and looked straight at Peter (v. 61). His reference to Peter remembering 'the word of the Lord' underlines his portrayal of Jesus as a prophet, and accentuates the fulfilment of his prophecy at this point. The insults of those who mock Jesus are also a fulfilment of an earlier prediction that he has made (18.32); his delivery to the Romans and the punishment that they will give will fulfil the rest of this prediction. Jesus has not been taken by surprise, nor is he cowed by the questions put to him by the Jewish leaders (vv. 66–71).

No false witnesses are brought to testify against Jesus (these are kept until Stephen's trial in Acts 6.13–14; cf. Mark 14.56–58; Matt. 26.60–61). The high priest does not rend his robes nor explicitly accuse Jesus of blasphemy; rather it is the whole Sanhedrin who question and are answered – albeit obliquely – by Jesus (vv. 67, 70, 71). Thus the entire Jewish leadership is implicated in his death. Jesus is asked separately if he is the Christ and if he is the Messiah, whereas the questions are combined in Mark and Matthew. Jesus answers neither question directly; he does not accept the title of Messiah (cf. 23.2) but refers only to the Son of Man. There is no mention of the Son of Man coming on the clouds (cf. Mark 14.62; Matt. 26.64), so Jesus' reference to him 'seated at the right hand of the power of God' is presented as a prophecy of his post-resurrection and ascension state in glory (v. 69; cf. 24.26; Acts

2.33; 7.55–56). Luke's emphasis is christological. The questions put and answers given recall the prophecies of Gabriel to Mary (1.32, 35). Both the prophet and the one who sent him remain firmly in control.

The trial before Pilate is also brief, and the political charges brought against Jesus are patently false (23.2; cf. 20.20–25; 22.67–69). Thus Pilate shows little interest. His statement that he finds no basis for any accusation against Jesus, even though he is accused of sedition, anticipates his later findings (23.22) and also the centurion's declaration of Jesus' innocence (on which see further below).

Pilate's discovery that Jesus is a Galilean allows him to pass Jesus on to Herod (23.6–12). This scene is found only in Luke. Its absence from other Gospels raises questions of a historical nature, but the literary and apologetic functions that it fulfils are clear. It demonstrates the fulfilment of Scripture concerning God's anointed being brought before kings and rulers (Ps. 2.1–2; cf. Acts 4.25–28) and it shows also the fulfilment of Jesus' own words at 18.32. Herod was an Idumaean, a non-Jew and a virtual Gentile, and he mocks and abuses Jesus (v. 11) in a way that Pilate does not. It also allows Luke a further opportunity to emphasize Jesus' innocence of any charge brought against him, and a second witness to corroborate Pilate's conclusion on this point (v. 15). Pilate declares Jesus' innocence a third time, now in the face of an angry mob ('all', v. 18; probably referring back to the crowds as well as to their leaders – see vv. 4, 13). Lest his readers miss the irony of the release of an insurrectionist and murderer in place of a man against whom no charge can be upheld, Luke makes the point in his own authorial voice (v. 25).

Simon of Cyrene is known also from Mark and Matthew, but the depiction of the daughters of Jerusalem following and being addressed by Jesus are found only in Luke. Although on the way to his own death, Jesus shows compassion to them, warning that they too, although innocent of his death, will be caught up in the violence to which it will lead (vv. 28–31; cf. 19.41–44; 21.20–44). Luke shows the fulfilment of Simeon's words about a people divided (2.34). These women are part of a larger crowd who follow Jesus – a verb usually associated with discipleship – and others besides his own acquaintances mourn his death (23.48–49). Not all the people are to be blamed for Jesus' death; the people merely watch, but the leaders continue to sneer, even at the foot of the cross (v. 35).

Jesus' words from the cross are distinctive to Luke. He prays for forgiveness for those who act out of ignorance against him (v. 34; cf. Acts 3.13–19), offers solace to a repentant sinner (v. 43) and entrusts his spirit to God (v. 46; cf. Ps. 31.5; Acts 7.59–60). Jesus' self-control is evident to the very end; he prays before he dies.

Luke 23.1–49

See above, on 22.14—23.56.

Luke 23.33–43

See above, on 22.14—23.56.

Luke 24.1–12

Luke's account of the empty tomb is the first of the four scenes of which his resurrection narrative is composed. He shares with Mark and with Matthew the story of the women's discovery of the empty tomb and the announcement to them that Jesus has been raised from the dead, and there are also parallels with the account of the empty tomb in John 20.1–10. But much of Luke's account shows the way in which he has presented his narrative in accord with the distinctive way in which he presents his story of Jesus and those who would proclaim his resurrection.

When first introduced, the women are not named, but their piety is emphasized in Luke's comment that on the sabbath they rested according to the commandment (23.55–56). It is only after they are prompted to remember Jesus' words that they are named (vv. 8–11). Previously they were named when they were first introduced (8.1–3). Now we are reminded of their identity when they bring their service of Jesus to a climax by proclaiming the resurrection to the apostles. The first witnesses to Jesus' resurrection are those who had been with him in Galilee and had seen him be crucified and buried (23.49). They have followed him every step of the way. These women come to faith before Peter (he wonders at what he has seen, but is not said to believe that Jesus is alive, v. 12; such belief appears to come only after Jesus has appeared to him; cf. 24.34) or the eleven, yet find that their testimony is treated with disdain (v. 11).

The condescending male superiority felt by the apostles is neither defensible nor securely based. According to Mark and to Matthew, the angel gives the women a message to bring to the disciples. According to Luke, he gives them the dignity of explaining to them what has happened, and it is they who take the initiative to share the good news of the resurrection with others. Yet the incredulous response of the apostles gives room for a certain amount of Lukan apologetic. These disciples will themselves be witnesses to the resurrection (Acts 1.22; 2.32; 3.15; 10.41; 13.31). Their initial reluctance to believe offers assurance to Luke's readers that it was not without good reason that they came to proclaim the resurrection.

Luke's interest in presenting Jerusalem as the place where Jesus' ministry reaches its climax and from where he is taken up (9.51; 24.51) means that the angels refer to Galilee as somewhere he taught in the past, not somewhere that he will go to now (v. 6; cf. 24.49; but see Mark 16.7; Matt. 28.7). Yet the remembered past is important for understanding the present and the future. It is through Jesus' own words that the women and the others are to understand what they experience now (vv. 6–8). The angels' words that they should remember what Jesus taught serve also as a prompt for readers and hearers of the Gospel to recall what Jesus said.

Luke 24.13–35

The second part of Luke's resurrection narrative consists of a long, dramatic account of one resurrection appearance that tells how two individuals move from despair to hope, from unbelief to belief (vv. 13–33, 35), and the brief report of a second appearance of which no further details are given (v. 34).

When Cleopas and his companion set out for Emmaus their hearts and minds are filled with disappointment and despair. Turned in on themselves, they try to figure out the meaning of all that has happened. Deep in earnest conversation, their eyes are kept from recognizing Jesus when he draws alongside. When Jesus asks what they are talking about, the dramatic irony in their reply (vv. 19–24) is unmistakable. The travellers do not realize that it is Jesus to whom they speak, yet they accuse him of not knowing what has happened. They have given up on their cherished hope that Jesus would redeem Israel, yet this is what the one to whom they speak has done. They knew that Jesus was a prophet, yet they (like the women at the tomb) have not remembered and understood what he had taught and they had seen fulfilled.

Cleopas and his companion had heard that Jesus had been raised. But they did not believe, and their focus remained on his death. A death understood in the only way, humanly speaking, that it could be – as a public and abject failure for all in Jerusalem to see. God could not work like this. How foolish you are, Jesus tells them (vv. 25–27). You may know the scriptures, but you fail to see what they say.

Luke frustrates our wish to know to which scriptures Jesus referred, though perhaps there are clues in Acts (e.g. Acts 7; 8.32–35). His point seems to be that the whole of Scripture points to Jesus and to his cross and resurrection. That the whole pattern of God's activity points to, foreshadows and culminates in the suffering and glorification of his Son.

On the road (vv. 32, 35; cf. 15, and see above on 9.51–62) Jesus walks with his disciples and teaches them the scriptures. But only at the table do they find themselves in a context in which understanding and recognition can come – in the breaking of the bread (vv. 35, 30; cf. 9.16; 22.19; Acts 2.42, 46; 20.7, 11; 27.35).

Luke 24.36–53

Luke's description of Jesus' final encounter with his disciples is presented in a second extended narrative which has clear structural parallels with the preceding account of Jesus' appearance on the road to Emmaus (see above on 24.13–35). Jesus is not recognized when he appears, and his disciples believe only after he has taught them from the scriptures. Jesus then departs. A meal scene is included, but it is used to demonstrate the physical nature of the risen Jesus, not to reveal his identity.

Luke's account of the ascension has no parallel in the earlier narrative, but is clearly linked to the appearances that precede it, and takes place on the same day (24.1, 13, 29, 33, 36, 50). Luke alone offers a narrative account of the ascension, although Jesus' exaltation is assumed throughout the New Testament. Only in his second volume does Luke put Jesus' final departure 40 days later (cf. Acts 1.1–11); perhaps here he places it on Easter Day in order to provide a neat and fitting climax to his first volume, and to emphasize his conviction that Jesus' trial, crucifixion, resurrection, entering into glory and ascension are all part of the one departure (9.22, 31, 51, on each of which see above; 24.6, 26, 51) that was the divinely required reason for his journey to Jerusalem. (Similar overlapping between volumes may be seen in 1 and 2 Kings, and in 2 Chronicles and Ezra–Nehemiah.)

Luke's account of Jesus' appearance emphasizes the physical nature of his body, a concern shared also with John who has a similar appearance scene with an invitation to touch and see (John 20.24–29). Luke stresses the reliability of traditions about Jesus' resurrection by making clear that he ate (vv. 41–43; cf. Acts 1.3; 10.41). According to certain Jewish traditions angels did not eat, even when they appeared to do so, so Luke may wish to rule out the possibility that Jesus has taken on some sort of angelic nature similar to that of the men at the tomb (24.4). Perhaps already some had claimed that Jesus only appeared to have been raised from the dead. The fact that Jesus ate fish may be a further echo of the story of the feeding of the five thousand (vv. 42–43; cf. 24.30; 9.16); in John the risen Jesus offers bread and fish to others (21.9–13).

After eating, Jesus instructs his disciples from Scripture. At first the ground covered is similar to his teaching on the road to Emmaus (vv. 44–46; see on 24.13–35 above). Here resurrection on the third day seems to be parallel to the earlier statement about the Messiah entering into his glory (vv. 46, 26; cf. 9.31). But then Jesus' words look forward, in a programmatic prophecy that anticipates (and is fulfilled by) the narrative that follows in Acts (vv. 47–49). Thus Luke's use of the proof from prophecy once again supports the reliability of traditions about past events that he presents (see above on 2.1–14 (15–21)).

Luke links the story of Jesus with the story of the Church that continues to proclaim him, and anticipates the gift of the Spirit at Pentecost (v. 49; cf. Acts 1.4–5; 2.4, 33). Jesus departs, but he does not leave the disciples alone.

Luke 24.36–48

See above, on 24.36–53.

Luke 24.44–53

See above, on 24.36–53.

The Gospel according to John

HENRY WANSBROUGH

Introduction

In the arrangement of the Lectionary, the Gospel according to John has a special place. The three synoptic Gospels, similar in pattern and purpose, each have a year allotted to them. John is reserved mostly for special liturgical seasons, especially Lent and Eastertide. On the Lenten Sundays of Year A it wins a special place with the great stories of water (the Samaritan), light (the man born blind) and life (the raising of Lazarus), preparing for the mysteries of Easter and especially for the celebration of baptism at Easter. Traditionally, also, the Johannine passion account is read on Good Friday, and the resurrection stories again have a special place among the readings for Eastertide. Apart from that, John 6 with its eucharistic symbolism has a special slot in the summer of Year B, using the space made possible by the brevity of Mark, the Gospel of that year.

Such an arrangement in the Lectionary corresponds to the special nature of this Gospel. Unlike the short, succinct episodes and isolated sayings of the synoptic Gospels, John has fewer incidents, all presented more expansively in order to bring out their meaning and symbolism. Similarly, the succinct sayings are replaced by, or expanded into, long, reflective discourses by Jesus. For this reason John has sometimes been called 'the spiritual Gospel', both because it is more elevated in tone and because the Spirit, the agent of deeper understanding, receives greater prominence. This is nobly expressed by Augustine: 'John, as though scorning to tread upon earth, rose by his very first words not only above the earth, above the atmosphere, above the heavens, but even above the whole army of angels and all the array of invisible powers' (*Homilies on John* 36.1).

Such an elevated tone must not, however, be taken to imply that John is historically less reliable, for it rests on equally good factual knowledge, as is shown, for example, by John's detailed knowledge of the city and surroundings of Jerusalem. Where there is difference between John and the synoptics (one visit to Jerusalem or several? cleansing of the Temple at end or beginning of Jesus' ministry? healing of the centurion's boy or of the royal official's son?) it is difficult to assess which is more likely to be original. At any rate, John should not be considered an attempt either to correct or to supplement the synoptic accounts, but rather as an independent account using some of the same oral traditions (e.g. the walking on the water, the multiplication of loaves).

The other great difference between John and the synoptic Gospels is John's concentration on the person of Jesus. While the synoptics show Jesus proclaiming the kingdom of God, in John he is concerned above all to reveal his own personality, the relationship between the Son and the Father, and his divine prerogatives of judging and giving life. The theme of judgement runs through the whole Gospel, so that the reader experiences the characters judging themselves by their reaction on meeting Jesus and either accepting or rejecting him; by this the reader also is encouraged to the same self-judgement. Elsewhere also the theme of judgement hovers in the background and the language of the lawcourts abounds: truth, falsehood, witness, condemn (see below, on 15.26–27; 16.4b–15). The theme of eternal life, given by Jesus and fostered by the presence of the Spirit in the life of the Church, has taken the prominent place of the kingdom of God; 'eternal life' barely appears in the synoptics, and 'kingdom of God' barely appears in John. The Gospel was written 'so that you may have life', and the climax of Jesus' ministry is the gift of renewed life to Lazarus – the incident which, with typical Johannine paradox, sparks the decision that he must be put to death.

The chief theme of the Gospel, however, to which it recurs time and time again, is the relationship of Son to Father. It is by this, from the Prologue onwards, that Jesus' divinity and humanity is expressed. The Prologue begins and ends with the Word being 'towards the Father' (1.1; cf. 1.18), but centres on 'the Word became flesh' (1.14). On the one hand, John insists that Jesus is human. In no other Gospel do we see Jesus tired (4.6), thirsty (19.28; cf. 4.7), and weeping at the death of his friend Lazarus (11.35). Yet on the other hand his knowledge is beyond that of any human being. He sees Nathanael under the fig tree (1.48–50). He speaks of his own pre-existence (8.58). He knows all about his future passion (8.21–28; 12.32–33; 13.1, 21–27; 18.4), maintains his sovereign control even when he is dying on the cross (19.26–28), and even in death has the power to take up his life again. This is because the purpose of his coming is to reveal the Father, for he and the Father are one: 'whoever has seen me has seen the Father' (14.9). Rather than by any static definition, this is made clearest by the dynamic equivalence of the Son with the Father; 'the Son can do only what he sees the Father doing, and whatever the Father does he does too' (5.19).

To whom do we owe this Gospel? Certain dislocations and repetitions suggest that it was not written at one thrust. The poetic style of the prologue has led some scholars to deny it to the main author; the dubious textual authority of the story of the woman taken in adultery (8.1–11) has led many to remove it altogether from the text; some un-Johannine features of John 21 have cast doubt on its authorship. There seem to be some clear repetitions, such as the three versions of the discourse after the Last Supper, put one after another (see below, on 14.1–4). The confrontation between the Baptist and the Jewish authorities looks like two independent versions intertwined. Nevertheless, there are traits of style running throughout the Gospel which show that the final version is the work of one mind. Very evident is a pattern of opposites: light and dark, sight and blindness, acceptance and rejection, lies and truth, above and below, Throughout, there is the technique of the puzzled question ('How can this man give us his flesh to eat?' (6.52)) to advance the dialogue, ambiguity (is 'living water' in 4.10 merely fresh water or the water of life? When Jesus is to be 'lifted up' (3.14; 8.28; 12.32, 34) is this lifted up on the cross or to heaven?) and above all irony. The Pharisees berate the man born blind, when all the time it is they who cannot see (9.13–34). Caiaphas proposes that one man should die to save the people, failing to grasp what he is really saying (11.49–52). The Roman soldiers mock Jesus as king of the Jews (19.2–3), which the reader knows to be really the case. Similarly, Pilate publicly declares Jesus king, refusing the plea of the Jewish leaders that Jesus merely claimed this title (19.19–22).

It would be helpful to know the origin of the Gospel in place and time. It has often been thought to be later than the synoptic Gospels because of its more developed Christology, but this assumes that theology developed uniformly in different places. The Gospel certainly stands against a background of tension between Jews and Christians, in particular a Jewish threat to ban from the synagogue any who profess the divinity of Christ. Such hostility, seen also in Matthew, fits well the atmosphere at the end of the first century; it is, however, also present in the earliest of Paul's letters, 1 Thessalonians (2.14–16). The knowledge shown of Jerusalem suggests a close link with that city at some stage of its composition.

Granted that one author is responsible for the final edition of the whole Gospel (though using material which was not necessarily formed by him), the identity of this author remains mysterious. Tradition associates the Gospel with John the Apostle, son of Zebedee. The two sons of Zebedee feature strongly in the synoptic Gospels, but are mentioned only in John 21, which is probably an addition to the original Gospel (see below, on 21.1–19). Traditionally this has been explained as self-denying reticence by John, who merely gives himself the code-name 'the Beloved Disciple'. It has, however, been asked why this disciple occurs only in the Jerusalem stories, how he was 'known to the High Priest', if he was a Galilean fisherman. It has even been suggested that the disciple whom Jesus loved, who is at the origin of the tradition of the Gospel, is Lazarus. Others suggest that the Beloved Disciple is a purposely faceless figure, standing for any disciple whom Jesus loves, close to Jesus at the Eucharist, sharing the passion with Jesus and with his mother forming the first Christian community, believing in the resurrection, and custodian for ever of the Christian message. Even if we do not know his identity, he makes clear for us his purpose: 'these things are written that you may come to believe that Jesus is the Messiah, the Son of God, and that through believing you may have life in his name' (20.31).

Commentary on the Sunday readings from John

John 1.1–18

This prologue to John's Gospel is like an overture to an opera which contains all the themes to be developed later. It has been thought to have been composed by an author other than the writer of the Gospel itself, since it is in a poetic and reflective style. It is an overture in the form of a hymn. But the vocabulary and verbal techniques, quite apart from the grasp of the same theological themes, are so similar to the rest of the Gospel that it is better to posit the same author, writing in a different mode. It subsumes ideas which will reappear again and again in the Gospel, and is itself opened up by the idea of the Logos or Word.

The shape of this overture is a parabola, beginning in heaven, descending to earth and finally again returning to heaven. Thus it starts with the Word with God, is centred on the Word made flesh (v. 14), and ends with the Son close to the Father's heart. The relationship between Word/Son and Father expressed at beginning and end is closer and more dynamic than any simple translation of the Greek can convey: 'with God' (v. 1) is really '*towards* God', and 'close to the Father's heart' (v. 18) is really '*into* the bosom/embrace of the Father', both expressing a vibrant and active exchange. The structure is more complicated than this, being in the form known as *chiasmus*, after the Greek letter X. On either side of the centre come the themes of rejection (vv. 10–13) and acceptance (v. 14), which will feature so importantly throughout the Gospel; rejection by 'the Jews', acceptance by the disciples, play an important part in the process of judgement which continues throughout the Gospel. On either side of these are the little passages about John the Baptist (vv. 5–8 and 15), less poetic passages, which link the prologue to the narrative which is to follow. Without the elaborate prologue the Gospel might once have started, like so many other biblical stories, 'A man came, sent by God. His name was . . .' (v. 5).

The prologues to the other Gospels also all tell the reader who Jesus is: Mark shows Jesus as Son of God at the baptism. Matthew and Luke go further back, to show that Jesus was Son of God from the beginning of his conception. John goes further back still, to show that from the beginning and before time the Word existed in God.

Hence he deliberately begins his Gospel with the first words of Genesis, 'In the beginning...', to situate the affirmation before time began.

For Israel the Word of God was a life-giving revelation of God's nature and his loving care for Israel, particularly embodied in the Law, and most of all in the 'Ten Words' or ten commandments. This Word is now seen to be embodied or made flesh in Jesus. But the Genesis context gives a further dimension, for God created by his word, 'God said, "Let there be light" and there was light', etc. In the final centuries before Christ Judaism had such an exalted sense of God's majesty and awesome remoteness from the world that it was difficult to see how he could have, so to speak, dirtied his fingers by forming the world. So it was by the mediation of his Wisdom that God created. Of divine Wisdom it was said, 'The Lord possessed me, first-fruits of his fashioning, before the oldest of his works. From everlasting I was firmly set' (Prov. 8.22–23). God's Wisdom is not identical with God, but is intimately and utterly related to God. God cannot be conceived without the divine Wisdom, nor can the divine Wisdom exist apart from God. In the Book of Wisdom this is expressed, 'She is a breath of the power of God, a reflection of the eternal light, untarnished mirror of God's active power and image of his goodness' (Wisd. 7.25–26). The imagery of Law, Word and Wisdom fall together.

Already there was the tradition that in some sense this Wisdom had found its place in Israel, for Ben Sira, in his lovely poem about Wisdom, sings: 'I came forth from the mouth of the Most High. From eternity, in the beginning, he created me. In the holy tent I ministered before him' (Ecclus. 24.3, 9–10).

In Hellenistic Judaism, as represented by the influential Jewish philosopher Philo of Alexandria at the time of Jesus, the divine *logos* is what makes sense of the world, gives it that rationality which was so important to the Greek mind. Philo uses the word more than 1,200 times in explaining Jewish wisdom and good sense to his non-Jewish audience.

All these overtones come together when John brings the Word and Wisdom to earth with the central statement, 'the Word became flesh and dwelt among us and we saw his glory'. The last two elements of this statement have their own awesome sense. The word for 'dwelt' could be translated 'tented', suggesting the Tent of Meeting, where God dwelt in Israel during their wanderings in the desert. Its sound, *eskenosen*, further suggests the majestic *shekinah*, or awesome divine presence, the glory of God before which human beings can only cower in terror and unworthiness. So 'we saw his glory' is a strikingly bold claim to have received the full intimacy of revelation, to have experienced in Jesus the divine presence itself.

John 1.29–42

The first reading after the Prologue gives us initial reactions to Jesus from those who meet him. First of all comes John the Baptist. His testimony in this Gospel almost suggests that Jesus was a follower of John, who did not recognize him as 'the one who was to come' until the descent of the dove upon him, perhaps on the occasion of the baptism, though there is no account of a baptism of Jesus in the Fourth Gospel. John hails Jesus as the Lamb of God, but the overtones of this title are not clear. It probably does not coincide with the Lamb Standing as though Slain in the book of Revelation, for this is expressed by a less gentle and more lordly Greek word, a noble ram rather than a meek lamb. When we come to the passion narrative, this Gospel stresses the symbolism of the paschal lamb (Jesus dies at the same hour as the paschal lambs were being slaughtered in the Temple, and the Gospel notes that no bone is broken in him). There may also be some allusion to the Suffering Servant of Isaiah's prophecy, 'led like a lamb to the slaughter' for the sake of the world.

The positive reaction of the Baptist is followed by a more questing reaction from the first disciples. This encounter with two disciples begins a series of encounters, carefully spaced out over days, with individuals who come to Jesus. The tone is set by this first pair. As they follow him, he asks them the question which will be so frequent in the Gospel, 'What/whom do you seek?' (18.24; 20.15). Then they give the example of the disciple by staying with him, resting with him in tranquillity to learn from him. Although the first two named disciples are the brothers Andrew and Simon, it would be a mistake to harmonize this story with that of the call by the lakeside in Mark and Matthew. Here we are still in the Jordan Valley in the Baptist's territory.

John 1.43–51

As the crowd of followers increases one by one, they attribute to Jesus in a crescendo titles sacred in Judaism, first 'Rabbi', then 'Messiah', then, 'him of whom Moses wrote', finally 'Son of God' and 'King of Israel'. These are the revered figures of Jewish history and expectation. Even 'Son of God' is not yet a divine title, for it pairs with 'King of Israel', and the prophet Nathan had promised David that God would always be a father to his royal heirs. In the Fourth Gospel Jesus is treated on two levels. One is the climax of the hopes of Judaism, for he takes up into himself all the great institutions and figures of Judaism. The other goes beyond this to the level which many of the Jews consider blasphemous, putting him in the closest of all relationships with God.

Jesus in his turn gives names to his disciples: Simon is the Rock, and Nathanael the true Israelite. The giving of such a nickname is not only a gesture of friendliness and of profound assessment, but it creates a person, for names are always significant in Hebrew culture, and are frequently the subject of puns. So Jacob is named 'Israel' (= 'man who sees God') after his encounter with the angel of God at the ford of the River Jabbok (Gen. 32.28), and Abram is renamed 'Abraham' as 'father of a multitude' (Gen. 17.5). Peter was a rather wobbly Rock, and got his stability from the Spirit rather than his personal dependability.

Finally Jesus makes his own claim, to be the source of revelation. In the final verse he speaks not to any single individual, but to all. This Jacob's Ladder, on which the angels ascend and descend over the Son of Man, is an open pathway in two directions, a channel of apocalyptic revelation from heaven to earth, and a pathway from earth to heaven.

John 2.1–11

The change of water into wine at the wedding-feast is the first of the signs given by Jesus in chapters 2 to 12, which has been named 'the Book of Signs'. They are signs which reveal Jesus' glory for those who will open their eyes to see it. This is in itself a tremendous concept, for glory belongs properly only to God. It is the awesome and terrifying aspect of the deity which Moses experienced on Mount Sinai and Isaiah in the Temple of Jerusalem at his vocation. When the disciples 'saw his glory', does this already hint at the divinity of Jesus?

Why is it a sign? Because Jesus takes the water for the Jewish rites of purification (six water-pots, the number just short of the perfect number seven, signifying radical imperfection) and changes it into the wine of the messianic wedding-banquet. Water had always signified the Jewish law, for each in its own way is the means to life, without which no life is possible. The prophets from Hosea onwards had looked forward to the joyful wedding of God and his people Israel. Now the wine for the messianic wedding-banquet is provided in generous quantity: it multiplies out at 120–180 gallons, at most, nearly 700 bottles!

What of the part of the mother of Jesus? She is not named either here or at the foot of the Cross, but is simply called 'Woman', perhaps as though she were the archetypal woman or mother. Initially Jesus refuses to help, on the grounds that his 'hour' has not yet come, the hour of completion of his work and of his glorification on the Cross, to which both Jesus and the reader are looking forward with increasing expectation throughout the narrative. Nevertheless, her trust in his devotion to her gives her the confidence that he will somehow move forward his 'hour' and the revelation of his glory.

John 2.13–22

When did it happen, at the beginning of Jesus' ministry, as here, or at the end, as the other Gospels relate? Perhaps it was the climax, the last straw which moved the authorities to dispose of Jesus. Perhaps it was the initial proclamation, stating firmly Jesus' position right from the start. After that, the authorities would be continually watchful of Jesus, ever more hostile to him, waiting at each of his visits to Jerusalem for the moment to pounce.

Jesus had to show, on his first appearance in Jerusalem, that Judaism as it was currently being lived was an empty show. Like the ancient prophets, he expresses this by an attack on the sacrificial system which was the heart of the Jewish identity.

The vast, ornate and magnificent Temple made Jerusalem – in the words of the Roman author Pliny – 'far the most distinguished city

of the East', so that an attack on its ritual was an outrage to the authorities, quite apart from being bad for the pilgrim-and-tourist trade.
Jesus' reply to their protest is the claim quoted in the other Gospels
at his trial, but read by the evangelist in the light of later understanding:
the true Temple is his body, the Christian community. The community
at Qumran which wrote the Dead Sea Scrolls made the same claim,
that the true Temple in which God dwelt was their community.

The Gospel of John reads like a great debate in which people are
divided on one side or the other by their reaction to Jesus. It is full
of legal language, like 'witness', 'truth', 'judge' and 'condemn'. In
these first two incidents the disciples fall on one side, 'the Jews' on
the other, by acceptance and rejection of Jesus. The debate and divide
will become ever more bitter until finally, before Pilate, 'the Jews' reject
Jesus and God at the same time: 'We have no king but Caesar!'

John 3.1–21

After these first two incidents of acceptance and rejection of Jesus
comes the dialogue with Nicodemus, 'a leader of the Jews'. He seems
to sit on the fence, for he comes by night, perhaps out of fear; certainly the symbolism is that he is emerging from the darkness (cf.
13.30), as he is reminded in v. 19. In the end he commits himself
to Jesus to the extent of risking the opprobrium of his fellows by
taking part in the burial of Jesus (19.39).

The dialogue is very carefully and symmetrically shaped, each of
the three major statements by Jesus starting with the characteristic
phrase which occurs only in John, 'Amen, amen I say to you' (vv. 3,
5 and 10 – the Hebrew root of 'Amen' signifies firmness and reliability, so that the double 'Amen' denotes very strong emphasis).
Each renewed statement is provoked by that other Johannine feature, the puzzled question (3.4, 9; cf. 4.9; 6.34, 42, etc.). The whole
process rests, typically, on Nicodemus' misunderstanding in v. 4 of
the ambiguous Greek word 'anew/from above'. Nicodemus takes
one meaning, Jesus intends principally the other, though without
excluding the idea of being born again.

There are, however, two puzzles about the dialogue. First, to what
extent is Jesus supposed to be speaking? It is of course in Johannine
style, but how far is it presented as Jesus' own speech, or where does
the reflection of the evangelist start? Second, is it about sacramen-

tal baptism? Rebirth 'through water and the Spirit' is mentioned once (v. 5), but otherwise there is no mention of water, even in the seemingly repetitious v. 8. It is entirely possible that sacramental baptism may be in view, for, as so often in John, the text expresses not only the thought of Jesus but the reflection of a later age, when Jesus has already been 'lifted up' and the Jews have rejected 'our' evidence.

The whole burden of the dialogue is, however, that natural birth and natural life are insufficient. It is a strongly trinitarian statement. First is explained the part of the Spirit in this rebirth (3.5–8). To the Jews this idea of rebirth through the divine Spirit would already have been familiar through the prophets, and especially Ezekiel 36.25–27 and 37.1–14. It is also eagerly awaited in the texts of Qumran (1 QS 4.19–26: 'He will cleanse him of all wicked deeds with the spirit of holiness like purifying waters. He will shed upon him the spirit of truth').

Next comes the role of the Son as revealer (3.11–14). By contrast to the synoptic Gospels, John mentions the kingdom of God only twice (3.3, 5) in the whole Gospel. His favourite equivalent expression is the more personal and individual 'eternal life' (3.14), for which the only condition is belief. Taking up the Moses-symbolism of the prologue – it will feature again especially in the Bread of Life discourse and in the death of Jesus at the moment of the slaughter of the Passover lambs – John sees salvation in the lifting up of the Son of Man like the serpent in the desert of the Exodus (Num. 21.4–9). Another ambiguity: does he mean the lifting up onto the Cross or lifting up to heaven? John plays on this ambiguity frequently (8.28; 12.32).

Finally the Trinity is completed because the initiative of all salvation is seen in the Father who out of love sent his only Son into the world. The themes of judgement and darkness again return: God sends his Son not to judge but to save. It is those who refuse to believe who judge themselves by turning away from the light.

John 4.5–42

This light-hearted scene of Jesus with the Samaritan is one of the most delightful and wittily told stories in the New Testament. Just as the synoptic scene of Jesus with the Syro-Phoenician or Canaanite woman, whose request he grants as a reward for her neat and cheeky riposte (Mark 7.24–30; Matt. 15.21–28), it shows Jesus' confident and open relationship with women – a strong contrast to Pharisaic and rabbinic insistence that a man should not even look at a woman, let alone converse with one alone. It is striking that it occurs when Jesus is at his most human, resting, tired from the journey, while his disciples go on into the town to buy food. There is something suspect about the woman from the very start: why wait till the heat of the day, and come at noon, on her own, to draw water? All the stranger that Jesus should initiate contact with a Samaritan, whom any Jew should be expected to shun and despise – as she is quick to point out. He plays with her by his punning talk of 'living water'. She duly misunderstands as 'fresh water' what Jesus means as 'water of life'. Yet she somehow divines that there is something elevated going on, by her startling comparison of Jesus to the great forefather Jacob. When Jesus provocatively presses her further by his challenges to her to produce her husband, she sparkles back with her cheeky suggestion that he is a prophet. For the Christian reader all this is further spiced by the knowledge that, with typical Johannine irony, the Samaritan may blithely misunderstand, but there is a deeper layer of truth lurking under each playful riposte. So there is a deep satisfaction when the woman's third outrageous suggestion, that he is the Messiah, is accepted by Jesus. Due release of tension follows, as the woman trips off into the town to brag to her fellow townsfolk and share her discovery with them.

The underlying import of the scene is progressive and twofold. First, Jesus is the source of the divine wisdom promised in the Old Testament. Wisdom is often represented as living water, as in Proverbs 13.14, 'The teaching of the wise is a life-giving fountain', or Proverbs 18.4, 'a gushing stream, the utterance of wisdom'. Wisdom herself cries out in Sira 24.21, 'they who drink me will thirst for more'. Against this background Jesus' offer of living water must be seen as the offer of divine wisdom, the fullness of revelation. This makes sense of the progression from Jacob to prophet to Messiah, especially in Samaria, where the *Taheb* (the 'Returner', as the Messiah was there called) is conceived as the revealer of all truth.

Second, the exchange about worship in spirit and in truth, rather than in any particular place, be it Jerusalem or Samaria, must be understood against the same background. The message is not against the exterior expression of worship, claiming that true worship can only be deep within the human heart or spirit, for there is plenty of evidence of exterior expression of worship in the New Testament Church. Rather, it is a claim that true worship must be according to the Spirit of truth ('worship in spirit and truth' should be understood as a hendiadys, a figure of speech in which one idea is expressed by two words). This is another expression of the dichotomies already familiar in John between 'above' and 'below', 'heavenly' and 'earthly'. The same call for a community in the Spirit of truth may be found in the Rule of the community of Qumran (1 QS 4.19–22; 9.3–5, 'they shall establish the spirit of holiness according to everlasting truth').

The final section, after the return of the disciples, is also sparked off by a ludicrous misunderstanding, this time over food. Jesus uses it to allude to the harvest of the messianic times, so pressing and so generous that 'ploughman will tread on the heels of the reaper and the treader of grapes on the heels of the sower of seed' (Amos 9.13). The fields are white for this harvest.

John 5.1–9

This healing miracle is as close as John comes to the stories of Jesus' miracles in the synoptic Gospels. In fact it has often been suggested that it is the same miracle as the healing of the bedridden man in Mark 2.1–12, transposed from Capernaum to Jerusalem. There are similar elements in the controversy with the authorities, the mention of sin and the instructions to the cured man to pick up his mat and walk. The pool with five porticoes near the Sheep Gate (the current eastern gate of the Old City of Jerusalem) has been excavated, and numerous pagan healing shrines found in its vicinity. There was more corruption of religion and superstition at Jerusalem than the Bible indicates, and indeed the process which the healed man describes seems pretty superstitious.

As often in John, the most important point about this miracle is the controversy and discourse which follows it. This constitutes the high point of the revelation of the relationship of Jesus to the Father. The miracle occurs on the sabbath, which gives Jesus occasion to point out that only God works on the sabbath. God must work on the sabbath, even though it is a day of rest, for God's two special works are to give life (and babies are born on the sabbath) and to judge (and people die on the sabbath, so must proceed to judgement). Jesus outlines on this occasion that the Son gives life to anyone he chooses, just as the Father gives life (5.23), that the Father has entrusted all judgement to the Son. Above all, the Son does nothing but what he sees the Father doing. This is in fact a dynamic definition of the equality of Father and Son, not in terms of persons and natures but in terms of powers. The powers of the Son are those of the Father, exercised in perfect union with the Father, but derivative to the Son from the Father.

John 5.36–47

Jesus has been speaking, to those 'Jews' who objected to his working a cure on the sabbath, about his power to give life and to judge. Now, at the end of this chapter, the judgement theme continues, but in reverse: Jesus is being judged, and the witnesses to him are cited. The forensic atmosphere of a great judgement-scene continues.

The first witness was John the Baptist (just before this reading begins). The Jews sent messengers to him; he bore witness to the truth, and for a time they respected him.

The second witness is the deeds of Jesus, the miracles described in this Book of Signs. In the synoptic Gospels the many miracles of healing, exorcism, and so on, are seen as fulfilling the promises of Scripture, signs of the coming of the kingdom of God promised in Isaiah and the other prophets. In John fewer miracles are related, and the significance of each is brought out by the discourse which follows – as here, or the discourses on the Bread of Life (John 6), Christ the Light (John 9), Christ the Resurrection and Life (John 11).

The third witness is the Father, perhaps because it is the Father who gave the Son his works to do. In the synoptics this could refer to the voice from heaven at baptism or transfiguration, but in John neither of these scenes occurs, which may be the meaning of 'you have never heard his voice' (5.37).

The final witness is the scriptures, and in particular Moses bears witness to Jesus. Here the Gospel is fiercely critical of the Jews, who pore over the scriptures, yet refuse to recognize Jesus and draw life from him. The strength of the criticism may well reflect the bitter tension towards the end of the first century between those Jews who accepted Jesus and those who rejected him.

John 6.1–21

Discussion has been intense whether John 6 has been accidentally displaced. A reversal of the order of chapters 5 and 6 avoids a rapid transition Galilee–Jerusalem–Galilee–Jerusalem. But such an accidental displacement is difficult to explain, and it is more likely that geographico-chronological sequence was of less interest to the author than theological coherence. John 6, with its two Moses-like miracles, provision of food in the desert (cf. Exod. 16) and a crossing of the sea (cf. Exod. 14), followed by the weighty discourse contrasting Moses' and Jesus' gift of manna in the desert, is more probably seen as a follow-up of the mention of Moses in 5.45–47.

Provision of food in the desert is the only miracle of Jesus' ministry recounted by all four evangelists. It shows Jesus as the prophet like Elisha (the way it is told follows closely the account in 2 Kings 4.42–44) and ultimately like Moses, whom Elisha in his turn was imitating. John stresses the comparison with Elisha by the boy who provides the bread, and by presenting the bread as barley loaves. Perhaps more important is his stress on the eucharistic pattern of a meal of Jesus and his followers; in just the same way as at the Last Supper, Jesus gives thanks (the Greek word *eucharistein*) and personally distributes the loaves to those sitting around him.

The story of Jesus walking on the sea is not unlike that of the synoptic Gospels; only in John there is no element of calming of the storm, and all the emphasis falls on the wondrous action of Jesus. Only God walks upon the sea (Psalm 77.19, 'Your way led over the sea, your path over the countless waters'). To the awe of the disciples at seeing him Jesus replies with the mysterious phrase which can be understood either as a simple self-identification, 'It's me!', or as the divine name revealed to Moses, 'I am.' In view of the stunning effect of this expression later in the Gospel (8.28, 58; 18.5) John surely at least hints, here too, at a divine claim.

John 6.24–35

The significance of many of Jesus' signs is brought out by a discourse that follows, and this of course draws on the sign of the multiplication of loaves. The discourse itself is preceded by two important interventions of Jesus. First he complains that they are looking for him not because they have seen the signs, but simply because they have had their fill to eat. This must mean that they have not seen the correct significance of the signs. They had indeed wanted to carry him off as king, so they had seen some significance, but only that of a material, earthly kingship. Jesus challenges them to see the deeper significance. Second, Jesus stresses, as so often in this Gospel, that life comes from faith in him. Believing is not accepting any particular propositions about Jesus. Putting one's trust in Jesus alone is the condition of life and the purpose of the Gospel, 'that believing you may have life through his name' (John 20.31).

The discourse in the synagogue at Capernaum is modelled on a type of contemporary synagogue-sermon. It starts from a quotation from the Law (v. 31, from Exodus 16.15), and has a booster-quotation from the prophets half-way through (v. 45, from Isaiah 54.13). Each phrase is meditated upon and explained in turn. The earlier sections consider the bread from heaven from the point of view of Wisdom and revelation, and then 'to eat' is commented in vv. 51–58. As in the six antitheses of the Sermon on the Mount (Matt. 5.21–48), the basic technique of this kind of sermon is to correct an accepted reading, so 'it was not *Moses* who *gave* you bread from heaven; it is my *Father* who *gives* you bread from heaven'. (In Hebrew 'gave' and 'gives' are written the same, though pronounced differently.) The manna given by Moses was provisional; the revelation given in Jesus and confirmed in the Eucharist is of lasting value.

John 6.35, 41–51

The discourse of Jesus here is bracketed at beginning and end by his declaration, 'I am the Bread of Life', and the contrast to the bread given by Moses in the desert. But what is meant by 'the bread of life'? The puzzled question of 'the Jews' (and such a puzzled question is a device frequently used by John as a means of advancing the discussion) is not out of place. The tone is set by the allusion at the beginning: in Sirach 24.21 Wisdom cries out, 'They who eat me will hunger for more; they who drink me will thirst for more.' To this, 'No one who comes to me will ever hunger; no one who believes in me will ever thirst' is a direct comparison and contrast. Coming to Jesus and belief are the keynotes, repeated in almost every verse, underlining that the bread of life is the revelation given by and in Jesus. Hence also the central quotation from Isaiah, 'They will all be taught by God' (v. 45, from Isa. 54.13). In the background also is the repeated invitation of Wisdom to come to her banquet (Prov. 9.5), the messianic banquet (Isa. 55.3).

Who are 'the Jews' who object so hostilely? John often designates Jesus' opponents as 'the Jews', and attempts have been made to avoid the implication that John is anti-Judaic by suggesting that he means 'the Judaeans, the inhabitants of Judaea'. This is unlikely here, for if they were visitors from Judaea they would not know the details of village life in Galilee. In 8.44 Jesus calls the Jews to whom he is speaking 'sons of the devil', yet in 4.22 he insists that 'salvation comes from the Jews'. There certainly lurks behind this treatment of the Jews the hostility, tension and even persecution with which the followers of Jesus were treated by their fellow-Jews. By the standards of controversy and abuse of the times (compare Qumran) the language is, however, mild.

John 6.51–58

Scholars are divided whether this is the final section of a long Bread-of-Life discourse, or an independent, short version; the latter view is attractive. Just like 35–50, it is bracketed at beginning and end by statements about the bread of heaven which will give life for ever. Similarly, it is punctuated and moved forward by a puzzled question of 'the Jews' (v. 52, as vv. 41–43). As we will see later, the subsequent section seems to refer back over this passage to 6.35–50.

All the emphasis, however, is now on eating the bread, not on wisdom and belief. This is expressed with repeated realism. The word translated 'eat' really means 'chew' or 'munch'. The realism of drinking the blood is startling, especially in view of the Jewish horror of consuming blood, for blood (the symbol of life) belonged to God alone, and all meat had to be drained of blood before being eaten (cf. Gen. 9.4; Lev. 17.11; Deut. 12.23; etc.). This gives all the more significance to drinking in the blood, so the life, of Jesus. Jesus stresses the effect of permanent intertwining with his divine life: Jesus will remain in the recipient, and the recipient will draw life from Jesus (vv. 55–57). So is indicated a vibrant and vivid union of lives through the Eucharist.

There is also strong allusion to Jesus' sacrifice: it is no longer the Father who gives the bread (v. 32), but Jesus gives himself, and for the life of the world (v. 51). This statement is so close to the words of institution of the Eucharist in the other Gospels (there is no such narrative in John's account of the Last Supper), that it may be a Johannine version of this. It is indeed difficult to understand this whole passage without this Last Supper background; it would have been almost unintelligible to listeners by the lakeside, and is probably best understood as a meditation enriched by later Christian developments.

John 6.56–69

Acceptance and rejection of Jesus run through the Gospel as those who approach Jesus either come to him in belief or turn away in disbelief. This is how those who meet him judge themselves, though they think they are judging Jesus who is truth itself. Here the bitterness is that those who cannot accept the teaching have been already followers of Jesus. What is it that they cannot accept? Is it the eucharistic teaching (vv. 51–58) or the revelation of Jesus as the Wisdom of God (vv. 35–50)? In either case it may indicate a background of difficulty or division in the Johannine community about the relevant doctrine, eucharistic or christological. We have put forward above the possibility that vv. 51–58 are a distinct version of the discourse, inserted later, and indeed 59–66 seem to refer back over these verses to the earlier section. There is the same 'complaint' of the opponents and reply of Jesus in 60–61 as in 41–43. The stress is on belief, not on eating. The flesh – far from being necessary food – has nothing to offer, and is to be understood not as linked to the blood of the Son of Man, but as purely human endeavour, in opposition to the Spirit. In this case it is the Christology rather than the eucharistic doctrine which is the sticking-point.

There is an uncanny likeness between this passage and the declaration at Caesarea Philippi in Matthew: Jesus challenges his followers and Peter affirms his faith in the Holy One of God, here using, of course, the Johannine terms of belief and eternal life. As at Caesarea Philippi Jesus says that flesh and blood have not revealed this to Peter, so here he says that 'the flesh has nothing to offer' (v. 63). As the Caesarea Philippi passage ends with the prophecy of the passion, so this ends with the mention of betrayal by Judas.

John 7.37–39

The difficulty about this passage is the punctuation of the Greek. Of course in the early manuscripts there is no punctuation. It is possible to attach 'anyone who believes in me' either to what precedes or to what follows. The question affects who the source of living water is, Jesus or the believer. The Greek could be read, 'Let anyone who is thirsty come to me! Let anyone who believes in me drink.' This implies that Jesus is the source of living water. The NJB opts for 'Let anyone who is thirsty come to me! Let anyone who believes in me come and drink. As scripture says, "From his heart shall flow streams of living water."' This stands in the middle, perhaps suggesting that the believer, having drunk the living water, is in turn the source of living water for others. The NRSV opts for 'Let the one who believes in me drink. As the scripture has said, "Out of the believer's heart shall flow rivers of living water."' By substituting 'the believer's' for 'his' in the scriptural quotation, the NRSV leaves no doubt that the believer is the source of living water. This should, however, be called an interpretation rather than a translation.

The occasion of this cry by Jesus is the Festival of Tabernacles, when fresh water was fetched from the Spring of Gihon below the Temple as a symbol of the fruitful autumnal rains. In the Jewish tradition water had always been the symbol of the Law, for both sustain life. As we have seen with regard to the Samaritan, water was also the symbol of wisdom, and Jesus is represented as the source of wisdom and of revelation. In an arid land water has a quite different connotation. If you have not been lost and parched in the desert, you cannot know the joy of water. So plentiful water was the sign of messianic times (Ezek. 47.1–12; Zech. 14.8). By this cry Jesus again shows that he is taking up and perfecting all the institutions of Judaism.

John 8.1–11

It is now universally accepted that this story was not originally part of John's Gospel. In some modern versions (e.g. NRSV, GNB) it is bracketed out. It is lacking in the most important Eastern textual witnesses, although it has now long been part of the Fourth Gospel as it was received in the Western Church, for it was included in the

Vulgate by Jerome. It interrupts the flow of the controversies in the Temple about Jesus' person. It is more Lukan than Johannine in style and vocabulary (in the first couple of verses 'the Mount of Olives', 'the scribes' occur only here in John, but the scene perfectly fits at Luke 21.38). Nevertheless, the attempt of the Pharisees to trap Jesus, the dignity and delicacy of Jesus and his mercy to sinners, are highly characteristic of the Gospel stories. It may well be a story mentioned in the early second century by Papias about a woman 'accused of many sins before the Lord'. It is perhaps a stray ancient story about Jesus which found its place here in the Gospel as a comment on John 7.51.

This story was not perhaps originally included in any of the Gospels because Jesus' refusal to condemn might have seemed to condone adultery. Yet repentance and forgiveness are important Gospel themes, perhaps less central in John and more stressed in Luke. One is reminded of the story of the Woman at Simon's House (Luke 7.36–50), and especially of Jesus' gentleness to the woman without in any way condoning her sin, or of his welcome to Zacchaeus (Luke 19.1–10). What was he writing on the ground? The Greek word can also mean 'draw'. Could Jesus in fact read and write? Was he writing some scriptural verse which would stir their consciences, or was he simply doodling to give them time for reflection?

John 9.1–41

In this scintillating and witty story Johannine irony is used to its full advantage. Like other Johannine signs, after the miracle itself (which resembles a number of synoptic miracles), its lesson is brought out by discussion. The basic lesson is that Christ is the light of the world. Paradoxically and ironically, the Pharisees, self-importantly protesting that they can see ('*we* know, *we* are disciples of Moses'), gradually get blinder and blinder, at first accepting the fact of the healing, but eventually simply abusing the man as a sinner and denying that the miracle ever could have happened. By contrast this 'sinner', under their pressure, gradually grows in enlightenment and understanding, at first simply obedient to Jesus, then proclaiming him a prophet, finally worshipping him as Lord.

His scared and timid parents, contrasting so amusingly with his articulate, outspoken and eventually angry self, reveal an important background to the story. Here and in 12.42 and 16.2 mention is made of being banned from the synagogue on grounds of recognizing Jesus. This fear surely reflects the hostility between Christian Jews and the Pharisaic party at the time of writing. Such tension and even enmity also lies behind passages in Matthew. In the synoptics disagreement is normally linked to questions of legal observance, but here (though the sabbath does enter into the story) it is specifically referred to Jesus' divine claims. The same lethal conflict occurs in John 8.28.

There may well be allusion in the background also to Christian baptism, which was called 'enlightenment' in the early Church. As in Christian baptism, anointing and washing with water lead from blindness to enlightenment. Jesus is the initiator and instrument, and the Pool of Siloam ('sent') is close to the Johannine idea of Jesus as plenipotentiary envoy of the Father. After this there is a gradual increase in loyalty, understanding and commitment to Jesus.

John 10.1–10

By contrast to the synoptic Gospels, where parables abound and are widely used to teach a variety of lessons, the sheep parables are almost the only developed parables in John. Certainly there are other *meshalim*, for the Hebrew concept of *mashal* is wider than the Greek concept of parable. A *mashal* includes any riddle, proverb or imaged saying, whereas 'parable' requires a certain elaboration or story-element. 'The bridegroom's friend is filled with joy at the bridegroom's voice' (John 3.29) or 'The fields are white for the harvest' (4.15) are *meshalim* but not parables.

The first parable (10.1–5) centres on the shepherd himself, trusted and let in by the gatekeeper. The immediate background and allusion is Ezekiel 34, where the leaders of Israel are castigated as lazy and self-indulgent shepherds, neglecting the well-being of the sheep, dressing themselves in wool, slaughtering the fattest sheep but failing to feed the flock. Jesus contrasts himself with these shepherds. There is also an implicit further claim, for the true shepherd of Israel is God himself, 'The Lord is my shepherd' (Ps. 23.1–4). Jesus may be presenting himself as the delegate of God, but there is also a claim to divinity implicit in the title of shepherd.

A second parable (10.7, 9–10) diverges significantly from the first, while remaining on the subject of sheep. Here Jesus is the gate of the sheepfold. Verse 8 returns to the former image, for the thieves and bandits who come must be contrasted with the shepherd rather than with the gate. Counterfeit leaders do seem to have been a problem in the early Church (Acts 20.28–29; 2–3 John). Then, in vv. 9–10, the meaning of the gate-image is made clear. Jesus is no longer the guide but provides the way of life through which the believer must pass in order to live. Elsewhere in John (14.6) Jesus calls himself the way, and the same image of the gate through which a person passes is used in Matthew's alternative images at the end of the Sermon on the Mount, the narrow gate and the broad way (Matthew 7.13–14).

John 10.11–18

After the brief image of the gate John returns to that of the shepherd, explaining its meaning. The emphasis is threefold. First, the image of the caring and devoted shepherd is expanded to include a willingness to die for the sheep. This dimension is entirely new to the shepherd image, so widely used of God and of kings in the Old Testament. It is allegorical, shaped by awareness of Jesus' willing sacrifice. In real life it is not sound pastoral policy, nor to the advantage of the sheep, that a shepherd should sacrifice his life in defence of his sheep against a predator. Still less is this the case on the waterless hills and in the precipitous valleys of Palestine. In fact a wolf does not attack a human being, though in a pack they might try to scare away a human shepherd who stood between them and their potential prey.

A second extension touches knowledge. Sheep, often thought to be hopelessly witless and contrary creatures, will respond individually, at least to a caring and affectionate shepherd who treats them individually. It is indeed the contrast between the witless unpredictability of the herded sheep and the individual response to the care of a shepherd which gives this image its point. When the mutual relationship of knowledge and trust is compared to that of the Son and the Father, this must be read against other passages in John where the latter is described. In John 5.19–30 the dynamic unity of purpose, power and will between Father and Son is presented; the

185

Father and the Son look towards each other. This is now offered as a model for the relationship between Jesus and his own sheep. Similarly a recurrent theme of the Last Supper Discourse is the mutual indwelling of Father and Son, echoed by the indwelling of Jesus in his followers.

A third aspect is the extension to 'sheep that are not of this fold'. One may doubt to what extent the historical Jesus articulated a mission beyond Israel, but by John's time this implication of his mission was becoming fully clear.

John 10.22–30

The different chronologies of John and the synoptic Gospels give different pictures of Jesus' ministry in Jerusalem. According to Mark, followed by Matthew and Luke, Jesus spent only a brief four days in Jerusalem between Palm Sunday and Maundy Thursday before his arrest. That was enough to show the authorities that he had to be removed before the Passover crowds arrived. According to John, however, who certainly seems to know Jerusalem better, he made four separate visits to Jerusalem, with the cleansing of the Temple during the first visit. So after that the authorities would have been thirsting to arrest him, with increasing bitterness each time he came. They were frustrated by the awe in which he was held by the crowds, or – as John puts it – because 'his hour had not yet come'. After this confrontation in the Portico of Solomon (a covered colonnade, suitable for teaching in winter) they got as far as trying to stone him, but again he walked away.

Jesus' teaching on this occasion combines two themes we have already met, the Son of the Father (5.36–47) and the shepherd of the sheep (10.1–18). Now he goes further on each of these. Not only is he the shepherd, but he gives life which is eternal. This is the Johannine equivalent of the synoptic kingdom of God. By the gift of eternal life, received simply by knowing and acknowledging Jesus, he brings his followers within the kingdom, into the new, expanded kingdom where there is no more death, fear, alienation or contempt, but where all can serve God in freedom and joy. However little this may seem to be the case amid the stresses and strains of life, that is the basic reality which the followers of Jesus need to make real for themselves.

It is Jesus' final statement, 'The Father and I are one,' which detonates the bomb. As before, when Jesus used the divine formula, 'Before Abraham was, I am,' so now when he says frankly, 'The Father and I are one,' they immediately took up stones to throw at him. It is the claim to divinity which bursts the parameters of Judaism.

John 11.1–45

The raising of Lazarus from death is the climax of the Book of Signs, John's account of the ministry of Jesus. It is the climax not only because it is the final incident but because raising from death to life is the greatest of Jesus' miracles. Jesus came 'that they might have life and have it more abundantly' (John 10.10). Furthermore, with typical Johannine paradox, it is this gift of life which leads directly to Jesus' death, for as a result of the attention won by the miracle (the Jews going out to visit the raised man and coming to faith in Jesus) the high priest and his associates decide to liquidate Jesus (11.45–50).

The sisters Martha and Mary appear in Luke (Luke 10.38–42). Lazarus also features in a Lukan parable (Luke 16.19–31; cf. above p. 145), in a quite different role though also concerned with death and return from death. Since the incident of the raising of Lazarus occurs nowhere in the synoptics, and appears to be cavalierly inserted in John after the conclusion of 10.42, like an independent and removable block, some have suggested that the story is spun from the Lukan episodes. It is thoroughly Johannine in character, full of irony, different layers of meaning, and misunderstanding through deliberate ambiguity. It is built on contrast, light and dark, withdrawal and appearance, life and death, sorrow and joy. Jesus is at once vibrantly human in his affection for the three family members, and at the same time divinely exalted in his knowledge, power and control. He knows that he will wake Lazarus. He knows that his prayer is always heard by the Father. He declares, with the solemn expression 'I am', that he himself is Resurrection and Life. The one feature unusual for John is that 'the Jews' stands in this story not for the opponents of Jesus, who are here accurately characterized as the chief priests and Pharisees, but for the inhabitants of Judaea and Jerusalem, not opposed but rather sympathetic to Jesus.

It has been said that in the synoptic Gospels Jesus reveals the kingship of God, while in John he reveals himself. In the course of this Gospel Jesus several times uses the expression 'I am' or 'I am he' – both translate the Greek *ego eimi*. This can be simply a self-identification, like 'It's me!' Repeatedly, however, Jesus uses it to claim for himself mysterious and awesome titles, frequently of special significance in Israel: 'I am the bread come down from heaven' (6.41, the gift of the Father, greater than Moses), 'I am the light of the world' (8.12, when normally in Judaism the Law is the light of the world), 'I am the gate of the sheepfold' (10.7), 'I am the good shepherd' (10.11, when God is the shepherd of Israel), 'I am the way, I am truth and life' (14.6, when God is truth and is the Master of life), 'I am the true vine' (15.1, when Israel itself is the vine of the Lord). Here at 11.25 Jesus makes the solemn claim, 'I am the resurrection.' By this stupendous claim Jesus puts himself in the position of God at the last day, for that was the moment when God would raise the dead to life again. On three occasions Jesus uses *ego eimi* with special solemnity and without a predicate. This 'I am' claims the divine name revealed to Moses at the Burning Bush (Exod. 3.13) or in the great monotheistic declarations of Deutero-Isaiah 43.10; 51.12. The Jews recognize that this is a divine claim which they regard as blasphemy (John 8.24, 58). At the arrest this expression occurs three times (18.5, 6, 8), and each time the arresting party involuntarily falls to the ground in reverence. By this expression, then, Jesus both posits and explains his divine claims.

John 12.1–11

This story of the anointing at Bethany is a fascinating example of a loose unit of tradition which serves different purposes in different Gospels. Placing ointment on the head at a banquet was a ceremonial custom (frequent washing is a phenomenon of the modern, Western world); anointing of the feet, however, serves only to make them sticky and gather more dust. In Mark and Matthew the anointing of Jesus' head is placed after the triumphal entry into Jerusalem, two days before the Passover; it is part of the lead-up to the passion, stressing that Jesus is being anointed for burial. Anointing was an important part of the respectful leave-taking of death, whereas in Mark 15.46 Joseph of Arimathaea simply unceremoniously 'wrapped him in the shroud' – Matthew stresses that it was a clean shroud. The anointing by the woman was seen as a significant substitute.

In John the incident is carefully linked to the previous scene by the mention of Mary and Lazarus – no mention of the Simon at whose house it occurs in the other Gospels. It occurs a little earlier, 'six days before the Passover' (not two days, as in Mark 14.1). The anointing serves the same purpose, though Jesus' instruction to 'keep it for the day of my burial' is puzzling; there is no sign of anything being kept for later. The scene also serves to inform the reader of Judas' poor reputation; he attracts more blame as the Gospel tradition develops.

The strange feature of anointing Jesus' feet rather than his head, and then wiping off the ointment, is very likely to be contamination from the Lukan story. There the anointing at Simon's house by the woman of bad repute is coherent: she weeps on his feet, wipes off her tears and then anoints those same feet, not for his burial but as an expression purely of penitent affection.

John 12.12–16

In the synoptic Gospels Jesus' festive entry into Jerusalem for the first time leads directly on to his demonstration in the Temple; it shows the Messiah taking possession of his city and Temple. In John the sense is quite different. It is not Jesus' first entry into Jerusalem; during the last few chapters he has seldom been far distant from Jerusalem (Lazarus' home at Bethany is a 20-minute walk from the Temple). The scene starts with great nationalistic enthusiasm. The palm-branches are a nationalist symbol, familiar from the Maccabean revolts and later to be blazoned on the coins of the Jewish Revolt of AD 66–70; the term used for 'went out to receive him' (v. 13) is a technical term for the solemn reception of a Hellenistic monarch; they greet him as 'king of Israel'. It is the arrival of the messianic kingdom in the popular sense of the word.

However, just as Jesus rejected their enthusiastic attempt to make him king after the feeding miracle in John 6.15, so now he rejects this surge of nationalism. Verse 14 begins, '*But* Jesus . . .'. So Jesus prophetically reinterprets his entry. His choice of a donkey, that delicate, sure-footed mount, is utterly unmilitaristic. The meaning is clarified by the evangelist through the quotation of the two prophets. The first line, from Zephaniah 3.16, inspires gentle, not aggressive, confidence: in the following verses the Saviour will gather together the weak and the strays, and will receive the praise of all peoples. It is a message of healing universalism. The other two lines, from Zechariah 9.9, introduce an unpompous king who will banish war and bring peace to the nations. The evangelist tells us that the disciples misunderstood the scene at the time and understood it only after the glorification of Jesus, that is, his death and resurrection were necessary before even they could appreciate the true meaning of his messianic kingship.

John 12.20–33

The Greeks who approach Jesus in vv. 20–23 provide further confirmation of the importance at this stage of the universalistic theme which was so carefully hinted in the messianic entry into Jerusalem. They presumably are 'god-fearers', that is, members of the circle around Judaism, drawn to the purity of monotheism by contrast to the uninspiring and unedifying gods of the Gentiles, but not yet fully embracing Judaism with circumcision and all its restrictions. However, after they have made this initial approach to Jesus through Philip – his Greek name suggests that he was a Greek-speaker – they are mentioned no more.

The principal subject of this passage is the hour of Jesus. Since the marriage feast at Cana, when Jesus excused himself on the grounds that his hour had not yet come (2.4), the hour has been lurking mysteriously in the shadows: 'the hour is coming when . . .' (4.21; 5.28). They could not arrest him because his hour had not yet come (7.30; 8.20). Now the hour has at last come for the Son of Man to be glorified.

The image of the grain falling into the earth and dying so that it may yield a rich harvest gives rise to the Johannine equivalent of the Agony in the Garden. As in that scene, Jesus' soul is troubled as he faces death. Conscious that he came into this world for this hour, he cannot pray that the cup should pass him by. As in Matthew's account he prays to his Father the third petition of the Lord's Prayer, 'Your will be done', so now he prays the second, 'Father, glorify your name.' To glorify God's name is the Johannine equivalent of hallowing the name of God by the coming of the kingdom. With the clear knowledge which is characteristic of Jesus in this Gospel, he even hints at the crucifixion, 'when I am lifted up from the earth', a phrase which at the same time hints at his exaltation to heaven.

John 13.1–17, 31b–35

The Johannine scene of the Last Supper is very different from the synoptic account. Notoriously, the date is different: for John it is important that Jesus dies as the paschal lambs are being slaughtered (John 19.13), which puts his own final supper at least 24 hours before the official Passover meal. (Did Jesus follow a different calendar? Was the supper not a paschal supper at all? Did they simply celebrate a quasi-paschal meal? Each of these views has its supporters.) In the account itself we are told of no institution of the Eucharist, no new covenant. Almost the only element shared with the other Gospels is the story of the identification of Judas as the betrayer. In John the supper is principally the locale of the great final discourses. It begins, however, with Jesus' action of washing the feet of the disciples.

The foot-washing has been regarded chiefly as an example of humility. This lesson is made explicit in the commentary of vv. 12–16, and it is pointed out that John often gives us an action which is later explained in a commentary. However, it must also be a prophetic action, prophetic of the self-sacrifice of the passion which is about to begin. So much becomes clear from the repeated stress on Jesus' knowledge of what is about to happen, 'knowing that his hour had come' (v. 1, setting the tone of the whole passion narrative), 'knowing that he was returning to the Father' (v. 3). After the Judas-episode Jesus returns to the point, 'now has the Son of Man been glorified'. This also sets the tone for the Johannine passion narrative, which is a story not of humiliation and suffering but of triumph. Jesus not only knows what is to happen but controls it in every detail.

The stress in the foot-washing on the personal cleansing of the disciples necessary for company with Jesus, the need for a bath, also suggests an overtone of baptismal symbolism.

John 13.21–32

All the accounts of the supper include the identification of Judas as the betrayer of Jesus. Yet the accent is not upon the identification but on the treachery after sharing the meal with Jesus and especially after the intimacy of sharing the same dish. Everywhere, but especially in the orient, such sharing of hospitality creates a special bond. When once I had an Israeli soldier's gun pointing at me, I asked for a cup of water before explaining myself; it wonderfully defused the situation. The treachery is enhanced by the deceit of the impression that Judas was leaving with Jesus' approval to perfom his official duty as treasurer of the group. It is confirmed by 'Satan entered him' and by the symbolic blackness of night (vv. 27 and 30), for John is sensitive to the powers of night (1.5; 11.10; 20.1).

This is also the first appearance of the Beloved Disciple. Four times this mysterious disciple comes to the fore (and three times in partnership with Peter), but he is never named. Tradition guessed that he was John the evangelist. Some scholars have guessed that he was Lazarus, for Jesus is said to have loved Lazarus, and the proximity of Bethany to Jerusalem would explain why he appears only in the Jerusalem chapters, and why he was known to the High Priest. Alternatively, the fact that he is never named is significant, and he is presented (whether or not he is founded on one individual disciple) as any disciple whom Jesus loves. He is close to Jesus at the supper (the Eucharist?). He is close to Jesus on the cross, so shares his passion. He, rather than Peter, comes immediately to faith in the resurrection. In John 21.23–24 he is said to be the tradent of and authority behind the tradition of the Gospel with the hint that he will remain for ever. Is this the portrait of the beloved disciple?

John 14.1–14

A helpful, but not the sole possible, way of considering the Discourse after the Last Supper is to see it as three separate versions put one after another (chapter 14; chapters 15–16; chapter 17). None of these is exactly as it left the lips of Jesus, but – just like the synoptic final discourse of Jesus on the future of his community (Mark 13 and parallels) – it is amply clear that a host of sayings of Jesus lie at its base and have been elaborated by the Johannine tradition. Features of the Johannine style are everywhere strong: puzzled questions, ambiguity leading to misunderstanding and further clarification. Strictly speaking it cannot be regarded as a speech of Jesus, but many of the sayings have parallels in the synoptic

Gospels; arguably the Johannine version is often the more primitive. It was a convention in both the classical and biblical worlds that before his death a great leader would gather his disciples, often at a meal, to prepare them for the future which he foretold. The fascination of this discourse is that it shimmers or hovers between several different points in time. At times the real Jesus at the supper seems to be speaking about the future, at times the risen Christ about the future, at times Christ present in the Spirit about the current situation of the Church.

This first segment begins and ends with assurance of Jesus' continuing presence in his disciples. He has gone away only to prepare a final place for them, to which he will gather them at the end of time (vv. 1–3). Even now, during their time on earth, his disciples are in him just as he is in the Father, and can do his works just as he does the Father's works (vv. 11–14). This is the basis of the whole life of the Christian community. In the middle (vv. 6–7) the statement, lapidary in its simplicity, of the central position of Christ: he alone is the Way; he alone is Truth and Life.

John 14.15–27

After the physical departure of Jesus would his followers be left deserted? Mark 13.11 gave the answer that the Holy Spirit would speak in them. Matthew 28.20 gave the answer that the risen Christ would be with them always, to the end of time. The present section of the Last Discourse gives the threefold promise of divine presence. The Father will send another Paraclete, the Spirit of truth (vv. 14–17). Jesus himself will be with them and reveal himself to them (vv. 18–21). Jesus and the Father will come to anyone who loves him and will make their home in him (vv. 23–26). In each section the condition of the divine presence is simply that the disciple should 'love me' and 'keep my commandments'. This is no emotional or sentimental feeling of love; it is a firm and practical commitment which issues in the obedience of love, for each time it is linked to observance of commandments. John does not give any detailed, practical moral teaching, but simply insists on this active love.

This is the first mention of the Paraclete, about whom there are several important passages in the discourse. The title literally means 'one called to the side', an 'advocate', a helper to support, a witness to convince, often a spokesman (1 John 2.1). The Paraclete makes Jesus present, so to speak, when Jesus is absent, to be with his disciples and lead them into all truth and full understanding. In this first passage about the Paraclete, this presence is the Paraclete's principal function, 'to be with you for ever'. Such pairs to carry on the mission of a great figure are common in the Bible, for instance Moses and Joshua, Elijah and Elisha. In first-century Judaism another antecedent is also the tradition of the Spirit of truth dwelling in and guiding the community of Qumran, making it the temple of God.

John 14.22–29

'Peace' was (and is) the normal greeting in Hebrew, but it has here a special prominence, reiterated in the repeated greeting of the risen Christ in 20.19 and 26. From the beginning of his mission Jesus brings peace. When he was with the wild beasts in the desert (Mark 1.13), this fulfilled the messianic prophecies of peace in nature by Isaiah 11.6–9, 'the wolf will live with the lamb'. In his miracles and his teaching he brings peace to troubled consciences, calling sinners and eating with them and freely forgiving them; to troubled minds by removing sickness, fear, alienation, bereavement and death. Now he passes this task to his disciples.

In this second of the Paraclete passages the stress is on the Paraclete's role in making clear the teaching of Jesus. Frequently we have heard that the disciples did not understand at the time and understood only later, when the Spirit had been given (2.22; 12.16; 13.7). Especially in the synoptic Gospels the disciples are often startlingly obtuse, but it was only after the resurrection that the pattern of Jesus' life and teaching became clear. The coming of the Spirit – in the upper room according to John, at Pentecost according to Luke – made a great leap forward, readying the disciples for their mission. This was, however, only the beginning of the Paraclete's teaching. Down the ages the real meaning and implications of the life and teaching of Jesus have needed to be assimilated and made clear to each generation, and it is by the Paraclete that this development of faith has been guided.

How is 'the Father is greater than I' compatible with the statements about the oneness of Father and Son? The Son exercises the same powers of judgement, of giving life as the Father. He does nothing but what he sees the Father doing. The powers are his own, and yet he is the one who is sent by the Father.

John 15.1–8

Apart from the sheep parables in John 10.1–18, the vine is the only extended parable in this Gospel. It is striking that this image (and the whole of 15.1–5) contains no reflection of the situation of the final discourse; it is far more like the synoptic parables. The *mashal* (an extended parable) may perhaps owe its position to the wine of the supper. Only in vv. 7–8 does the thought revert to the theme of asking what is necessary for the Christian life. The imagery of vine, vineyard and wine occurs frequently in Jesus' teaching: new wine in new wineskins (Mark 2.22), the wicked vine-dressers (Mark 12.1–12), the wine of the messianic wedding-feast (John 2.1–10); such imagery is natural in a wine-producing countryside. In the background, however, must always be Isaiah's parable of the vineyard of Israel, fostered by the Lord carefully but to no effect (Isa. 5.1–7). In more detail, Jeremiah 2.21 even uses the imagery of a 'true vine': Israel had been planted and cared for as a 'true vine' but had degenerated into a wild vine. If John is alluding to this, the parable suggests the failure of Israel.

As so often with John, the imagery must be read on at least two levels, christological and ecclesiological. The parable is another instance of Jesus focussing on himself the great institutions of Israel: the sabbath, the Temple, the light, the living water. Now, by claiming to be the true or authentic vine, he suggests that Israel was not itself the vine (if 'authentic' has this sense), but that he himself is the vine of which Israel is a reflection. On the ecclesiological level this *mashal* illustrates the teaching of the mutual lasting indwelling of Jesus and his disciples, with the additional touch of the tendrils drawing from Jesus their sustenance or their life-blood (to revert to the imagery of John 6: unless you drink my blood you cannot have life in you).

John 15.9–17

The present segment of the final discourse is concentrated entirely on love. There is a direct line both of example and of consequences, love of the Father for the Son, love of the Son for his disciples and friends, love of his friends for one another. The love of the Father for the Son is the model of the love of the Son for his disciples, which in turn is the model of the love of disciples for one another.

John is the apostle of love, which may be one reason why tradition fixed on the disciple who was so close to Jesus at the supper as being the author. Love is also the principal message of 1 John (especially chapters 4 and 5 on the mutual love of Jesus' disciples). While Matthew and Luke give detailed instructions about Christian behaviour, for example in the Sermons on the Mount and on the Plain respectively, in John the sole demand is love. So this word, *agape*, occurs once only in Matthew and Luke, but eight times in John. The Greek translators of the Bible virtually invented the word, for there was no equivalent in Greek thought for the biblical concept. It is a strong, unbreakable family commitment, generous and unselfish. If I love my brother in this sense, I may not get on too well with him, but I will never let him down.

There are two other valuable links: 'to bear fruit, fruit that will last' links this passage to the imagery of the true vine, showing that John still has this parable in mind, and that the love is still conceived as sap drawn from the stem of the vine which is Christ. The other valuable connection is with joy (v. 11). This becomes a dominant note of the discourse, especially joy in the progress of the mission (14.28; 17.13) and eschatological joy (16.21). In Luke there is constant stress on joy at conversion of the sinner; in John there is constant joy in the presence of the Lord (16.22; 20.20).

John 15.26–27; 16.4b–15

There will be opposition between Jesus' disciples and 'the world': 'the world hates you' is stated strongly and at length (15.18–22). Just as in the synoptic Gospels the Spirit will put words into the disciples' mouths when they are challenged and persecuted (Mark 13.9–11), so in John the Paraclete will be a witness to show the world how wrong it was. This is an aggressive role, to demonstrate the failure of 'the prince of this world' who has already been condemned. Very similar is the role of the Spirit of truth at Qumran, confuting the spirit of falsehood, a strife which will culminate at the coming of the Messiah with a war of annihilation between the sons of light and the sons of darkness.

Running through John is a theme of division and of judgement. It is almost like one great court-scene in which those who encounter Jesus judge themselves ('the Father has given all judgement to the Son', John 5.22) by their reaction to Jesus, falling either on one side (the disciples, the Samaritan, the man born blind) or the other (the 'Jews', the disciples who depart in John 6.66), perhaps sitting on the fence for a while (Nicodemus). The sole criterion is belief in Jesus. So law-court words abound, like 'witness', 'judge', 'truth', 'condemn', 'true' and 'false'. The height and climax of this typically Johannine process is when before Pilate the Jewish leaders think they are condemning Jesus when in fact they are condemning themselves. In the life of the community, when Jesus is no longer physically present, it is the Spirit of truth who leads this process. The process of judgement led by the Spirit of truth consists in a revelation and a grasping of who Jesus is. It therefore glorifies him by revealing that he and the Father are one.

John 16.12–15

See above, on 15.26–27; 16.4b–15.

John 17.1–26

A farewell discourse of a great teacher to his disciples often concluded with a prayer, just as this majestic prayer brings Jesus' final instructions to a climax. It has been named the High Priestly Prayer. There is more concentration on the role of Jesus as exalted intercessor than as offerer of himself as victim; the latter thought occurs only indirectly in v. 19, 'I consecrate myself'. There is no thought of suffering, but rather of glory. 'Priest' and 'High Priest' in the Christian sense occur in the New Testament only in the Letter to the Hebrews, with similar emphasis on Jesus standing to make intercession as High Priest according to the order of Melchizedek.

The prayer may be regarded as a meditation (technically a *midrash*, a Jewish term used for reflection on and developing of the message of Scripture) on the first three petitions of the Lord's Prayer. Like the Lord's Prayer, it begins with the invocation 'Father' (repeated in vv. 5, 11, 21, 24), which makes it the affectionate prayer of Son to Father. In Judaism it was not unknown to address God as 'Father', but this was normally wrapped in other, more formal and honorific titles. The special relationship established in the Christian use of 'Father', justified by adoption of the position of sons in Christ (Rom. 8.15; Gal. 4.6), is enshrined in the retention of the Aramaic word 'abba' even in the Greek writings of the New Testament. To keep Jesus' own word legitimates the boldness of the invocation.

The sanctification of God's Name (vv. 11, 12, 26) is reflected in the revelation of God's and Jesus' glory, for to the Hebrew mind the Name reflects the power and strength of the bearer of the name. It can be wielded as a talisman, expressing the power of the bearer. The Christian is inscribed with the name of God (Rev. 3.12), and Christians can be defined as 'those who call upon the name of the Lord' (Acts 2.21; 9.14). The sanctification of the Name of God (Ezek. 36.21–23) is one of the goals of the return from exile in Babylon, to be fulfilled at the completion of the ages; it means that God is to be recognized for what he truly is. An element in the recognition of God's glory is the glorification of the Son achieved and recognized at the resurrection.

The second petition of the Lord's Prayer does not appear overtly in John 17, but its place is taken by 'eternal life'. John avoids the expression 'kingdom of God' (used only at John 3.3, 5). In the synoptics Jesus came to bring the kingdom into being. The equivalent in John is the eternal life which Jesus came to bring. In this prayer eternal life consists in 'knowing you, the only true God, and Jesus Christ whom you have sent' (v. 3). Such knowledge does not, as in gnostic circles, release from the world and its cares, but transforms both the disciples and the world. The disciples of Jesus have an ambiguous relationship with 'the world', being in the world (v. 11), but hated by the world and not 'of the world' (vv. 14–16). Paradoxically, the Christian knows and understands God's love by understanding the expression of God's love, Father and Son, in the crucifixion and resurrection of Jesus, that is, the glorification of the Son. The obedience of Jesus on the cross is a revelation of the divine love of the Son for the Father. The love of Father for Son is revealed in the resurrection: 'God raised him high and gave him the name above every other name' (Phil. 2.9). It is this knowledge which consecrates the Christian (v. 17).

The prayer is shot through with the idea of the obedience of Jesus to his Father, Jesus fulfilling God's will, being one with the Father, keeping his disciples true to God's name, or doing God's will. This is equivalent to the third petition of the Lord's Prayer, and – by its timing – especially to Jesus' use of this petition in his prayer in the Garden, 'May your will be done' (Matt. 26.42).

This meditative prayer is conveniently divided into three parts, in widening circles, according to those for whom Jesus prays: vv. 1–8 are Jesus' prayer for his own glorification and the completion of his revelation. 'World' is here surely used in two different senses (typical of John), one in a neutral sense (v. 18, 'as you sent me into the world'), and one in the sense of the domain of the Evil One (v. 15). In vv. 9–19 Jesus prays for his disciples as they challenge the world with the truth; in vv. 20–26 for the wider circle of 'those who through their teaching will come to me'. But each section is centred on the Father and the glorification of God through the message of Jesus, mediated by his disciples.

A central emphasis throughout, but most clearly expressed in the third section, is concern for the unity of the disciples. This stands in marked contrast to the earlier sections of the discourse, especially chapters 15–16, where the principal concern is opposition from the outside. It has been plausibly suggested that the community context of the prayer is no longer one of persecution and opposition from those who rejected Christianity, but is the beginning of internal dissension within the Christian community, dissensions which become ever clearer in the later letters of the New Testament, the so-called 'catholic Epistles', especially 2—3 John, 2 Peter and Jude.

John 18.1—19.42
John's passion narrative and history

John's narrative of the passion is different from that of the synoptic Gospels in important respects. Some of these differences are matters of emphasis, others seem to rest on a set of different facts. The historical prelude is different, for according to John, Jesus has made several visits to Jerusalem, while in the synoptics he had spent only four days in the city before his arrest. On the Johannine schema the authorities seem to have been waiting to pounce during his series of visits since the Cleansing of the Temple. In fact the decision to

dispose of Jesus was made long before the arrest itself, after the raising of Lazarus (11.47–53). A significant detail is that already at the
arrest the Romans are involved in the form of a cohort of auxiliary
troops (18.3), which suggests that the governor has already been
brought into the picture. No Jewish trial-scene before the high
priest, no meeting of a Sanhedrin to prepare a charge to put before
Pilate, was therefore necessary. Instead John gives an interrogation
before Annas, the ex-high priest and father-in-law of Caiaphas. The
trial before Pilate may well be built on the same incident as that of
the synoptics, but in John it is highly elaborated for theological reasons. The scourging and mockery are built into this scene. The mockery fits less well here in the middle of the trial scene, for it seems
more suitable as a rough military pastime in the night; in John's narrative it finds its place here as part of the ironic declaration of the
kingship of Jesus. There are considerable minor differences between
all the accounts of the crucifixion itself; one option is to conclude
that the evangelists had little detailed knowledge of what occurred
on Calvary, and rather reconstructed what *must have* happened, each
somewhat differently.

It must be stressed that John's access to information is in no way
inferior to that of the synoptics. John – or the tradition behind
the Gospel – certainly knows Jerusalem (the Sheep Gate, the Pools
of Siloam and Bethesda) and its environs (Bethany, Bethphage,
Ephraim) better than they do. The synoptic Gospels betray no
detailed topographical knowledge of Jerusalem. There were connections to the high priest's household (18.15). The outline of John's
story is at least as probable as that of the synoptic writers.

Theological emphases

The Johannine account is not the story of a condemned criminal
being dragged to the disgraceful and tortured death reserved for slaves.
Jesus is the majestic king, who proceeds royally to his triumph in
death. From the beginning it is stressed that Jesus is fully aware of
what is to happen (13.1, 3). The whole process begins with his prophetic gesture of service in the washing of his disciples' feet. Before
he can be arrested his captors repeatedly fall to the ground in an
involuntary gesture of reverence at Jesus' pronouncement of the
divine name, 'I am.' Jesus commands them to let his followers go,

and is taken only when he gives the word (18.11). The humiliating elements of the other accounts, such as buffeting, spitting and the challenge to prophesy, have disappeared. Jesus is emphatically declared king in the three great world-languages by the very man who condemns him to death (19.20–22). John even notes that the proclamation was publicly acknowledged by 'many of the Jews'. Even as he hangs on the cross, Jesus is firmly in control, dying only when he is ready, has finished his task and has given his consent, 'It is fulfilled.'

Not only is Jesus king; he continues his role as revealer and judge as well. In the interview with Annas, the high priest is said to question Jesus (18.19), but it is Jesus who challenges and questions the high priest, reiterating his own teaching which he has given for all the world to hear. Similarly at the Pilate trial, Jesus questions the governor and shows his control, until Pilate collapses with the feeble evasion, 'What is truth?' – a humiliating self-condemnation in this Gospel of truth. The theme of judgement has run throughout the Gospel as one after another of Jesus' interlocutors judge themselves by their reaction to him. It now reaches its climax when the Jewish leaders, in a formal and balanced scene (a chiasmus, 18.28—19.16, alternating scenes inside and outside the Praetorium), condemn themselves before Jesus: he is enthroned on the judgement-seat as judge and crowned – with thorns – as king, still wearing the royal purple robe of his mockery, while they deny the very existence of Judaism by declaring, 'We have no king but Caesar' (19.15). If the God of Israel is not universal king, then Israel has no point or purpose.

From the very earliest tradition about the death of Jesus (1 Cor. 15.3) the puzzle of how the Messiah could be so rejected and humiliated was solved by seeing it as the fulfilment of Scripture. Hence the frequent quotations of Scripture in all the Gospel accounts (e.g. Jesus' last cry from the cross in Mark 15.34 or Luke 23.46, each quoting a different psalm). The scriptures expressed in a special way the will of God, and so prescribed how Jesus should suffer and die. This is exemplified also in John's account (19.24, 28, 36, 37). A particular emphasis is on Jesus as the paschal lamb, whence the stress that Jesus' death-sentence coincides with the ritual slaughter of the paschal lambs in the Temple (19.14), and the note that, like the paschal lambs, no bone of his was broken (19.36, quoting Exodus 12.46). His final drink is offered on a hyssop-sprig, a supple little twig used for sprinkling the blood on the doorposts (Exod. 12.22) but quite unsuitable for supporting any drink.

The death of Jesus

The final scene of course has special significance. Jesus carries his own cross, unaided, and is enthroned on it – no agonizing details of nailing and hoisting – between two attendants. There is no final psalm-quotation of seeming despair (as in Mark and Matthew) or of resignation (as in Luke), no wordless 'great cry' as Jesus expires. In John Jesus prepares the community of the future. In contrast both to the other Gospels and to verisimilitude, Mary (or rather his mother, nowhere named by John) and the Beloved Disciple stand at the foot of the cross and are entrusted to each other's care to constitute the first Christian community, the woman and the man, the mother and the ideal disciple. This is cemented by the gift of the Spirit, as Jesus – with typical Johannine ambiguity – 'gave over his spirit' (is this simply the last expiring breath or the gift of the Holy Spirit?). Only then does Jesus consent to die, with the words, 'It is fulfilled' (What is fulfilled? The Scripture, the will of the Father, his own purpose?). After this from his side flow blood and water, perhaps symbolic of the sacraments of Eucharist and baptism respectively. The Church and its sacraments for the future are constituted only – no institution of the Eucharist at the Last Supper – at the death of Jesus. After this, fittingly, instead of the unceremonious and hurried burial of the synoptic Gospels, the Jewish rites of burial are duly observed, and the quantity of spices prescribed for a royal entombment is administered (19.39).

John 18.33b–37

This reading is part of the dialogue between Jesus and Pilate, hardly in the tone one might expect between a Roman governor and a prisoner facing summary justice. They speak on equal terms, but it is Jesus who leads the discussion. The chief point of the dialogue as we have it is to stress that Jesus is king (see above), and king of a realm far superior to any earthly realm, with his own subjects who are devoted to the truth. Pilate acknowledges this kingship, but finally loses all credit and credibility by casting aside the value of truth. The irony is that Jesus is the Truth, the true Vine, the true Shepherd, the Way, the Truth and Life.

How accurate is the picture of Pilate? We know from one of the fullest external witnesses, the Jewish historian Josephus, that Pilate condemned Jesus 'at the instigation' of the Jewish authorities (*Antiquities*, 18.3.3). This ensures that such a scene occurred. The contemporary sources have little good to say of Pilate, representing his tyrannical behaviour as largely responsible for the discontent which led to the Jewish Revolt. It is, however, possible to read the same evidence as showing a well-intentioned but not very capable foreign governor making conciliatory moves to the provincials, but outwitted at every turn by their skilled exploitation of the Jewish law. Having three times stated 'I find no case against him' (18.38; 19.4, 6), he is finally pushed into condemning Jesus to death by the threat, 'If you set him free you are no friend of Caesar's' (19.12). Any hint to the authorities at Rome that Pilate was condoning a movement of revolt – as in the synoptics Jesus' messianic claims were represented by the Jewish authorities – would be sufficient to deprive him of his coveted title *amicus Caesaris* ('friend of Caesar'), if not his office and life as well.

John 19.25b–27

This episode in the narrative of the crucifixion is certainly considered by John to be of capital importance, for after it he comments, 'Jesus, knowing that everything had now been accomplished . . .'. He uses those two key terms, 'knowing', with which he constantly stresses Jesus' awareness and careful direction of the whole passion sequence, and 'accomplished', which is used again in v. 30 for Jesus' solemn final word. The importance of it stands out all the more because there is no corresponding scene in the synoptic Gospels, and because it is hard to believe that relations and close friends would ever be allowed near enough to the cross to make this scene possible in any realistic way: four soldiers keeping control of the execution and of five relations and friends?

In interpreting the scene the similarities to the appearance of Jesus' mother at the marriage feast at Cana must be held in mind. There too she is unnamed; there too she is addressed by Jesus with the unusual formula, 'Woman' (in Greek this is not bluff or discourteous, but it is strangely formal and impersonal); there too Mary plays a part at a significant point in Jesus' ministry, as though making him begin his saving activity before he is ready to do so. It is tempting also to bring into the interpretation the scene in Revelation 12, when the unnamed woman robed with the sun brings forth a son who is to rule over all nations. In the allusive apocalyptic genre of writing is this son Jesus or the Christian community?

In any case, the entrusting to each other at this critical moment of the mother of Jesus and the Beloved Disciple (on his identity, see commentary on 13.21–32) must signify that the death of Jesus is the moment of the foundation of the Christian community. Immediately afterwards Jesus 'gives over' his spirit, the Spirit which makes Jesus present in the life of the community, and blood and water flow from his side to symbolize the sacraments of Eucharist and baptism.

John 19.38–42

Two points stand out in this account of Jesus' burial. The first is the immense amount of spices brought to fulfil the burial rites, far more than was necessary. It is again an indication of honour paid to Jesus. The whole account of the passion and crucifixion in John minimizes the sufferings of and indignities to Jesus, and stresses the glory of his being 'lifted up', 'exalted', and so drawing all people to himself. Now this honour is completed by a supply of spices fit for a king's burial.

The second point made is that Nicodemus, who had come to Jesus earlier by night 'out of fear of the Jews', now comes openly to bury him. In the other Gospels the burial is done by Joseph of Arimathea alone, without any help mentioned. Mark calls Joseph a 'Councillor', and it has been conjectured that he was the Councillor in charge of the burial of criminals in a common grave. The fact that he was in fact a disciple would make all the difference, so that an impersonal official duty became a personal act of homage. However, the addition of Nicodemus must have a theological purpose. Throughout the Gospel of John people are judged, or rather judge themselves, by their reaction to Jesus, either for or against him.

Nicodemus had sat on the fence, uncertain and puzzled, interested but neither believing nor rejecting Jesus. Now he, 'the teacher in Israel' as Jesus described him (John 3.10), is prepared to commit himself to Jesus – and publicly, too. Perhaps Nicodemus becomes the type and example of those who need to reflect long and carefully before they act. Or is it a further demonstration that the death of Jesus is the act which forms the Christian community?

John 20.1–18

In John's account of the empty tomb two stories are combined, and somewhat clumsily at that! Mary of Magdala jumps to the conclusion that they have taken the Lord out of the tomb without even looking in to see whether it is empty. She merely sees that the stone has been moved away and runs off. She next appears standing patiently weeping near the tomb. It is only then that she stoops to look inside and sees the angels. Meanwhile Peter and the Beloved Disciple have inspected the empty tomb, and the latter at least has understood the message and believed – but still has not explained it all to Mary of Magdala.

Why did he believe? Was it the position of the grave-clothes, which is so fully described? Perhaps it was clear that the risen Christ had passed through them without disturbing or unravelling them. What was the risen body like? Paul, in 1 Corinthians 15.35–36, says that this is a silly question, and goes on (in vv. 42–44) to explain a transformation from corruptible to incorruptible, from contemptible to glorious, from weak to powerful, from enlivened by the soul to enlivened by the Spirit of God. Each of these expresses a transformation into the sphere of the divine. So the risen Christ (and consequently the risen Christian) is somehow transformed and transferred into the realm of the divine. It is not immediately clear what the physical consequences of this are. From the stories of the meetings with the risen Christ it is clear that he could enter or leave a room without doors, that his closest friends did not immediately recognize him, above all that they were filled with awe when they did recognize him. He carried the aura of the divine.

So in the touching story of Mary and the 'gardener', when she recognizes him by the sound of his voice, her first reaction is to blurt out 'Rabbouni'.

John 20.19–23

The first Christian community was established by Jesus on the cross, when he entrusted his mother and the Beloved Disciple to each other's care and breathed forth his Spirit. Now the risen Christ takes this up and carries it one further. By the gift of the Spirit he gives to the community the power of acting in his name. The scene is clarified by the similar promise in Matthew, made to Peter and to the community (Matt. 16.18 and 18.18), of binding and loosing: the decisions made by the community are valid in heaven as on earth, and all through the presence of Jesus among his disciples. In John, with his more explicit teaching on the Spirit (the Paraclete or Advocate who makes Jesus present when Jesus is absent) this permanent presence of Jesus in his community is through the Spirit which he here breathes on them.

This scene in the upper room must be consciously correlative to the prayer of Jesus at the Last Supper in John 17. There Jesus prayed for his followers, sending them into the world (17.18): now 'As the Father sent me, I am sending you.' He left them his peace (14.27): now he greets them 'Peace be with you' twice. He prayed that his joy might be fulfilled in them (17.13): now they are filled with joy. He prayed that they might receive the Spirit (15.6; 16.7): now he breathes the Spirit on them.

Striking is the silence of the disciples. Normally in John there is plenty of dialogue, even if it is only puzzled questions to advance the argument. The minor characters, the Nathanaels and Mary Magdalenes, Nicodemus and the Samaritan, have plenty to say. Now all the disciples are awestruck into silence at the presence of their risen Lord.

John 20.24–31

The final scene of the Gospel (if we accept that John 21 is an addition, an epilogue) both rounds it off and opens the way to the future. It rounds it off with Thomas's confession, the most explicit acknowledgement in the four Gospels of Jesus' divinity, but pairing with John's opening verse, 'The Word was God'. So, as Mark is bracketed or book-ended by the title 'Son of God' (at the baptism and on the centurion's lips), so John is bracketed by the unequivocal assertion that Jesus is God. And as the prologue told us that 'in him was life', so now the objective is stated, 'that believing you may have life through his name'.

At the same time, Thomas's doubt is the believer's charter. All the way through the Gospel the accent has been on believing the signs and wonders, on believing because you have seen the works of the Father, on believing because you have seen me. Now this is reversed, and the blessing is on those who have not seen and yet believe. This is opening the way to the believers of the future. The final physical evidence is given: despite the transformation of the risen Christ, now given life by the Spirit rather than by the mere human soul, it is still possible to touch him physically; but for the future, belief is to rely on the witness of the disciples of Jesus.

This belief is subtly nearer to the belief about which Paul writes. In Paul belief is simply trust in God's promise to Abraham, an unwavering acceptance that God in his unwavering fidelity will fulfil those promises. In John the belief of the onlookers is based on evidence that Jesus is the fulfilment of God's promises. Henceforth belief will be trust rather than acceptance of evidence.

John 21.1–19

The clue to the understanding of this story of the meeting with the risen Christ at the lakeside lies in its similarity to the story in Luke 5.1–11 of the earlier meeting of Peter and the disciples with Jesus on the lake. Each is the story of a call and a mission, the Lukan story at the beginning of Jesus' ministry, the Johannine story at the end. In each there is the fishing all night without success, in each the command of Jesus which brings success in fishing, in each the admission of sin (in the present story Peter's triple declaration of love undoes his triple denial of his Master during the passion), in each the mission to carry on the work of Jesus. Only our present story is coloured and enriched by the atmosphere of the post-resurrection meetings.

Which is the original version and position of the story we cannot now determine. In John the story is an epilogue, attached to the Gospel loosely, suddenly starting again after a deliberate conclusion to the Gospel (20.30–31), and still showing traces of its pre-Johannine origin (for example, the sons of Zebedee appear here but nowhere else in John; on the other hand the expression 'Simon Peter' is distinctively Johannine, but occurs in Luke only in his version of this story, Luke 5.8, 10).

In any case, the purpose of the story is to convey the mission of Simon Peter and the Beloved Disciple. Simon Peter, with his vigour, reckless enthusiasm and impulsive eagerness, is to feed Christ's sheep and suffer martyrdom for it. The Beloved Disciple, the faceless, deliberately unnamed, type of all the disciples whom Jesus loves, is to carry on his mission 'till I come'. This mission is to be – as in the four scenes in which he has occurred in this Gospel – close to Jesus at the Eucharist, to share his cross and passion, to believe in the resurrection and to be tradent and guarantor of the tradition.

Select bibliography

The Lectionary

The Revised Common Lectionary: The Consultation on Common Texts, Nashville, Tenn. / Norwich: Abingdon / Canterbury Press, 1992.

West, Fritz, *Scripture and Memory: The Ecumenical Hermeneutic of the Three-Year Lectionaries*, Collegeville, Minn.: A Pueblo Book, published by the Liturgical Press, 1997.

Jesus, the four Gospels and the fourfold Gospel

Barton, Stephen C., *The Spirituality of the Gospels*, London / Peabody, Mass.: SPCK / Hendrickson, 1992 / 1994.

Bock, Darrell L., *Jesus according to Scripture: Restoring the Portrait from the Gospels*, Leicester / Grand Rapids, Mich.: Apollos / Baker, 2002.

Bockmuehl, Markus and Donald A. Hagner (eds), *The Written Gospel*, Cambridge / New York: Cambridge University Press, 2005.

Burridge, Richard A., *What Are the Gospels? A Comparison with Graeco-Roman Biography*, Grand Rapids, Mich.: Eerdmans, 2nd edn, 2004.

——, *Four Gospels, One Jesus?*, London / Grand Rapids, Mich.: SPCK / Eerdmans, 2nd edn, 2005.

Gregory, Andrew F., *Four Witnesses, One Gospel? Reflections on the Fourfold Gospel and the Revised Common Lectionary*, Cambridge: Grove Books, 2005.

Griffith-Jones, Robin, *The Four Witnesses: The Rebel, the Rabbi, the Chronicler and the Mystic*, New York: HarperCollins, 2000.

Hooker, Morna D., *Beginnings: Keys that Open the Gospels*, London / Harrisburg, Pa.: SCM Press / Trinity Press International, 1997 / 1998.

——, *Endings: Invitations to Discipleship*, London / Peabody, Mass.: SCM Press / Hendrickson, 2003.

Houlden, Leslie, *The Strange Story of the Gospels: Finding Doctrine through Narrative*, London / Cleveland, Ohio: SPCK / Pilgrim Press, 2002.

Morgan, Robert, 'The Hermeneutical Significance of Four Gospels', *Interpretation* 33 (1979), 376–88.

Schnackenburg, Rudolf, *Jesus in the Gospels: A Biblical Christology*, Louisville, Ky.: Westminster John Knox Press, 1995.

Stanton, Graham N., *The Gospels and Jesus*, Oxford / New York: Oxford University Press, 2nd edn, 2002.

——, *Jesus and Gospel*, Cambridge / New York: Cambridge University Press, 2004.

Wansbrough, Henry, *The Passion and Death of Jesus*, London / Nashville, Tenn.: Darton, Longman & Todd / Abingdon, 2003.

——, 'The Four Gospels in Synopsis', in J. Barton and J. Muddiman (eds), *Oxford Bible Commentary*, Oxford / New York: Oxford University Press, 2001.

Matthew

France, Richard T., *Matthew: Evangelist and Teacher*, Exeter / Eugene, Oreg.: Paternoster / Wipf & Stock, 1989 / 2004.

Gundry, Robert H., *Matthew: A Commentary on His Handbook for a Mixed Church under Persecution*, Grand Rapids, Mich.: Eerdmans, 2nd edn, 1994.

Harrington, Daniel J., *The Gospel of Matthew*, Sacra Pagina, Collegeville, Minn.: Liturgical Press, 1991.

Kingsbury, Jack D., *Matthew as Story*, Philadelphia: Fortress, 1988.

Luz, Ulrich, *The Theology of the Gospel of Matthew*, Cambridge / New York: Cambridge University Press, 1995.

Proctor, John, *Matthew: The People's Bible Commentary*, Oxford: Bible Reading Fellowship, 2001.

——, *Matthew's Jesus*, Cambridge: Grove Books, 2004.

Senior, Donald, *What Are They Saying about Matthew?* Mahwah, NJ: Paulist Press, 2nd edn, 1996.

Stanton, Graham N., *A Gospel for a New People: Studies in Matthew*, Edinburgh / Louisville, Ky.: T&T Clark / Westminster John Knox, 1992 / 1993.

Mark

France, Dick (= Richard T.), *Mark: The People's Bible Commentary*, Oxford: Bible Reading Fellowship, 1998.

Hooker, Morna D., *A Commentary on The Gospel according to St Mark*, London / Peabody, Mass.: A. & C. Black / Hendrickson, 1991 / 1992.

——, *The Message of Mark*, London: Epworth, 1983.

Juel, Donald H., *The Gospel of Mark*, Nashville, Tenn.: Abingdon, 1999.

Matera, Frank J., *What Are They Saying about Mark?*, Mahwah, NJ: Paulist Press, 1987.

Rhoads, David M., Joanna Dewey and Donald Michie, *Mark as Story: An Introduction to the Narrative of a Gospel*, Minneapolis: Augsburg Fortress, 2nd edn, 1999.

Telford, William R., *The Theology of the Gospel of Mark*, Cambridge / New York: Cambridge University Press, 1999.

Thurston, Bonnie B., *Preaching Mark*, Minneapolis: Fortress, 2002.

Luke

Cadbury, Henry J., *The Making of Luke–Acts*, Peabody, Mass.: Hendrickson, 1999 (originally published by Macmillan, 1927).

Fitzmyer, Joseph A., *The Gospel according to Luke*, 2 vols, Anchor Bible, New York / London: Doubleday, 1970, 1985.

Green, Joel B., *The Theology of the Gospel of Luke*, Cambridge / New York: Cambridge University Press, 1995.

Johnson, Luke T., *The Gospel of Luke*, Sacra Pagina, Collegeville, Minn.: Liturgical Press, 1991.

Lieu, Judith M., *The Gospel of Luke*, Epworth Commentaries, Peterborough: Epworth Press, 1997.

Powell, Mark A., *What Are They Saying about Luke?* Mahwah, NJ: Paulist Press, 1989.

Tuckett, Christopher M., *Luke*, T&T Clark Study Guide (previously published as Sheffield New Testament Guide, 1995), London / New York: Continuum, 2004.

Wansbrough, Henry, *Luke: The People's Bible Commentary*, Oxford: Bible Reading Fellowship, 1998.

John

Brown, Raymond E., *The Gospel according to John*, 2 vols, Anchor Bible, New York / London: Doubleday, 1966.

Burridge, Richard, *John: The People's Bible Commentary*, Oxford: Bible Reading Fellowship, 1998.

Edwards, Ruth, *Discovering John*, London / Cleveland, Ohio: SPCK / Pilgrim Press, 2003 / 2005.

Harrington, Wilfrid J., *John, Spiritual Theologian*, Blackrock, Co. Dublin: Columba Press, 1999.

Sloyan, Gerard S., *What Are They Saying about John?* Mahwah, NJ: Paulist Press, 1991.

Smith, Dwight M., *The Theology of the Gospel of John*, Cambridge / New York: Cambridge University Press, 1995.

——, *John among the Gospels*, Columbia, SC: University of South Carolina Press, 2nd edn, 2001.

Wansbrough, Henry, *The Gospel according to John*, London: Catholic Truth Society, 2002.

30000130